the great medieval heretics

the great
medieval heretics

Five Centuries of Religious Dissent

MICHAEL FRASSETTO

BlueBridge

Jacket design by Stefan Killen Design

Cover art top by The Bridgeman Art Library International: Ms 722/1196 fol.372r St. Dominic and the test by fire of the heretic books and the orthodox book, from Le Miroir Historial, by Vincent de Beauvais, French School (15th century), Musee Conde, Chantilly, France

Cover art bottom by The Bridgeman Art Library International: The Last Judgement (detail of the entrance of the damned into hell), by Rogier van der Weyden (1399–1464), Hotel Dieu, Beaune, France

Copyright © 2007, 2008 by Michael Frassetto
Published in Great Britain under the title
Heretic Lives by Profile Books Ltd.

ISBN 978-1-933346-12-0

First published in North America in 2008 by
B l u e B r i d g e
An imprint of
United Tribes Media Inc.
240 West 35th Street, Suite 500
New York, NY 10001

Printed in the United States of America
Book Club Edition

CONTENTS

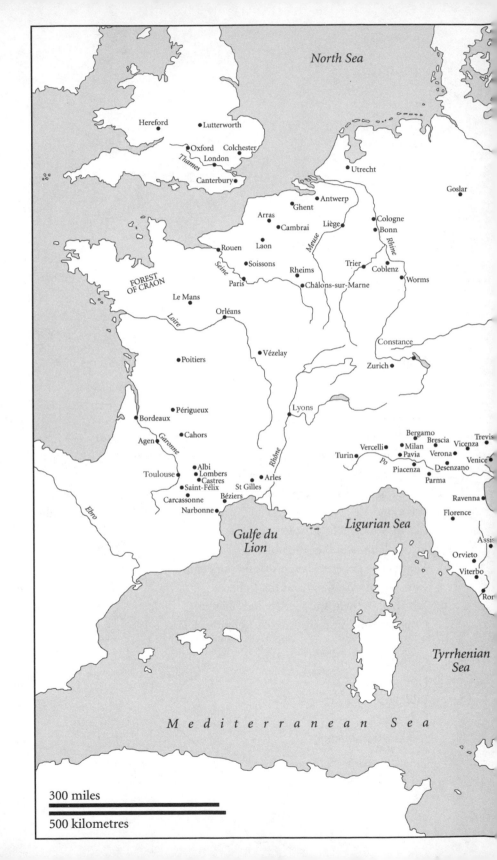

Cities and Centres of Heresy in Medieval Europe

1. Northern French knights, with the support of the pope, force heretics from Carcassone, the great stronghold of Albigensian heretics during the Albigensian Crusade. The crusaders would not only weaken heresy in the south but would also damage southern French culture and help the kings of France extend their authority in the region. (HIP/Art Resource, NY.)

2. *One of the greatest of medieval popes, Innocent III was an aggressive opponent of the Cathars and all heretics. He launched the Albigensian Crusade against the Cathars of southern France and laid the foundation for the Inquisition. He also approved the order of St. Francis in order to bring one of the most powerful religious impulses under the control of the Church. (HIP/Art Resource, NY.)*

3. One of the great tools at the disposal of the Church for the suppression of heresy was the public display and execution of unrepentant heretics. This highly stylized image depicts St. Dominic, founder of the Dominican order, presiding over one such display. Heretics, including Pierre Autier, the last of the great Cathar leaders, would come to an unhappy end at a public execution, which, despite the presence of Dominic here, was carried out by the secular authority. (Scala/Art Resource, NY.)

4. *Although not the all-powerful institution it is often said to be, the Inquisition was one of the most effective weapons the Church had in its war against heresy. The inquisitors, often members of the Dominican and Franciscan orders, were given the authority to root out heretics. One of the most successful of the inquisitors, Bernard Gui, left a valuable manual of the work of inquisitors and recorded the beliefs of many heretics, including Fra Dolcino. (Erich Lessing/Art Resource, NY.)*

5. *Since the time of Constantine and the Council of Nicaea (325), ecumenical councils like this one held at Vienne (1311) were called to resolve the great issues facing the Church. Pope Clement V held this council to discuss a wide range of issues, including a new crusade, the dispute within the Franciscan order, and the fate of the Knights Templar. It was also at Vienne that the great mystic Marguerite Porete was condemned for heresy and then burned. (Scala/Art Resource, NY.)*

6. The Oxford theologian John Wyclif, whose teachings inspired religious revolution in England and on the continent and prefigured the teachings of Martin Luther. (HIP/Art Resource, NY.)

7. *Despite assurances of safe conduct and other promises, Jan Hus was given little chance to defend his views at the Council of Constance and was burned for heresy. His charismatic leadership of the Bohemian Church attracted a great following, however, and his death at Constance inspired a revolt against church and state that led to recognition of a semi-independent church in Bohemia. (Snark/Art Resource, NY.)*

HERIBERT'S WARNING

'*a* new heresy is born in this world and in our days.'

So declared the Monk Heribert at the turn of the first millennium. Addressing himself to 'all Christians in the Orient and in the Occident, North and South, who believe in Christ,' he warned that a new heresy was being spread throughout Périgord in France by 'men of iniquity' who claimed the authority of the Apostles.[1] Displaying a horror soon to be characteristic of the members of the established Church, the 'orthodox' throughout Europe, Heribert sought to secure their well-being from the, in his view, perilous doctrines advanced by these new preachers of iniquity.

The heretics Heribert had discovered were, as he saw them, pseudo-apostles bent on undermining the integrity of the faith and on converting people to their error. Though false apostles, they seemed to live chaste and pious lives, which was all the better for undermining the Church. Pretending to follow the apostolic life, they did not eat meat, did not drink wine except on the third day, and refused to accept money. They were often found in prayer, genuflecting a hundred times a day, and were active and successful missionaries and preachers. Heribert alleged that they had 'corrupted and brought to them numerous people, not only laypeople, who have given up their belongings, but also clerics, monks, and nuns.'[2] In their simple life of preaching and poverty, the heretics might seem to be following the core teachings of the Church, in a resumption of the apostolic life, but, he contended, the appearances were deceiving. The heretics might have adopted the apostolic life, but they followed it imperfectly because they had rejected the core teachings of the Church itself. They were 'perverse' and 'hidden and deceptive,' and entered churches only to corrupt others. They denied alms had any value and, rejecting all property, held all wealth in common. The heretics also rejected the mass, maintaining that the Eucharist was nothing more than a piece of blessed bread. They might attend mass, but only as a pretense and so that they might corrupt others and lead them to turn their backs on the altar. They took communion but threw the host behind the altar or placed it in the missal instead of eating it, like good Christians. They rejected the cross and accused those who honored it of being idol-worshipers, and they refused to pray like the 'orthodox' and proclaim: 'For yours is the Kingdom, and you rule all creatures for ever and ever, Amen.'[3]

Beyond their rejection of Catholic doctrine and adoption of unorthodox teachings, the heretics were able to 'perform many wondrous feats.'[4] Not only could they convert members of the laity and priests, monks, and nuns to their ways; once converted, the new heretics could not be turned back to the true faith. 'No one,' Heribert asserted, 'no matter how rustic, adheres to their sect who does not become, within eight days, wise in letters, writing and action, [so wise] that no one can overcome him in any way.'[5] Heribert then goes on to describe a spectacular miracle, which he claims to have witnessed himself. A group of heretics were bound in chains and placed in a wine barrel which was open at the bottom and shut at the top. The barrel was then turned over and guards were set over it. On the following morning, the heretics were gone, and, inside the barrel, a vase which had had but a little wine in it was found to be full.[6] The letter concludes with references to numerous other marvelous deeds and a final warning that the heretics were invading Périgeux and other areas.

Heribert does not identify the leader of the group of heretics in the region of Périgord. In this respect his account differs from the reports of many later writers on heresy, but it features numerous of the central themes in the development of heresy in the Middle Ages, as well as some of the challenges facing those who attempt today to find out about the lives of medieval heretics.

Some of the most serious challenges concern the documents themselves: Heribert's letter demonstrates, better than almost any other one from the Middle Ages, the difficulties of using these documents. On one level, like most of the available sources, the letter was clearly written by a good Catholic, a monk who clearly sought to warn his fellow Christians against 'heretics.' The letter was written by one of the victors in the great struggle between heresy and ortho-doxy in the Middle Ages and bears the mark of the biases held by members of the established clergy. It was the clergy who possessed the truth; the doc-trines and dogmas sanctioned by the Church were the only true teachings, and those perceived as offering something different, even if that was based on the Gospels, were deemed to be in error. Moreover, the heretics are not allowed to speak for themselves; their teachings, and the motivations they had for accept-ing and spreading those teachings, are based on the interpretations of Heribert, and these were in all likelihood based on a stock collection of beliefs drawn from St. Augustine of Hippo and other earlier writers, who had outlined what the heretics were supposed to believe. Although Heribert did not ask the leading questions that the inquisitors would raise in the thirteenth and fourteenth centu-ries, he was influenced in his account by literary traditions which described the beliefs of the heretics from the earlier history of the Church.

Ancient sources, especially those of Augustine, described a number of reli-gious dissidents. Augustine spoke against the Manichaeans, condemning their dualism and rejection of the Hebrew Scriptures. He also denounced the Dona-tists, who believed that the validity of the sacraments depended on the priest's morality, and the Pelagians, who emphasized personal responsibility for obtain-ing salvation. Other early texts recorded the heresy of Priscillian, a Chris-tian dualist who was executed in 385. Also of concern to ancient writers was Arianism, which maintained that the Son of God was created by the Father, and was not coequal with the Father. Denounced at the Council of Nicaea (325), Arianism was adopted, but later rejected, by many of the Germanic peoples who reigned after the fall of the Roman Empire.

Even though the sources themselves are often problematic, they can never-theless offer important information about the emergence and nature of heresy, as does the letter of Heribert. The letter, known for some time from a twelfth-century copy but recently found in a manuscript of the eleventh century, provides evidence concerning the origins of medieval heresy. It has tradition-ally been taken to demonstrate the influence of Bogomil missionaries on the emergence of heresy in western Europe, and it has been suggested that the arguments which apply to the twelfth-century document hold just as well for the eleventh century. Arguments in favor of reading the letter as an authentic eleventh-century document remain controversial, but, if the letter of Heribert is accepted as a reliable account, it would provide evidence for the early arrival of the Bogomils and would reinforce the opinion of those who accept Bogomil's influence on the heresy of Stephen and Lisois. Even if these leaders of the heresy at Orléans were not influenced by the Bogomils, it is generally held that missionaries from Bulgaria, preaching a message first taught in the tenth century by the simple village priest Bogomil, helped to shape the teachings of the Cathars, whose popularity in southern France had a dramatic impact on the career of Count Raymond VI of Toulouse.

Heribert's letter is also suggestive about the nature of the heretics' beliefs in his day and throughout the later Middle Ages, and it indicates the possibly dualist nature of medieval heresy. Bogomil and generations of his followers taught a Christian dualism that emphasized the transcendent nature of God and the authority of the devil over the world. The rejection of meat and wine by Heribert's heretics may well reveal a Christian dualism which identified the material world as inherently evil. Their prayer recalls that of dualists of the eastern Mediterranean, and their rejection of images of Christ on the cross and of the Eucharist is also indicative of a rejection of the material world. These teachings gained increasing prominence among heretics in southern France, Italy, and other parts of Europe in the mid-twelfth century and were among the core beliefs of the Cathars, whose movement was perceived as the greatest threat to the Catholic Church in the Middle Ages. The Cathars' challenge was deemed to be so serious that it inspired the Church to launch a crusade and the Inquisition to destroy their movement. These efforts ultimately proved successful, even though it is sometimes said that the crusade did more to damage southern French culture and independence than it did to destroy heresy. The Cathar heresy, however, proved to be attractive to many Christians throughout the thirteenth and fourteenth centuries despite the extent of the persecutions it provoked, and one final flourishing of the heresy took place under the direction of Pierre Autier and his followers in the early fourteenth century.

Even if the heretics in Heribert's letter were not Christian dualists, they did seek to live the apostolic life and did base their teachings on the Gospels. Devotion to the scriptures and the life of Christ and the Apostles was promoted by all the leading heretics, whether dualist or not. The evangelical life was the most important model of Christian piety throughout the Middle Ages, and the heretics of Périgord adopted this model in their ascetic lifestyle, refusal to accept money, attention to prayer, and active missionary work. Indeed, the life of active preaching and poverty emerged as a core value for heretics from Bogomil to Pierre Autier. The great leaders of heresy of the twelfth century, most notably Henry the Monk, took up the life of missionary preaching, condemning the failures of the Church and seeking to promote a more pure and pristine version of the faith. Attracting a large, although short-lived, following, Henry sought to restore the Church to its original, apostolic purity, and the power of his preaching encouraged many to give away their worldly possessions. More successful and long-lasting was the movement initiated by Valdes of Lyons, whose heresy was firmly based on the Gospels and the apostolic life. The very essence of his heresy involved the life of preaching and poverty, and his and his followers' unwillingness to give up the practice of preaching led to their denunciation by the Church and ultimate condemnation as schismatics and heretics. Heribert's group at Périgord may be said to have also anticipated the radical and violent apostolic movement of Fra Dolcino, whose extreme devotion to the apostolic life led to the outbreak of attacks on the Church and its representatives. Despite their strict adherence to the apostolic life, Valdes, Henry, and the sectaries of Périgord were deemed heretics because of their rejection of Church authority and criticism of ecclesiastical materialism – being too good a Christian was at times as big a problem as not being Christian enough.

Heribert's letter, in reviewing the nature of the heresy at Périgord, thus traces the basic outlines of heresy, especially popular heresy, in the Middle Ages. It reveals the essential problems the documents pose, and it illustrates the basic character of heresy from the eleventh to the fourteenth centuries. It also hints at the emergence of a different kind of heresy in its report on the miracles and prodigies associated with the heretic movement of Périgord, which had an apocalyptic flavor.[7] Apocalyptic and prophetic sentiments were very important in the development of medieval religious beliefs, both orthodox and heterodox. Apocalypticism fueled the violent movement of Fra Dolcino and the Apostolici or Apostolic Brethren in the early fourteenth century. Their eschatological expectations drove them to renounce both material possessions and the authority of the Church and to open warfare between members of the movement and the Church itself. A rough contemporary of Dolcino, Marguerite Porete also cultivated a prophetic and mystical belief that undermined the traditional role of the Church in society and in the plan of salvation. Marguerite Porete was a member of the Beguine movement, which adopted an apostolic lifestyle, and her *Mirror of Simple Souls* was a handbook of the spiritual life and mystical path to God that offered a means to salvation independent of the Church. Her execution was a reminder of how sternly the Church was prepared to deal with those who questioned or undermined its authority.

The dedication to the apostolic life and the desire to return to the true Christian path revealed by the heretics at Périgord also found expression in learned circles. Indeed, leading heretics in the Middle Ages were found not only among the 'rustics' mentioned in Heribert's letter but also among the most educated members of society. Two of the greatest and most influential of the medieval heretics were the trained and learned theologians John Wyclif and Jan Hus. Their teachings examined some of the central doctrines of the Christian faith and came to conclusions that anticipated the teachings of Martin Luther. Motivated by many of the same concerns that inspired earlier heretical leaders, Wyclif and Hus applied their vast learning to questions of religious belief and practice and to the proper ordering of the Church in society. Their conclusions, like those of their many predecessors, rejected the teachings of the established Church and led to their eventual break with it or even, in Hus's case, to a fiery end.

The outlines of the history of heresy in the Middle Ages can be seen in the letter of Heribert. Driven by concerns of proper belief and practice, many Christians in the Middle Ages were condemned as heretics by an increasingly hierarchical and powerful Church. Responding to the call of the true faith, heretics sought to create a more pure Church and a religious experience that followed the teachings of Christ more faithfully. From Bogomil in the tenth century to Jan Hus in the late fourteenth and early fifteenth, religious leaders outside the boundaries of the Church provided an alternative to the normative Church and its teachings. They offered a challenge to its authority and, at times, faced the full fury of the religious and political leaders of their day. The heretics also contributed to the growth of the medieval Church and influenced the development of orthodox belief and practice. Although many of the heretics faded from the pages of history or suffered a dramatic end, they were a pivotal part of the history of the Church in the Middle Ages and important agents in the evolution of medieval religious belief and practice.

CHAPTER ONE

POP BOGOMIL AND COSMAS THE PRESBYTER: THE TENTH CENTURY

One of the earliest, most influential, and most elusive of all medieval heretics made his appearance first in tenth-century Bulgaria. This was the preacher Bogomil. The themes and tenets of his teaching mark a clear break from the great heresies of the ancient world and echo down throughout the whole of the Middle Ages. Living in an area heavily influenced by the Byzantine Empire and by the Orthodox Church so closely associated with it, Bogomil developed a large following throughout the eastern Mediterranean. The impact of his ideas was felt far beyond his homeland and the Byzantine Empire, and during the centuries following his death reached the countries of Germany, France, and Italy. Yet despite being the founder of a lasting legacy of religious dissent, and despite his prominence in the history of heresy in the Latin and Greek worlds, we know of his teachings only through the writings of orthodox ecclesiastics, whose evidence must be interpreted with care. The most important of these ecclesiastics was the priest Cosmas.

As with many other medieval heresies, the emergence of Bogomilism – as this one came to be known – was the result of a complex mix of religious and social developments, in this case in Bogomil's native Bulgaria. Although perhaps Bulgaria at the time of the emergence of the heresy was not a land of chaos, as it is sometimes depicted, it was a region that was undergoing a profound and important transformation.[1] Not the least of these changes, of course, was the

Christianization of the Bulgarians, which began under their great King Boris (ruled 852–89). The confusion that would affect Bulgarian religion in the tenth century was already manifest during the reign of Boris, who, for both political and religious reasons, sought to convert to Christianity. His retirement to a monastery in 889 reveals that he truly accepted the new faith, even if it is unclear how early this inner conversion occurred. In 864, when he was baptized, the Bulgarian ruler may well have believed in the Christian faith, but he was also concerned with the independence of his kingdom and his own authority. Under the new faith, Boris would be recognized as king by the grace of God and would stand in a more exalted position than the boyars (nobles) in his kingdom. He also sought to move out from under the shadow of the Byzantine Empire, and thus his conversion involved negotiations with the pope in Rome and western missionaries, who were powerful exponents of Latin Christianity. He turned to them because the pope and his allies would grant certain organizational concessions to the Church in Bulgaria without being in the position to impose any political authority over the king and his Church. The emperor in Constantinople and the Byzantine Church saw the threat of western interference in its neighbor, Bulgaria, and worked to ensure that Boris converted to Orthodox Christianity. Boris did, in fact, accept baptism at the hands of the patriarch of Constantinople, and his baptismal sponsor was the emperor Michael III. Despite this, later on Boris made overtures again to the pope and his representatives; the latter moved into Bulgaria and replaced the Greek priests and missionaries, who had begun the process of establishing the Church there. But when the pope refused to grant Boris's request for an archbishop, the Bulgarian ruler turned again to the Byzantine Empire and its Church. The competition and polemic that developed between Latin and Greek missionaries surely confused a newly converted and nominally Christian people and undermined the authority of the representatives of the Church, either Roman or Byzantine.

This complex and often ambivalent relationship with the Byzantine Empire and Orthodox Church continued into the tenth century, when Boris's successors, Symeon (ruled 893–927) and Peter (ruled 927–67), fought against, and then accepted, the Byzantines. Further complicating matters was the continued attraction of the traditional Bulgarian religion, to which a large part of the nobility and peasantry still adhered during Boris's lifetime and after. Boris faced a revolt of the nobles, inspired in part by their rejection of Christianity, and his immediate successor, Vladimir (889–93), repudiated and persecuted the new faith until his overthrow by Symeon, aided by Boris. The lingering attraction of paganism at all levels of Bulgarian society was complemented by animosity toward the Byzantines and their Church. During his reign, Symeon adopted an aggressive policy toward Constantinople and even sought to have himself crowned as Byzantine emperor. He promoted an independent Bulgarian Orthodox Church and cultivated hostility toward the Byzantine Empire, its culture, and its religion. His successor, Peter, at first also followed an anti-Byzantine policy, but his initial success against the Empire led to his receiving important concessions, including the hand in marriage of a member of the imperial family. This led to yet another dramatic influx of Greek clergy into Bulgaria and to the growing influence of Byzantium at the Bulgarian court and, possibly, on the whole Bulgarian culture and society. Greek clergy and Bulgarians influenced by them became increasingly important, and monasticism, which had first entered Bulgaria during the reign of Boris, grew substantially during the reign of Peter. Renewed Byzantine influence thus brought a new group of clerics and Byzantinized the leadership of the Bulgarian Church. It also renewed Byzantine influence on monastic life, which rested upon the establishment of large-scale plantations, worked by many peasants, and advocated a highly ascetic and world-renouncing lifestyle. For many, though, this new influence was not particularly welcome and, according to one scholar, contributed to the rise of a religious nationalism in Bulgaria that would lead to the emergence of heresy.[2]

The matter of religious nationalism remains, however, debatable. But the confused religious and socio-political environment of tenth-century Bulgaria opened the way for an alternative form of Christian belief and practice, which would be deemed heretical by the official Church. The first recorded mentioning of the heresy that would become known as Bogomilism is in a letter from the patriarch Theophylact Lecapenus, which has been dated between 940 and 950. The patriarch noted the appearance of this heresy during the reign of Tsar Peter.[3] Although he did not call it Bogomilism, he described it as 'a mixture of Manichaeanism and Paulianism'; in this way he identified its fundamental religious dualism and suggested that it originated in an ancient eastern Mediterranean dualist tradition.[4] He associated the new heresy with the Persian religious leader Mani (216–74? CE), who had developed a faith that drew on Christian teachings, gnosticism, and Persian religious traditions, posited the existence of two gods – a good and an evil one – and rejected the material world as the creation of the evil god.

Mani was seen in the Middle Ages as the originator in a long chain of heretics, which stretched to the Bogomils and even to the Cathars of western Europe. This view is now generally discredited, but it was upheld by serious scholars until well into the twentieth century.[5] The chain of dualist heresies comprised Theophylact's 'Paulians,' a designation which may refer to the followers of a heretic named Paul, or to those with a special devotion to the Apostle Paul. They are, however, generally identified as the Paulicians of Armenia, a group which was transferred to the Balkans by the Byzantine emperors; most likely they held dualist notions which contravened orthodox Church teaching.[6] As Peter of Sicily notes in his history, the Paulicians actively proselytised in Bulgaria, possibly already in 869–70.[7] This was a time when the religious situation there was most unsettled; hence their appearance would not have seemed out of place when Greek and Latin missionaries were also preaching in Bulgaria, but it complicated matters further, as the two Churches competed with each other for the devotion of the nominally Christian Bulgarians. The preaching of the Paulicians is often thought to have either introduced dualist teachings or reinforced dualist notions that already existed in the culture.

The new heretics in Bulgaria were most certainly not the heirs of the third-century prophet Mani and may not have been directly influenced by the rather militaristic Paulicians. They were, however, clearly dualist Christians, according to the anathemas Theophylact included in his letter.[8] He condemned, namely, those who believed in two ultimate principles and held the view that the devil created the world and ruled over it. Those who rejected the law of Moses, opposed lawful marriage, and denied that Mary was the mother of God were also declared anathema. Theophylact further condemned anyone who denied that the Son of God assumed the flesh, suffered physically, and died on the cross, together with all those who taught that the body and blood given by Christ to his disciples was the Gospel.

The various teachings denounced by Theophylact in his letter to Tsar Peter are those most generally associated with Christian dualism throughout the Middle Ages, and his letter may be little more than a catalogue of teachings of previous heretics, which he used to discredit the new movement. His identification of them as 'Paulians' and 'Manichaeans' has been questioned by scholars, but Theophylact's instincts were sound even if he had little direct knowledge of the heretics: he captured well and correctly the nature of the heresy emerging in tenth-century Bulgaria.

Theophylact's letter, which makes no mention of the movement's founder, contains the first reference to the emergence of what would be termed Bogomilism. The most important early source for the heresy, however, is the eyewitness account in the sermon of the Bulgarian presbyter Cosmas. The earliest extant manuscript of this work comes from the fifteenth century, and it has been argued that Cosmas wrote it in the thirteenth century. It is most likely, however, that the sermon was composed c.970, possibly in eastern Bulgaria, and, as suggested by certain of Cosmas's comments, certainly after the death of Tsar Peter. Such a dating would make the heresy several decades old by the time of the writing of the sermon. Thus Cosmas's work would reveal a more developed Bogomil heresy than the one which appears in Theophylact's letter.[9] Cosmas's account was also less dependent on earlier theological traditions than that of Theophylact. Rooted firmly in his personal experience of the new heresy, Cosmas's sermon against the Bogomils therefore provides a much more accurate depiction of the beliefs and practices of the early heretics and of the original teachings of the founder of Bogomilism. The sermon itself was very influential in later generations; it was adopted by members of other Slavonic Orthodox Churches and used by the Russian Orthodox clergy to denounce new heresies.

Little is known about Cosmas himself, except what can be discerned from his sermon on the Bogomils. There is little evidence concerning the dates of his birth and death, or when he entered priesthood. There is general agreement that Cosmas was a priest, as the accepted title of his work indicates, but exactly what kind of priest he was is uncertain. On the one hand, it has been said that, because he did not make reference in his sermon to the great ancient heresies, he was not a 'sophisticated theologian': such absence would suggest a more modest background.[10] On the other hand, it has also been conjectured that Cosmas was no simple village priest but rather held a position of some prominence in the Bulgarian Orthodox Church; and it has even been suggested that Cosmas was a bishop, on the grounds that his work was addressed to other bishops of Bulgaria.[11]

Although his exact rank remains uncertain, Cosmas was surely a devoted son of the Orthodox Church, leaving this first-hand account of a new heresy in Bulgaria. His work was written in Old Slavonic — a language promoted by King Boris, who patronized the missionaries introducing into Bulgaria a translation of the Bible in Old Slavonic — and it clearly supports the established eastern Orthodox Church. The sermon contained not only the warning about the Bogomil heresy and its condemnation, but also a defense of the 'orthodox' faith and a call for its reform. A substantial portion of the work addresses the failures of the Bulgarian Orthodox Church, which is blamed for allowing heresy to appear in the first place. Cosmas, in some ways, is not that far removed from his nemesis, Bogomil: the Orthodox presbyter was as critical of the Church as was his heretical opponent. He was most particularly critical of those who took up the monastic life without adequate preparation.

Monasticism had become increasingly popular during the reign of Peter, and many believed that the only way to gain salvation was to become a monk, living their life in celibacy. As Cosmas asserts, however, many of those who joined monasteries were hypocritical and failed to leave the world behind in the way monks should. Many monks lived unchaste and drunken lives, devoting themselves to their own bellies and wasting time in idle gossip. Others would break their vows by wandering from monastery to monastery, instead of staying in their original community in obedience to the rule and their abbot. For Cosmas, who may have indulged in rhetorical hyperbole on the theme of the corruption of the monks, this behavior was one of the key factors in the success of Bogomil's movement, and the priest drew strong links between the failures of the monks and the rise of heresy in Bulgaria. Like other ecclesiastics in the coming centuries, Cosmas urgently called for a reform of the Church, to stem the tide of heresy and to improve religious life overall.

The life of Bogomil is as shrouded in the mists of the past as is that of Cosmas, and what little we know of that life comes from the sermon written against him, and from his teachings. The founder of the heresy is mentioned only once in Cosmas's sermon and receives no direct reference in any other contemporary document. One indication of his status, however, is revealed in that lone mentioning by Cosmas, who identifies his rival as Pop Bogomil. The title 'pop' was used for ordinary village priests, and so it is likely that Bogomil was a simple priest, preaching at first to the small community in which he lived.

His name, which he may have adopted later in life, is a translation of the Greek name Theophilos, which was fairly common in Bulgaria at the start of the tenth century. The name probably means 'beloved of God,' or (depending on the placing of the accent) it can also be translated as 'worthy of God's mercy,' 'one who entreats God,' or, in the most recent translation, 'worthy of God's compassion.'[12] Cosmas offers a play on Bogomil's name by declaring that he is not Bogomil but 'Bogunemil, "unworthy of God's compassion".'[13] The descriptive nature of his name has led some modern commentators to argue that the name indicates that there was no individual founder of the movement and that only tradition dictates that he existed; but it is perhaps a case of excessive skepticism to deny Bogomil's existence, even if his personality and other elements of his biography are difficult to discern.

Beyond the name of the founder, Cosmas provides no other direct references for Bogomil's biography. He does, however, offer important insights into Bogomil's teachings and even hints concerning his life. The various criticisms he ascribes to Bogomil are suggestive of the way he lived. His rejection of marriage indicates that he led a celibate life, and it is probable that he lived simply, in accordance with the teachings of the Gospels, and adopted a life of poverty. Cosmas admits as much in his description of Bogomil's early disciples, which is most likely applicable to their mentor. The heretics, and most assuredly Bogomil himself, 'are gentle and humble and quiet. They seem pale from their hypocritical fasts, they do not utter vain words, they do not laugh out loud, they do not show curiosity, they take care not to be noticeable and to do everything externally so that they may not be told apart from orthodox Christians.'[14] Of course, Cosmas declares that they are ravening wolves inside, but he cannot fail to notice the simple piety of the Bogomils, which is much more similar to the behavior of true monks and Christians than that of the Orthodox monks whom Cosmas also condemns. This monastic lifestyle, inspired in part by true monastic practice and by the Gospels – which Bogomil himself very probably knew in an Old Slavonic translation – clearly reflects the behavior of the founder of the Bogomil movement.

Bogomil must also have been a charismatic and successful preacher, if we are to judge by the growth of the movement he founded. It is generally believed that he attracted a substantial following with his preaching – especially among the peasantry, as most would agree. The success of his preaching can be discerned from two passages in Cosmas's treatise against the heretics. The Orthodox presbyter notes in one section that people 'approach them [the heretics] and take their advice about their souls' salvation … and when they see anyone simple and ignorant, there they sow the tares of their doctrines.'[15] And later in the work he explains that the 'heretics cloak their poison under hypocritical humility and fasts, and again they take the Gospel in their hands, and, giving it an impious interpretation, they try to catch men this way and lead them to perdition.'[16]

Bogomil's disciples, following his example, spread throughout Bulgaria and the Byzantine Empire within a generation of the founding of the heresy. His teachings found a receptive audience among his country-men, many of whom believed, like the Orthodox Cosmas, that the clergy of the established Church were not fulfilling their obligations of living holy lives and preaching the Gospel. Indeed Bogomil, by the probity of his life, stood in stark contrast to the corrupt and worldly monks, the Byzantinized clergy, and the distant and powerful hierarchy that lived in Bulgaria at the time. Although there is almost no direct evidence concerning his life, what little there is suggests, therefore, that he was a zealous preacher who lived simply and piously. His very mode of life stood as an indictment of the established Church, which failed the newly Christianized people of Bulgaria. Understandably, the Orthodox Church was filled with a growing concern about his teachings.

Along with such suggestions concerning Bogomil's life, Cosmas also provides the earliest commentary on the teachings both of the founder and of the early practitioners of the heresy. His treatise clearly reveals that, from its very inception, Bogomilism was a dualist faith. This fundamental feature was to affect the teachings and practices of the Bogomils for centuries to come. In religion, dualism is a type of doctrine which involves belief in two gods, one good and one evil. At its heart, Bogomil's dualism was one that rejected the material world, identifying it as a place of evil. Hence Bogomil and his followers refused the physical pleasures and the material aspects of cult in the Orthodox Church, notably the water in baptism and the bread and wine of the Eucharist. As Bogomilism evolved and spread into the Byzantine Empire and even into western Europe, this dualism of matter and spirit would remain the sect's essential feature, even if the theology behind it became more sophisticated and the Bogomils became divided over the exact understanding of what their dualism entailed.

Although Cosmas argues that the Bogomils were not consistent in their terminology concerning the devil, he plainly asserts that 'they claim the devil as creator of mankind and all the divine creation.'[17] Indeed, Cosmas expands on this central tenet of Bogomil's teaching later on in the treatise: Bogomil and his followers say that 'it is by the devil's will that all exists; the sky, the sun, the stars, the air, mankind, the churches, the cross; all that belongs to God they ascribe to the devil; in short everything that moves on the earth, whether it has a soul or not, they ascribe it to the devil.'[18] Moreover, the devil was given the name Mammon, by which they refer to the 'creator and architect of things terrestrial.'[19] It is Mammon who ordered 'men to take wives and eat meat and drink wine,' and those who live in the world and marry are servants of Mammon.[20] This is clearly an echo of the biblical passage stating that one cannot serve God and Mammon, and in this way Bogomil identified himself and his followers as the true believers in God and his revelation.

The Bogomils, according to Cosmas, corroborated this belief by references to the scriptures. They found support, for instance, in the Gospel according to Matthew, where the devil says to Jesus, 'All these things I will give you, if you will fall down to worship me' (4: 9). They believed that the devil offered Jesus things in the world that he, the devil, had created, and therefore the devil was master of the world. The heretics cited John's Gospel as well, including the verse in which Jesus declares, 'Now the ruler of the world is coming, and has no power over me' (14: 30), which they took to mean that the devil was the lord and creator of the world. Cosmas may dispute the Bogomils' biblical exegesis, but it is important that they turned to scripture to support their beliefs – Bogomil and his followers always claimed to be true Christians – and it is equally important that they believed the scriptures taught that God did not create the world but the devil did.

The belief that the devil was the world's creator had important consequences for Bogomil belief and practice, but his own teachings about the devil were shaped by a further passage from the scriptures. According to Cosmas, Bogomil and his followers believed that the parable of the prodigal son (Luke 15: 11–32) was about the devil. On this reading, the younger son, who deceived his father, was the devil, and the older son was Jesus. This made God the father both of Jesus and of the devil, who were then brothers. Thus Bogomil taught what is called 'mitigated dualism,' rather than 'absolute dualism.' In mitigated dualism the devil or creator of the world is himself a created being, or at least subordinate to the one true God, whereas in absolute dualism the good and evil deities are equal powers existing in all eternity.

Later on in the history of the sect, some Bogomils would adopt absolute dualism. The founder of the heresy, however, seems to have taught a mitigated dualism, which reveals another possible influence on the emergence of the heresy as well as his own creative powers.

Although the Paulicians are often seen as an influence on Bogomil, his dualism was distinctly different from theirs. According to one recent scholar, the trinity of God and his two sons Jesus and the devil, which featured in the teachings of the early Bogomils, is reminiscent of the Zurvan Zoroastrian trinity of Zurvan, Ahriman, and Ohrmazd, and there is some evidence to suggest contacts between the Bulgars and the Iranian Zurvanites (third to seventh centuries CE).[21] This link is, however, rather tenuous; Bogomil's mitigated dualism and understanding of the relationship between God and the devil reveal the independence of his thought, thus testifying to the originality of his teachings. Whatever his sources, Bogomil promoted the belief that the devil was both the son of God and the creator of the world with everything in it. This view of our world had a profound influence on all the other beliefs and practices of the Bogomils.

Bogomil's teachings on God and the devil had a direct impact on his understanding of Christ and of his presence on earth. Later accounts state unambiguously that Bogomil heretics had a Docetist Christology, namely that they upheld the belief in a non-human, celestial Christ, who only seemed to assume the flesh and suffer on the cross in his humanity. Docetist beliefs would fit in well with the dualist cosmology taught by Bogomil, but Cosmas, in this discourse on the heresy, offers only one suggestion that the founder might have held such beliefs and that his Christology was Docetist, yet that testimonial is not conclusive. This happens in a passage where Cosmas claims that the Bogomils deny that Christ performed any miracles because they believe that the devil was the creator of all things. The founder and his disciples, Cosmas explains, say: 'Christ did not restore any blind person's sight, he cured no cripple, he did not raise the dead; these are only parables.'[22] Indeed, to do so would be to accept the goodness of creation and the power of Christ in an evil material world. Rather, the Bogomils would contend that the Evangelists presented the sins as diseases; they would explain that the five loaves of bread Christ used to feed the masses were really the four Gospels and the Acts of the Apostles. This allegorical interpretation of Christ's miracles could support a Docetist Christology, as it could be predicated on the belief that the material world is the kingdom of the devil.

Bogomil's teachings on the person of Christ, or at least those of his disciples as recorded by Cosmas, are indeed a bit confused. The rejection of Christ's miracles is in line with a Docetist view, but Cosmas's discussion of the heretics' refusal to venerate the cross suggests that Bogomil may not have fully worked out his Christology. Denial of the cross was a feature of early Bogomilism; Cosmas notes that the heretics 'chop up crosses and make tools of them,'[23] but this seems to be in line with their general rejection of material objects rather than emerging from some Christological viewpoint. Moreover, the Bogomils refused to adore the cross because the son of God was crucified on it and therefore 'the cross is even more the enemy of God.' They argued further, 'If anyone killed the king's son with a cross of wood, would the wood be dear to the king? The same is true of the cross of God.'[24] This argument against the veneration of the cross suggests that they viewed it as the place of Christ's actual suffering and death; but such a view, in turn, presupposes that Christ assumed the flesh, because Christ in his divinity cannot suffer and die. The Bogomils would eventually work out an elaborate Docetist Christology, in which Christ very clearly did not assume the flesh and was not born of the Virgin Mary – they taught that he entered her body through her ear and only appeared to have been born of the Virgin – but the earliest Bogomils and the founder himself appear to have preached a somewhat mitigated and confused Christology. Or at least they failed to work out the full implications of their Docetism, as it applied to various aspects of their teaching.

One doctrine which seems, however, to have emerged as a consequence of a Docetist Christology is – quite apart from the Bogomils' essential dualism – their attitude toward the Virgin Mary. In his letter, Theophylact makes the rejection of the Virgin one of the main features of the heresy, but Cosmas pays only passing attention to it. He notes that 'they do not honor the most glorious and pure mother of Our Lord and God Jesus Christ, and utter madness against her.'[25] He qualifies this statement, however, by remarking that this error is greater than all their other evils, and he notes that he cannot 'record in this book their words and their insults with regard to her whom the prophets foretold.'[26] In this way, perhaps, he indicates the extent to which Bogomil offended

Orthodox sensibilities concerning the Blessed Virgin, and in a later section of the treatise he accuses his followers of claiming that 'the most holy mother of God sinned.'[27] It is possible, moreover, that Bogomil's 'insults' included the rejection of the virgin birth of Christ as it was taught by the established Church, or the denial of that veneration which the Orthodox bestowed on Mary as the mother of God. In any case, Cosmas seems clearly disturbed by Bogomil's attitude – so disturbed, in fact, that he cannot discuss it at any length. And Bogomil's refusal to honor Mary reinforces the belief that he taught a form of Docetism in which Christ would not have been born of the flesh. The rejection of Mary is also part of a broader repudiation of the prophets and saints venerated by the Orthodox Church.

Consistent with their dualist cosmology, Bogomil and his sectaries, like all dualists since Mani and others from the earlier history of Christianity, rejected the prophets of the Hebrew scriptures. In later generations of Bogomils, the devil would be associated with the God of the Old Testament, which offered them justification for rejecting the Hebrew scriptures. Cosmas, however, does not make that connection in his treatise, even though he denounces Bogomil and his followers for refusing to accept the law of Moses and the teachings of the prophets and blames their rejection of the law on the devil. They 'spurn the law God gave to Moses' and 'reject what the holy prophets prophesied about Him [Christ].'[28] Cosmas notes, specifically, that Abraham, Azarias, and David were rejected, and that Bogomil and his sect called John the Baptist 'the precursor of antichrist.'[29] In casting aside the Hebrew prophets, John the Baptist, and the Hebrew scriptures, Bogomil asserted his exclusive preference for the books of the New Testament and for the teachings of Christ. According to Cosmas, the heresy was based solely on the false interpretation of the Gospels and Acts of the Apostles. False or not, Bogomil's understanding of the scriptures discarded both the importance of the Old Testament and the scriptural exegesis of the Orthodox Church.

In fact Bogomil imparted to his followers a much broader rejection of the teachings and institutions of the Orthodox Church; as Cosmas noted, 'they insult every law which is part of the tradition of God's Holy Church.'[30] This attitude toward the Church and its teachings most plausibly derived from Bogomil's repudiation of the material world, but also from a general dissatisfaction with the Church, which is shared by Cosmas and revealed in his critique of it and of its clergy. The Bogomils refused to honor the saints recognized by the Church. They did not respect their relics and denied that miracles were performed by them through the power of the Holy Spirit. In accordance with the belief that the devil rules over the world and everything in it, they argued that '[t]he miracles did not take place according to the will of God, but it was the devil who did them to trick mankind.'[31] Not only did they repudiate saints and relics held sacred by the Orthodox, but they also refused the veneration of icons, one of the central expressions of religious devotion in the Ortho-dox Church. Just as they derided the practice of honoring the cross, the Bogo-mils mocked those who honored holy icons and denounced the latter as idols; and this, according to Cosmas, made these heretics worse than the demons, who feared icons. The Bogomils denounced the practice of honoring religious images by declaring that 'those who venerate icons are like the pagan Greeks,' who worshiped false idols.[32] Cosmas offered a spirited defense of both practices in his treatise, which demonstrates the importance of the matter both to the orthodox and to the heterodox.

Bogomil most probably rejected the entire sacerdotal and sacramental struc-ture of the Church. In his discourse, Cosmas notes that the heretics attacked the priests, 'yapping at them like dogs following a mounted man.'[33] They criticized not only those who deserved to be condemned on the grounds of their immo-rality, but also those who deserved respect for the quality and purity of their lives. They did not honor the clergy as God intended, concluded Cosmas; and he also observed that the heretics could not be Christians because they did not have any priests. Along with their rejection of the clergy, Bogomil and his dis-ciples denied the validity of the sacraments offered by the Church. For them, the Eucharist was 'a simple food like all others,' and the sacrament of commun-ion, or the mass itself, were not instituted by divine command but rather by the teachings of men.[34] Moreover, Bogomil understood the scriptural passages concerning Christ's sharing of the bread and wine at the Last Supper in an alle-gorical sense, which was markedly different from the teaching of the Church. Cosmas wrote: 'You tell that they [the words of the Gospels] refer to the four Gospels and the Acts of the Apostles, not to holy communion; by "body," you understand the four gospels and by "blood," the Acts of the Apostles.'[35]

The rejection of the sacrament of the bread and wine may have stemmed from their dualism and abhorrence of the material world, an attitude clearly revealed by their rejection of the Orthodox practice of baptism with water. The belief that the world, with all the things in it, was created by the devil led all Bogomils to reject the use of any material substance like water in any of their rituals; they would replace the baptism with water by a spiritual baptism, even though Cosmas does not specifically mention this in his discourse. From the very beginnings of the movement, however, Bogomil and his adherents found baptism with water so distasteful that they loathed baptized children. Indeed, so profoundly did they oppose this form of baptism, that if 'they see a young child,' wrote Cosmas, 'they shrink from it, as if from some evil smell; they spit and cover their faces, when they themselves are filth to men and to angels.'[36] The Bogomils denied that baptism was instituted by God; the rejection of John the Baptist was rooted, in part, in John's practice of baptism with water.

Along with a cosmological dualism and rejection of the Orthodox Church, Bogomil most likely taught a number of positive doctrines, which Cosmas only grudgingly recorded. His followers were taught to live simple and pious lives. Cosmas describes them as 'gentle and humble and quiet,'[37] and he notes that they fast frequently. Bogomil and his followers rejected the practice of marriage; he encouraged celibacy – the hostile reaction to children may have been the result of the belief that they were the devil's own and that procreation contributed to the extension of the devil's realm. Bogomil may also have taught his disciples to pray the Lord's Prayer four times a day and four times a night, and he may have instructed them not to make the sign of the cross when they prayed.

It is also likely that the basic organizational structure of the sect was established during Bogomil's lifetime, or at least by the time when Cosmas was writing. Cosmas condemns members of the sect who 'go about in idleness and are unwilling to employ their hands with any task; they go from house to house and eat the goods of others, those of the men they have deceived.'[38] The fundamental division of the Bogomils was between the 'perfected' and the ordinary believers, those who were sympathetic to the sect without having joined the heresy. In later generations a more complex organization emerged involving bishops, but it is likely that a two-fold division was established right from the outset – between those who preached the message of the sect and those who heard it and offered support to the preachers in the form of food and shelter. Although this simple structure was established very early on, the followers of Bogomil, citing the letter of James (5: 16), were taught to confess their sins to each other. Indignant over this violation of orthodox practice, Cosmas was all the more exercised because it was 'not just the men who do this, but the women as well.'[39] And it is a commonplace in the history of heresy, and of religion, that women often played a crucial role in a new development.

Finally, Cosmas notes that the Bogomils were instructed to deny their beliefs, a practice to be repeated by heretics over the next several centuries in both eastern and western Christendom. In the opening passages of the treatise, Cosmas declares that the heretics appear to be as gentle as sheep, but in fact are ravening wolves; in other words, they hide their true nature behind a false appearance, in order to capture otherwise unsuspecting souls. He notes in a later passage that, when someone confronts their actual beliefs, they deny them 'so forcefully that you would think that there was no harm in them.'[40] They defend this practice by citing the passage from the Gospel according to Matthew, where Jesus tells his followers not to pray like the hypocrites. It was a means of protecting themselves from the persecution of the secular and religious authorities and of ensuring the continued success of Bogomil's teachings.

Although a shadowy presence to the extent that some historians question his actual existence, Bogomil was the founder of the first great heresy of the Middle Ages. Preaching his version of the Christian faith early in the reign of Tsar Peter, Bogomil attracted a substantial following in Bulgaria at a time when most Bulgars were only nominally Christian and exposed to a wide range of religious influences – Paulician and Roman and Byzantine Christian – and buffeted by cultural and socio-political turmoil. Within a generation or two, the teachings of Bogomil had spread to a sufficiently large number of people, so that the Orthodox Cosmas recorded them in his treatise. He revealed a Christian heresy rooted in cosmological dualism and in the rejection of the established Church. It was this combination that proved to have great impact on the development of the Church in Bulgaria, the Byzantine Empire, and, most importantly, western Europe.

CHAPTER TWO

STEPHEN AND LISOIS: HERETICS IN THE ELEVENTH CENTURY

*t*he emergence of the Bogomils signaled the revival of heresy throughout the Mediterranean and heralded its reappearance in Latin Europe
for the first time since late antiquity. Religious dissent was breaking
out in several places in western Europe at the turn of the millennium. The most
important and most dramatic of all the occurrences of heresy in the early eleventh century took place in Orléans. Its improbable leaders were two pious and
respectable canons. Their names were Stephen and Lisois.

The heretical developments at Orléans in 1022 were, in some ways, foreshadowed in Aquitaine and other regions. In the year 1018, 'Manichaeans
appeared throughout Aquitaine seducing the people. They denied baptism and
the Cross and every sound doctrine. They abstained from food and seemed
like monks; they pretended to be chaste, but among themselves practiced
every sort of vice. They were messengers of Antichrist and caused many to
turn away from the faith.'[1] In this way Ademar of Chabannes (*c*.989–1034),
a monk of southwestern France, announced the rebirth of heresy in western
Europe in the Middle Ages, after more than five centuries when it had lain
dormant.

Although, as we have seen, heresy had already emerged in Bulgaria and
in the Byzantine world in the tenth century and had subsisted there almost
continuously, in some form or other, since late antiquity, this was a relatively

new phenomenon so far in the medieval West. Ademar's announcement of the sudden resurgence of heresy – or religious dissent, as it is sometimes called – heralded important changes for western Christendom. It also raised the possibility that the phenomenon was due to contact with Bogomil missionaries and was broad enough to spread, beyond Ademar's native Aquitaine, across all of western Europe.

Ademar described the heretics who appeared in his homeland as Manichaeans because he believed that they advocated a dualist religious heresy. The heretics' beliefs and practices, as recorded by Ademar, recall those adopted by Bogomil and his followers. Indeed, Ademar's description of the heretics as simple, pious folk who secretly indulged in debauchery offers a further echo of the behavior of the Bogomils as Cosmas explained it, and forms part of a long tradition of demonizing heretics and others outside the bounds of society. Consequently, some scholars have argued that the influence of Bogomil missionaries on the origin and growth of heresy in western Europe was felt already in the early eleventh century.[2] The Bogomils from Bulgaria were active missionaries, as the founder encouraged them to be, and some have suggested that it was their appearance in the early decades of the eleventh century that focused the inchoate opposition to Church teachings and to the clergy which could be registered throughout society at that time. On this traditional view, the Bogomil missionaries, who lived ascetic and devout lives, may well have been seen by those in France and other parts of western Europe as the true representatives of Christianity, as many Bulgarians had seen them, and they were thought to offer an attractive alternative to the religious life dictated by the established Church. The eleventh-century arrival of the Bogomils in the West remains, however, a controversial point which most, though by no means all, recent historians do not accept. But the issue is not whether the Bogomils helped to shape heresy in France and other parts of western Europe; it is, rather, when this happened. The importance of the Bogomils in the development of heresy in Latin Europe should not be understated even if the exact moment of their arrival may never come to be known.

On the now generally accepted view, the Bogomils only arrived in western Europe in the twelfth century, but the first expressions of heresy in Latin Europe took place in the years around the turn of the millennium, as Ademar reveals. And the phenomenon was manifest not only in Aquitaine but also in Italy, in the

German Empire, and in several other places in France, from the last decades of the tenth century until the middle of the eleventh, with a cluster of outbreaks from the late 1010s to the early 1030s. For Ademar of Chabannes and other 'orthodox' ecclesiastics throughout western Christendom, these heretics were part of a united front that swept across the continent. Indeed, a corridor of heresy has been identified, which began in Italy and worked its way north, into France and into the Low Countries. The heretics were believed to have been inspired by the devil and intent on destroying the Church and on perverting all good Christians. Nevertheless, just as we have seen in the case of the emergence of the Bogomil heresy, there were several more 'mundane' and less 'diabolical' causes of the birth of medieval heresy after the year 1000.

Like the Balkans in the tenth century, at the turn of the millenium western Europe was in a state of great economic and social turmoil: historians have identified the period from 950 to 1050 as the age of the feudal transformation.[3] Many places in Latin Europe, especially in what would become France, were racked by a violence which both contributed to, and was part of, the breakdown of the old socio-economic and political order. Since the ninth century, much of Europe suffered from foreign invasions, most notably those of the Vikings. During the tenth century Viking assaults increased in ferocity and duration, as many of the invaders from the north began to settle in parts of France and England. The traditional military machine, led by the king himself, Robert the Pious of France, often proved ineffective against these raiders from Scandinavia, and the authority of the king partly diminished as a result of his failure to protect his subjects. Local representatives of power such as the counts and dukes claimed the traditional rights of the king in his place and built up semi-private armies to defend their lands. But these great regional powers were not always up to the task, and an even greater decentralization of authority ensued. By the late tenth and early eleventh century – the very time when heresy reappeared in western Europe – a new form of power, that of the castellan, began to take shape in France and other parts of Europe. Emerging as a result of the failures of the great powers to protect the countryside, but also at a moment when foreign invasions were about to end, this new type of leader appeared to impose his will on local society simply because of his possession of a castle. Not only did the castellans exploit the local peasants by demanding payment in return for protection, but they were also involved in private warfare which destabilized society and terrorized the peasants.

In the face of the breakdown of political order, the people of western Europe had recourse to the other pillar of society, the Church. But, although it traditionally offered solace to the powerless and support to the powerful, the Church had suffered at the hands of invaders and castellans alike and had only modest success in limiting violence in society. Moreover, the Church itself was undergoing a profound transformation: this period laid the foundation for the so-called Gregorian Reform of the later eleventh century.[4] Around the year 1000, the old order of the Church was fading away, as new institutions and a new understanding of the Church and its place in the world was taking shape. The traditional understanding of the saints as local spiritual protectors was giving way, being replaced by a notion of the universal saints, such as Peter and Mary. At the same time, the very figure of Christ was being transformed: the focus came to be, increasingly, on the human Jesus. Locally prominent saints faced 'competition' from Jesus and the Apostles; nevertheless, the cult of the saints, local and universal, remained at the center of everyday devotion, and the number of pilgrims to their shrines increased. As a result of this mounting devotion numerous churches were built throughout Europe, to accommodate the throngs of pilgrims. So widespread was this construction that one contemporary writer declared that the world was clothing itself in 'a white mantle of churches.'[5]

While the central teachings of the faith were undergoing transformation and religious fervor was growing among the people of Europe, Church institutions were themselves being reformed and restructured. One of the main points of emphasis in this process of reformation was the improvement of the life and behavior of the clergy. Already in the early tenth century, monastic life had undergone a reform associated with the French monastery of Cluny. The leaders of that movement sought to restore monastic lifestyle to its original purity, stressing separation from the world and increasing the religious obligations of the monks. The latter were to spend their time praying, singing Psalms and doing the works of God. While the liturgical routine of the monks became increasingly complex and elaborate, their personal life was restored to apostolic simplicity; they lived chastely, ate simply, and owned nothing.

Gradually, this emphasis on apostolic simplicity and purity came to shape the lives of priests and higher secular clergy as well. Although this was technically against Church law, in the tenth century local priests often had wives or mistresses; some bishops even fathered children. But now, in the spirit of reform, the clergy were increasingly expected to live celibate lives, in imitation of Jesus and the Apostles. This demand for sexual purity arose, in part, from a growing attention paid to the sacraments, especially the Eucharist; and these were administered by the priests. The mass, at which the Eucharist was offered, became a more elaborate affair and was increasingly focused on the priest rather than on the congregation. The Church also enlarged the number of sacraments, exercising increasing claims to authority over marriage.

The changes that took place around the year 1000 laid the foundation for a real revolution in the life and structure of the Church, but their immediate effects were not always positive. The increasingly elaborate sacramental structure of the Church and the expansion of its claims to authority alienated many faithful at all levels of society. Others were further disenchanted with the Church because of its growing economic wealth; although they advocated personal poverty, even the most reform-minded members of the Church benefited from gifts of land and other wealth from pious nobles. This was presumably regarded as a failure of the Church to live up to its own ideals, as it would be deemed in later generations. Moreover, the increasing focus on the priest as the central figure in Church life only heightened attention to the failures of many priests. Indeed, priests were often appointed by local counts and dukes, who built churches on their land as acts of religious devotion. The priests they appointed were frequently simple peasants subject to ducal authority, and they were generally unqualified for the priestly office. They were ignorant of the scriptures and the rites of the mass; they were also usually married, and often acquired a particular fondness for the sacramental wine used at the eucharistic rite. Their failure to live up to the newly emerging standards of priestly behavior only highlighted the religious values of chastity and poverty.

It should not be surprising that devout Christians at the time, dissatisfied with the failures of the local clergy but inspired by the ideals of apostolic purity and simplicity, and in the face of broader social transformations, sought an alternative religious life. The conditions they faced led to the outbreak of heresy in a number of places in western Europe during the closing years of the tenth century and the opening decades of the eleventh. In the generations

to come, the number of heretics and centers of heresy would increase expo-
nentially. But that should in no way diminish these relatively few episodes
of heresy around the turn of the millennium, especially since there had been
almost no outbreaks over the previous five centuries. Nor should this number
of episodes, which is smaller than the figures for the twelfth century, mini-
mize the seriousness of the matter for eleventh-century churchmen. In fact,
the response of the Church leaders was dramatic: it included the first offi-
cially sanctioned execution for heresy since antiquity. Indeed, according to
one account written in the mid-eleventh century, heretics who appeared across
Italy and Sardinia were hunted down and killed by the Catholics, and another
account records that the local populace gave them a choice between forsaking
heresy and being killed.

The harsh response from Church and state leaders, and even from the
average layperson, to the appearance of heresy was the result of their belief that
this was a widespread movement, inspired by the devil to destroy the Church.
The breadth of the movement is open to much modern debate, but at the close
of the tenth and opening of the eleventh century heretics emerged at various
points of western Europe, and at times their connections to other epicenters
of heresy were clear. The earliest of such outbreaks, which took place in 970,
is that of Vilgard of Ravenna, who was overly devoted to the great Roman
poet Virgil and other classical writers and taught many things contrary to the
faith, according to one contemporary author. It was said that many others in
Italy, Sardinia, and Spain were infected by his heresy and were exterminated by
orthodox Christians. Vilgard was followed by the peasant Leutard of Vertus, in
northeastern France, who spoke out against the Church in the year 1000. After
a swarm of bees had entered his body and instructed him on various matters,
Leutard returned home, put away his wife, and then destroyed the crucifix
at the local church and urged the people not to pay the church tithe. He was
denounced by the local bishop, and, overwhelmed by the learning and authority
of the bishop, he committed suicide by throwing himself into a well (an anti-
social act which parallels the false accusations against Jews of poisoning wells
later in the Middle Ages).

As Ademar of Chabannes noted, heretics who denied the teachings of the
Church appeared in Aquitaine in 1018, and most likely continued to operate
in that area throughout the 1020s, and possibly into the 1030s. The powerful

bishop of Arras-Cambrai in northern France, Gérard, discovered such a sect in his diocese in 1025 – a sect which, among other things, denied baptism and legitimate marriage and accepted only the books of the New Testament. The heretics of Arras returned to the fold upon receiving the benefit of an extremely long sermon by Gérard, in which he denounced their errors and defended the orthodox faith. They may well have been persuaded to re-convert also as a result of their three-day prison stay, in which they were quite possibly tortured, combined with the stately magnificence in which the bishop gave his sermon. Whatever the reason, the heretics signed a confession of the faith with a simple X, accepting the teachings of Gérard.

The episode at Arras is important, among other things, because it revealed connections between heretics in northern Europe and elsewhere. Gérard himself wrote a letter chastising a fellow bishop in Chalons for allowing heresy to fester, and the group Gérard discovered claimed to be followers of a certain Gundolfo, a missionary heretic from Italy. In some ways the likelihood that heresy percolated from Italy is confirmed by the discovery of heresy in Monforte, near Turin, in 1028 and by the increasing number of trade contacts between northern and southern Europe. Heresy also appeared at Périgord in the 1020s, at Toulouse in 1022, and at Goslar in Germany in 1051. At Monforte the heretics were killed in a popular rising and at Goslar, having identified themselves by refusing to kill a chicken, they were hanged at the order of Emperor Henry III (ruled 1039–56). The emergence of heresy was clearly seen as a serious threat by the orthodox Church and its supporters.

The number of outbreaks of such episodes and the degree to which the various sects rejected the teachings of the Church indicate the extent of people's dissatisfaction with the state of the Church in western Europe; on the other hand, the attention paid to these heretics throughout western Europe reveals that Church leaders of the time regarded heresy with utmost seriousness.

In 1022 a sect of heretics was discovered at Orléans, which sent a tremor through the ecclesiastical establishment. The group itself, according to a contemporary account, may have been in existence for several years before it was exposed. This outbreak of heresy, which involved, according to the various chroniclers of the event, from ten to fourteen of the most pious and holy men and women of the region, was such a profound shock to 'orthodox' Christians that the authorities condemned its leaders, Stephen and Lisois, and their followers to death. Unlike most of the other occurrences of religious dissent in the first half of the eleventh century, which had only one commentator or at most two, the heresy of Stephen and Lisois at Orléans was recorded by no fewer than five independent contemporary and near-contemporary witnesses. The heresy at Orléans attracted the attention of contemporaries for several reasons, including the high rank and status of its members and their tragic end at the stake. Moreover, Stephen and Lisois taught doctrines which, as some modern commentators have suggested, echoed the teachings of Bogomil, and one con-temporary described them as Manichaeans, suggesting that they were dualist Christians like the Bogomils. These heretical leaders also advocated many of the important themes that would characterize the popular heresies of the future, but at the same time their group comprised a clerical elite which in some ways foreshadowed the academic heresies of the later Middle Ages. Their heresy also involved the highest level of ecclesiastical politics, and their condemnation for erroneous belief was, in part, the result of their being on the losing side in this struggle. In this way Stephen and Lisois anticipated later religious innovators who found themselves on the wrong side in matters of ecclesiastical politics and organization and, like Valdès and John Wyclif, were declared heretics.

The heresy, according to Ademar, emerged as the result of the preaching of a rustic from Périgord, who carried with him a powder made from the ashes of children; anyone who ingested this powder was irrevocably turned into a Manichaean, rejected Jesus Christ, and 'practiced abominations and crimes of which it is shameful even to speak.' [6] Ademar's accusation foreshadows those brought against 'witches' in the early modern period. These were supposed to perform black masses and to worship the devil; but the partaking of the powder is clearly an inversion of the rite of the Eucharist, and it is similar to the alleged rituals of those 'witches.' Ademar not only accused the sect of indulging in the perversion of the eucharistic rite; he also claimed that they adored the devil in the form of an Ethiopian, or angel of light.

Although Ademar posited a diabolical origin for the sect at Orléans, the heresy originated in a circle of elite clerics, who had connections to powerful Church leaders and were in touch with some of the most important cultural trends of the day. The heretics at Orléans were men and women in the religious orders, esteemed for the piety of their lives, and they were led by the canons Stephen and Lisois. These two were especially well connected at the highest levels of religious and political society, even to the extent that they ministered spiritually to the queen of France. Despite the apparent respectability of the group and its leaders, the heretics raised enough suspicion to make themselves 'infiltrated' by the knight Arefast. It was this knight who exposed the group and helped to bring about their fiery demise.

The tale of Arefast and Stephen and Lisois was told by Paul of St. Pere de Chartres, a monk of the community who celebrated the memory of the former knight and benefactor of his monastery. This account was recorded some sixty years after the event but is regarded as reliable by many, who believe it was based on an oral history handed down over the years, possibly from Arefast himself.[7] According to Paul, the heresy was discovered by Arefast, a vassal of Duke Richard II of Normandy (ruled 996–1026/27), after his own chaplain, Heribert, returned from Orléans having been instructed by Stephen and Lisois and converted to their beliefs. Upon learning of the heresy, Arefast turned to his lord, Richard, and informed him of the group at Orléans. The duke, in turn, reported the matter to the king of France, Robert the Pious (c.970–1031), who ordered Arefast to go to Orléans, so that the error would be driven from the kingdom. Accepting this command from the king, Arefast first traveled to Chartres, where he hoped to get advice from the famed Bishop Fulbert (c.960–1028); but Fulbert had gone to Rome to pray. In place of Fulbert, Arefast found assistance from one of the clerics of Chartres, Everard, and was advised to prepare himself to do battle against the heretics by going to mass every morning, praying, and taking the Eucharist. Everard also told Arefast to protect himself with the sign of the cross; thus fortified he should go to the heretics, assume the role of a willing disciple, and learn all he could about their teachings.

Prepared in this way, Arefast approached the group led by Stephen and Lisois on the pretense that he wished to learn things from them about the faith. At first he was taught stories from the holy scriptures, and, when he seemed to submit to their teachings, he was told that he would be introduced to the higher teachings of the sect. They said that they would treat him like

a tree of the forest, which, when transplanted into a garden, is amply supplied with water until it is well rooted in the soil. It is then pruned of thorns and superfluous branches so that, after it is cut off near the ground with a hoe, it may be grafted with better cutting, which later will bear sweet fruit.

So you, in like manner, being transferred from the evil world into our holy companionship, will be well supplied with the water of wisdom until you are instructed and are strong enough to be shorn of thorns of evil by the sword of the Word of God, and when we have driven absurd teachings from the shelter of your heart, you can receive with purity of mind our teaching bestowed by the Holy Spirit.[8]

The heretics thus promised to bring Arefast gradually to the truth as they understood it, and to reveal the wisdom of the Holy Spirit to him. Revelation was central to the sect of Stephen and Lisois. Their followers were to receive a special gnosis: truth granted by the Holy Spirit itself. In other words, the heretics offered Arefast a special connection with God, and also the true understanding of God's word instead of the errors and rituals of the official Church.

Having been introduced to the basic elements of their belief, Arefast was taken further and led to higher teachings. The new faith rejected many basic doctrines of the 'orthodox' Church, several of which had also been repudiated by the Bogomils. The heretics of Orléans proposed a Docetist Christology. Christ, they told Arefast, was not born of the Virgin Mary; he did not suffer and die on the cross and did not rise from the dead in the flesh. Baptism did not cleanse the soul of sin and the sacrament of the Eucharist was worthless. Stephen and Lisois rejected the martyrs and confessors and denied the validity of all the teachings of the Church.

This denial prompted Arefast to ask how anyone could obtain salvation. The heretics responded that his eyes had been opened to the true faith by their instruction, and he would be granted further insights by the imposition of the hands. This rite would fill him with the Holy Spirit, who would teach him 'the profundity of divine excellence of all the Scriptures.'[9] Once this had happened, he would receive heavenly visions and be at one with God. The practice of the laying on of the hands, it should be noted, was reminiscent of the Bogomils' initiation and foreshadowed a similar ritual performed by the Cathars in the twelfth century. This was a rite in which the perfect literally placed his hands on the initiate, by way of conferring the powers of the Holy Spirit on to him. But it also recalled a rite of the Apostles, who were identified as the source and inspiration of all Christian belief and practice, be it orthodox or heterodox, throughout the Middle Ages.

Imposition of the hands and the secret initiation were at the center of the teachings of Stephen and Lisois, and Paul describes yet another new element in the process of initiation. The group would come together at night in a designated place, each member carrying a candle and chanting the names of demons. Upon the arrival of a demon, they would extinguish the candles, and each of them would grab the nearest woman and lie with her, even if she were a relative or a nun. Children born of these illicit unions would be burned, and the ashes were saved and venerated by the members of the sect. Anyone who ingested such ashes would become a permanent member.[10] Although it is most unlikely that the heretics indulged in the rites described by Paul (especially when it is recalled that the pagan Romans made the same allegations about the early Christians), the author of the account felt it necessary to include an incrimination of this kind, just as Ademar had done in regard to the same heretics, and just as the inquisitors and the chroniclers of later heresy would demonize the heretics they faced. In this way he managed to demonstrate the evil nature of the heretics led by Stephen and Lisois and to show that their true father was the devil. Their 'secret' sinful ways were thereby made to appear in sharper contrast to their apparent religious piety and chaste lifestyle – merely a front designed to capture simple souls and enroll them to serve the devil.

Despite the unlikelihood of the existence of such peculiar nocturnal rites, the heretics at Orléans clearly revealed a unique understanding of the faith, which ran counter to much of the orthodox teaching. Arefast had uncovered their false doctrine as he intended, and only awaited the opportune moment to expose them for the heretics they were. This opportunity arose at Christmas in 1022, when King Robert and Queen Constance arrived in Orléans, at Arefast's request, with several leading bishops, to join in uncovering the heresy. Upon their arrival, Arefast had arranged matters so that he and the heretics would be brought before the royal couple and the bishops in their attendance. Dragged before the council in chains, Arefast revealed his true identity and explained his secret mission to those in assembly. He then described his experience with the heretics and revealed their doctrines, including their Docetist Christology, repudiation of the Church's teachings, and denial of the sacraments.

Demurring at first, Stephen and Lisois eventually stepped forward as leaders of the group, to confirm that Arefast had explained their teachings correctly.

Their announcement, no doubt, shocked the royal couple and the bishops, since Lisois was a canon of the cathedral of the Holy Cross of Orléans, deeply loved by the king, and Stephen another respected canon, confessor to the queen herself. Their learning and piety, which may have tapped into the monastic spirituality that was becoming popular at the time, surely contributed to their heterodox understanding of the faith, and their status allowed them to develop their teachings without fear of persecution by other clerics.

Stephen and Lisois were further interrogated by the bishops in attendance. Having admitted that they did, in fact, teach the doctrines that Arefast attributed to them, they discussed their beliefs under further questioning from the royal couple's bishops. In this way, along with the more spiritual or Gnostic teachings they had already revealed to Arefast, they provided what some have considered to be a rationalist approach to the faith. When asked about the virgin birth, death, and resurrection of Christ, they declared: 'We were not there and we cannot believe that to be true.'[11] Although not providing an explanation for the Docetist Christology imparted to Arefast, Stephen and Lisois offered a defense of their rejection of official Church teachings and declared that they would not accept matters of faith on the authority of the Church, preferring their own inspired interpretation. When asked why they did not believe that Jesus Christ was born of the Virgin Mary by the power of the Holy Spirit, they responded: 'What nature denies is always out of harmony with the Creator.' In this way Stephen and Lisois asserted their unorthodox approach to matters of faith and provided a more rationalistic and individualistic approach to the scriptures and religious belief in general.

The most dramatic moment of the interrogation came when the two were asked whether they believed that God the Father created everything through the Son. Their reply provides great insight into the nature not only of the teachings of Stephen and Lisois, but also of heresy in the early eleventh century in general:

> You may spin stories in that way to those who have earthly wisdom and believe the fictions of carnal men, scribbled on animal skins. To us, however, who have the law written upon our heart by the Holy Spirit (and we recognize nothing but what we have learned from God, Creator of all), in vain you spin your superfluities and things inconsistent with the Divinity.[12]

This pronouncement made before a royal and episcopal gathering — a pronouncement which may have led one contemporary chronicler to suggest that the heretics believed in the eternity of the universe — confirmed the illuminationist or Gnostic nature of the sect, which Paul had revealed earlier in his account. Stephen and Lisois defiantly rejected the traditional teachings of the Church and its understanding of scripture. Although scorning the 'fictions … scribbled on animal skins,' they most likely did not repudiate the Bible itself, but rather what they saw as the flawed understanding of it by the official Church. Theirs was a more spiritual or mystical reading of the scripture; it was, as the Austrian historian Heinrich Fichtenau explained, a Pentecostal reading, which placed emphasis on the action of the Holy Spirit.[13] The true understanding of the faith came to those who received it from the Holy Spirit through the imposition of the hands, and not from the teachings or materialistic sacraments of the Church. Stephen and Lisois stood at the head of a spiritual elite which, they believed, had established a special connection with God.

Having revealed themselves and their beliefs fully to the council, Stephen and Lisois insisted that the meeting be brought to an end. They called on the king and bishops to do with them as they wished, declaring: 'For we shall see our King, reigning in heaven, Who will raise us in heavenly joys to everlasting triumphs at His right hand.'[14] Openly expressing their unorthodox teachings, Stephen and Lisois and their followers were recognized as heretics and were condemned by the king and his council. They were then clothed in the dress of their orders and deposed from their clerical offices. They were driven out of the assembly hall, care having been taken to ensure that the enraged multitude would not harm them, and Queen Constance struck out the eye of Stephen, her former confessor, with her staff, to display her displeasure and to disassociate herself from him. The entire group, with the exception of one cleric and one nun, who recanted their errors, were burned at the stake: this was the first recorded execution for heresy since ancient times. According to Ademar, the heretics 'showed no fear of the fire, predicted that they would emerge unscathed from the flames, and laughed as they were bound to the pyre.'[15] To complete the destruction of the sect at Orléans, the body of the cantor Theodatus, who had died three years earlier, was exhumed and left exposed. Although he appeared to be most pious during his lifetime, it was discovered that he, too, had been a heretic and should have been punished for his religious dissent.

Despite the very real and deeply religious convictions of Stephen and Lisois, the violent suppression of the heresy at Orléans by the king and queen of France has led R. H. Bautier to argue that religion had very little to do with the affair.[16] Stephen and Lisois appear to him not so much as the leaders of a new and dangerous religious sect but as the losers in a battle over ecclesiastical and royal politics which involved the royal couple and various nobles and bishops in northern France. It was this political struggle that formed the backdrop to the events involving Stephen and Lisois in 1022.

The city of Orléans itself was a great intellectual center and the focus of a power struggle between the king and the count of Blois, Eudes II. Competition for control over Orléans involved an appointment to the office of bishop, and candidates on the side of both Count Eudes and King Robert stood to ascend to the episcopal throne. Robert asserted his authority in order to make the appointment; this act was met by opposition from Fulbert of Chartres, who refused to consecrate Robert's candidate, Thierry. In 1022, Thierry was forced from office and eventually went to Rome. The council was held and the heresy, which had developed under Thierry's watch, was revealed in Thierry's absence, after Arefast had turned for help to Duke Richard and Fulbert, allies of Count Eudes and of his episcopal candidate. The leaders of the heresy, Stephen and Lisois, were closely associated with the king and queen and, indirectly, to the king's now departed candidate to the bishopric. And it was this close connection with the perpetrators of heresy that undermined the king's authority in Orléans. His condemnation of Stephen, Lisois, and their followers may well have resulted from the determination to emphasize his own religious orthodoxy and rightful claim to the throne. Bautier's analysis is a useful reminder of the importance of ecclesiastical politics in the history of heresy – that is, in deciding what counts as such. In the future, many, including members of the Franciscan order and Jan Hus, would be declared heretics for reasons that had to do with ecclesiastical politics as much as they had to do with genuine issues of belief.

Yet, even if Stephen and Lisois were indeed victims of power politics, their denunciation as heretics would have carried little weight, had there not been a real fear of religious dissent in the early eleventh century and had they themselves not held suspect beliefs. Their refusal to accept correction at the council of Orléans clearly put them outside the bounds of the faithful and marked them as heretics, just as the refusal to accept Church authority would mark later religious leaders as heretical. As Arefast revealed in his dramatic speech before the king and queen, Stephen and Lisois led a group that rejected Church doctrine on nearly every topic and, in many ways, foreshadowed the teachings of twelfth-century heretics. Their devotion to the scriptures in the way they understood them, as well as their Docetism, heralded the beliefs of Valdes on the one hand, of the Cathars on the other. Often described as an elitist sect, Stephen and Lisois surely accepted the call to spread their beliefs as all Christians should. Their acceptance of Arefast, and of Heribert before him, as disciples demonstrates the missionary zeal of the group, which had already begun to spread its beliefs from a clerical elite to the laity by the time of its destruction at royal order.

Despite being condemned as heretics by King Robert and the bishops, Stephen and Lisois and their followers very clearly represented an important development of the Church in the early eleventh century. Their understanding of the scriptures may have cast them beyond the pale of what was considered 'orthodox' at the time, but the importance they placed on the written word, and on the text itself, reflects the growing importance of literacy.[17] Indeed, the written word had begun to acquire a more exalted position in society as medieval civilization began to evolve away from a more strictly oral culture, and religious leaders, both orthodox and heterodox, adopted a new approach to the text of the scriptures. Even though many people were still unable to read Latin, they placed greater emphasis on the written word, and many were attracted to charismatic interpreters of it, like Stephen and Lisois. The group of those who could interpret scripture (or some other text) and the group of those who could not read Latin have been identified as 'textual communities' by the historian Brian Stock.[18] These 'communities' were bound together by a shared understanding of the text as interpreted by someone like Stephen and Lisois, or the Italian heresiarch Gundolfo in Arras, or orthodox figures such as Bernard of Clairvaux or Julian of Norwich. The gradual introduction of Arefast to the teachings of the group at Orléans and the unique interpretation of the scriptures adopted by this group provide insight into the ways such textual communities developed and functioned. The central role of the text is demonstrated not only by the evangelization of Arefast, but also by the declaration of Stephen and Lisois, before the king and his bishops, that the Holy Spirit had written the law on their hearts. Rejecting the Church's understanding of the scriptures, they believed they had received illumination from the Holy Spirit itself; that illumination allowed them to discover the true meaning of the scriptures, which subsequently they taught to the textual community that formed around them.

Brought to a fiery end, Stephen and Lisois nonetheless made an important mark on the history of medieval heresy; theirs was perhaps the most dramatic expression of religious dissent in the early eleventh century. Although distinct through their spiritual elitism, the teachings and organization of the sect reflected the religious and cultural developments of their times and contained the elements of many later heresies. Docetism and the practice of the imposition of the hands reflected beliefs and practices both of earlier and of later heretics. The intermingling of ecclesiastical politics and religious beliefs also prefigured later developments, and the emphasis on personal religious choice was echoed by religious dissidents from the twelfth century to the sixteenth.

The importance of Stephen and Lisois's sect lies not so much in its immediate impact, which was admittedly limited, but in its manifestation of religious beliefs and practices that would gradually be adopted, at least in part, by the mainstream Church. In the generations that followed, 'orthodox' reformers would adopt some of the tenets of Stephen and Lisois and of other heretics from the early eleventh century and incorporate them into the mainstream teachings of the Church. And the failure to implement these reforms, or the conviction that the established Church did not go far enough in reforming itself, set the stage for the next great wave of heresy. This would emerge in the early twelfth century, to make a more dramatic and more lasting impact on medieval religion and society.

CHAPTER THREE

HENRY THE MONK AND
THE EARLIER TWELFTH CENTURY

*t*he next great heresiarch is Henry the Monk, who not only inherited the mantle of earlier heretics but also adopted a more radical
program of religious reform than that of the Gregorians. Also
known as Henry of Lausanne or Henry of Le Mans, Henry had a profound
impact on his time and was perhaps the most important of the leaders of
heresy before the rise of the Cathars and the Waldensians at the end of the
century.

When heresy had appeared around the turn of the first millennium, it
elicited a dramatic response from the Church, as the tragic fate of the community at Orléans indicates. And it was not only the heretics at Orléans who
faced the sword of persecution, but also those in Italy and those at Goslar
where, as mentioned, in 1051 a number of heretics were executed. The views
of these people – as we have seen in the case of Stephen and Lisois – offered
a profound rejection of the teachings of the Church and introduced an alternative program of Christian belief and practice. Although the origins and
extent of heresy at this time remain disputed, it is quite clear that its emergence after the year 1000 was a great blow to Church leaders. The appearance of heresy also revealed the increasing Christianization of the people of
the Middle Ages and the seriousness with which they approached their faith.
Heretical leaders like Stephen and Lisois provided for many a truer Christian

faith, which rejected the inadequacies and excesses of contemporary belief and practice.

Even though the emergence of heresy marked a dramatic moment in the life of the Church and heretical leaders captured the attention and support of many among the laity throughout western Europe, heresy itself left the stage quietly by the middle of the eleventh century. While episodes had broken out repeatedly during its first decades, they ceased just as suddenly after the execution of the heretics at Goslar. Explanations for this abrupt disappearance vary. It could be that the foreign missionaries who, according to some scholars, were instrumental in the emergence of heresy, had ended their evangelical work in western Europe. Or the heretics may simply have gone underground for their own safety, as the Waldensians would in later times. Indeed, the very suppression of heresy by the Church, with its powerful allies among kings and nobles, may have put an end to the movement before it could blossom and last. At the same time, the institutional Church may have absorbed that movement by adopting many reforms the heretics had proposed – especially their focus on apostolic life and their emphasis on ritual and sexual purity.

Church leaders may not have consciously adopted the program of the heretics, but many ideas of the latter would be found in the Gregorian Reform movement, which took shape just as heretics reappeared in Latin Christendom. Itself part of a broader movement that stretched back to the tenth century and ultimately transformed much of medieval society – the heresies after the year 1000 could be regarded as the 'far left wing' of the broader reform movement – Gregorian Reform was an effort to restructure the religious life and the ecclesiastical organization of Christian Europe; it is most clearly identified with its most vigorous advocate, Pope Gregory VII (1073–85). Reformist ideas were first adopted by Pope Leo IX (1048–54) and promoted by each of his successors into the early twelfth century. The popes not only emphasized the necessity for improved moral and ethical behavior on the part of the clergy, they also redefined the nature of moral behavior, especially in regard to the matter of simony (the buying and selling of Church offices). The long tradition of exchanging money or gifts and swearing oaths of loyalty to secular overlords who often appointed the clergy to their positions came to a close as a result of the efforts of the Gregorians. Although this would create great difficulties between the clergy and the rulers of Europe, the new definition of simony would remain in place throughout the Middle Ages. Moreover, the Church hierarchy was reorganized so that the ultimate authority belonged to the pope, who claimed it as successor to the Apostle Peter, the first bishop of Rome; all the bishops, priests, abbots, and monks, together with all the Christians, were henceforth subordinate to the authority of the pope as the leader of Christendom.

The Gregorians' reforms also focused on the personal morality of the clergy. Clearly borrowing from the reforms of the early eleventh century and from the ideals of the heretics, the papal reformers stressed apostolic poverty for all the clergy. Indeed, one of the leading reformers, Peter Damian (c.1007–1072), embodied the ideals of apostolic poverty and was, in some ways, a forerunner of the wandering saints of the twelfth century. Of equal importance for moral reform was the emphasis on sexual purity, which was a means to distinguish the clergy from the laity and, especially, to establish a ritually pure clerical class.[1] Although rules existed against clerical marriage since antiquity, clergy of all ranks continued to marry and to sire. As late as the tenth century, there were examples of bishops fathering children, and lower-level priests appointed to the local church, themselves often simple peasants, had wives well into the eleventh century. One of the central goals of the Gregorians was to abolish this practice. Clerics could no longer marry or take mistresses; they were to live a life of celibacy and sexual purity. They would thus be able to approach the altar in a ritually clean state, the altar, that is, wherefrom they would preach and offer the sacrament of the Eucharist – the body and blood of Jesus Christ. Indeed, the awesome responsibility of handling the body of the Lord was an important justification for making clerical celibacy mandatory. The moral character of the priest at the altar became an important concern for the Gregorian reformers, as it had been for the reformers and heretics of the early eleventh century. Some of the advocates of papal reform even went so far as to declare that, if the priest was in a state of moral impurity, the sacraments he performed were not valid. This extreme position, which recalled the teachings of the Donatist heretics of late antiquity, was never adopted; but the movement as a whole focused on clerical morality and demanded improvement in the lives of all priests. The new code of purity, along with the new definition of simony, was confirmed by papal decree and by the decisions of the First Lateran Council in 1123.

Despite the profound and lasting impact of the Gregorian Reform on the history of Church and society in western Europe, its immediate effect in the early twelfth century was, at best, mixed, because of its successes and failures. The movement altered the internal structure of the Church and dramatically reshaped its relationship with secular power, but there were those who felt that reform failed to go far enough in purifying the Church and correcting the morals of its priests. The reform's focus on sacraments and clergy raised questions about the role of both in religious belief and practice, and the failure of clerics throughout Europe to adhere to the new regulations reinforced criticism of the Church. Among the critics were saintly figures like Robert of Arbrissel (c.1047–1116) whose personal example of piety and outspoken critiques of Church practices were equaled only by those of a new wave of heretics who challenged the teachings and authority of the established Church.

The new century opened in fact with numerous reports of religious dissent, heralding the beginning of an almost continuous stream of heresy, which lasted until the end of the Middle Ages. The earliest account, in the first decades, is that of Guibert of Nogent, who reported an outbreak in Soissons in which some have recognized evidence of Bogomil influence.[2] Not long after the appearance of that heresy, Tanchelm preached in Antwerp, denouncing the clergy and rejecting the sacraments. He married a statue of the Virgin Mary and his followers are reported to have venerated him as God; they are even said to have drunk his bathwater, just before his death at the hands of a priest in 1115. Toward the middle of the century, Eon d'Etoile preached heresy in Brittany, claiming that he was the Son of God, and attracted a number of followers from the peasantry before being imprisoned by the bishop. More representative of the heretics of the period, however, is Peter of Bruis in Provence, whose career lasted for some twenty years; he, too, has been seen as influenced by the Bogomils. He rejected baptism, church buildings, crucifixes, the Eucharist, and various good works. His protest was violent and his death, in 1139 or 1140, occurred when his enemies pushed him into a bonfire of crucifixes he had started.

Even within their brief periods of activity, the heretics of the first half of the twelfth century demonstrated significant dissatisfaction with the Church of the time. These heretics also reveal the influence that charismatic individuals such as these wandering preachers had on their contemporaries. Peter of Bruis in particular is noteworthy for his spell over those around him, and has been recognized as the ally and perhaps teacher of Henry the Monk. At the very least, in the words of the great abbot of Cluny, Peter the Venerable (c.1092–1156), Henry was the heir of Peter's wickedness. And it was Henry, more than Peter, who was seen as the great threat to the Church and attracted the attention of the greatest religious figure of the age, Bernard of Clairvaux (1090–1153).[3]

Henry's career, the longest among medieval heretics, can be broken down into three phases. The first started around 1116, when he first appeared as preacher of penitence and reform in the town of Le Mans and in the course of that year challenged the established social and religious order. The second phase started in 1135, when he reappeared in southern France, in the diocese of Arles, after an absence of some twenty years. Preaching heretical doctrines again, Henry was brought before the Council of Pisa in 1135; probably not long before that, he had engaged in debate with a monk named William, who left the most detailed record of Henry's teaching. The final phase began in 1139 and lasted until Henry's capture in 1145, when he was pursued by Bernard of Clairvaux. By that time he had spread his teachings in Languedoc, a region that would later become one of the great centers of heresy.

Henry first preached in the town of Le Mans, possibly having come from Lausanne in modern Switzerland; the probability is high that he was born in France or a French-speaking territory of the Empire. Little else is known of his origins or background, and there is much uncertainty about his status in life. He may have been a priest; most likely he became a monk in the mid-1130s or earlier, to judge by the comments of his rivals. Bernard of Clairvaux, the great Cistercian abbot, declared that Henry was learned and literate, but he may have acquired what learning he had later in life. Whatever his exact social status, Henry was a force to be reckoned with. He was one of many wandering preachers, who, like Robert of Arbrissel, marched 'barefoot through the crowds, having cast off the habit of a regular (e.g. a monk), his flesh covered by a hair shirt, wearing a thin and torn cloak, bare-legged, beard tangled ... only a club was missing from the outfit of a lunatic.'[4] Like Robert, Henry was a charismatic figure and a wandering holy man possessed of great rhetorical skills. Indeed, even Henry's rivals remarked on his apparent holiness, which was allegedly a false front, and on his preaching ability, of which one contemporary noted that by 'his speech even a heart of stone could be moved to repentance.'[5]

It was his appearance and reputation as a reform-minded and inspirational preacher that recommended Henry to Hildebert of Lavardin, bishop of Le Mans

(1109–25) and later archbishop of Tours (1125–33), when the future heretic first appeared in his diocese in 1116. Hildebert himself was a most pious shepherd of his flock and a devoted advocate of the ideals of the Gregorian Reform movement, as well as the founder of a number of new religious houses and patron of Robert of Arbrissel. The bishop was also one of the early medieval humanists and a talented poet, and thus represented the best of twelfth-century religious and intellectual life. At the time of Henry's arrival, Bishop Hildebert was preparing to make a trip to Rome and expected little more than penitential preaching from Henry, whom he welcomed with courtesy and friendliness. Before departing for Rome, Hildebert instructed the clergy to allow Henry free entry into the city and granted him the license to preach.

According to the chronicler of Le Mans, the good intentions of the bishop were betrayed by 'the deceits of a Trojan horse,' because Henry hid 'the madness of a ravening wolf under sheep's clothing.'[6] Indeed, the chronicler depicts Henry as a false prophet and a 'pseudohermit.' He notes that Henry appeared 'hair cropped, beard untrimmed, tall of stature, quick of pace … barefoot as the winter raged; easy of address, awe-inspiring voice, young in years, scornful of ornate dress.' Henry had a reputation for holiness and wisdom according to the chronicler, and seemed to set an example for all by his pious and celibate lifestyle. He seemed like one of the prophets and was able to 'declare the sins of mortal men which they hid from others.'[7] But all this was a clever ruse perpetrated by the wandering preacher, of whom the chronicler asserts that he enjoyed the pleasures of women and adolescent boys: they attended him and 'caressed his feet, his buttocks, his groin, with tender hands.'[8] But the very same allegations were made even against orthodox wandering preachers, and, where heretics are concerned, they were among the most commonplace accusations throughout the Middle Ages.

For all these allegations, it is most likely that Henry patterned his life after Jesus and the Apostles, if his entry into Le Mans and his pious behavior, which even the chronicler was forced to recognize, are anything to go by. Arriving on Ash Wednesday, Henry, just as Jesus had done on his entry to Jerusalem, sent two disciples ahead of him, to meet the bishop. Henry's followers appeared as penitents; each one bore a staff upon which a cross was fastened. Coming after them, and in the wake of the bishop's departure for Rome, Henry began preaching and attracted large and enthusiastic crowds. He spoke out against the abuses and excesses of the clergy, especially the more privileged and wealthy. His sermons were welcomed by the people of Le Mans, who had, at best, uneasy relations with the higher clergy of the town. Even some members of the clergy, mainly those in lower orders or those without land and wealth, supported Henry and looked up to him, as if he were an oracle. Although the chronicler of Le Mans left no account of Henry's exact preaching, it is clear that he spread a harshly anticlerical message, which provoked the people of Le Mans to violence against the ministers of the Church. At the very least, Henry most probably denounced their corruption; he may also have attacked the sacraments and the increasingly elaborate buildings of the Church. His sermons, which sounded as if 'a legion of demons were all making their noise in one blast through his mouth,'[9] exposed the hypocrisy of the clergy of Le Mans. His own example of moral purity and apostolic piety stood as an example which put the churchmen to shame. Henry's assault on the failings of Church and clergy alike was no doubt rooted in his own understanding of the Gospels and of the life of Jesus.

Despite the message of peace that Jesus himself taught, Henry's own preaching led to attacks on the clergy: they would surely have been killed or seriously harmed, had not the local count protected them from violence. In turn, some of the clergy sought to debate with Henry. Led by William Drink-No-Water – a name suggestive of less than ideal behavior – the clergy tried to approach Henry, but they were assaulted and pushed down into the mud and filth of the streets. Escaping with their lives thanks to the count, members of the clergy then wrote a letter to Henry, calling on him to stop his preaching. The letter, which was read out to Henry upon his refusal to accept it, declared that he had been welcomed to the city in a spirit of brotherly love, in the hope that he would spread the word of God. But instead of peace, the letter continued, Henry sowed discord, called the clergy heretics, and preached false words that denied the truth of the Catholic faith. Listening to the message, Henry shook his head and responded to each sentence by saying: 'You lie.'[10]

Rather than obey the demands of the clergy of Le Mans, Henry continued to preach and instituted his most dramatic reform so far. He proclaimed, as the chronicler noted, that 'women who had lived unchastely should, all unclothed, burn their garments, together with their hair, in the sight of everyone; that no one in the future should receive gold or silver, property, or betrothal gifts with his wife, nor should she bring him a dowry, but the naked should marry the nude, the ailing the sick, the pauper the destitute.'[11] As with much else that he said, Henry's teaching on marriage struck a chord and inspired the people of Le Mans to follow his lead. At this point, the chronicler once again denigrates his efforts, asserting that Henry admired the features of the women who appeared before him and collected large sums of gold and silver. Despite these allegations, it remains true that Henry was seeking to improve his followers' lot; at his request, the young men of Le Mans took in marriage those of the city's prostitutes who had given up their trade. Henry, to help the former women of the streets, gave each of them some money to buy new clothes – although not enough to make up for what they had lost, according to the chronicler.

Even if, as the chronicler joyfully points out, Henry's efforts failed, in that many prostitutes returned to their former profession and their husbands found new wives or mistresses, thereby committing adultery, attempts such as his, to rescue fallen women from a life of misery just as Robert of Arbrissel had done, would be deemed later on by Pope Innocent III (1198–1216) to be a most praiseworthy kind of work. Henry's new doctrine, however, was designed not only as pious good work but also as a challenge to new Church teachings on marriage. In many ways carrying on Gregorian ideals of piety and religious life, Henry repudiated the Church's recent encroachment on the rite of marriage; the Church had come to claim the authority to consecrate this bond, and designated marriage as one of its sacraments. The Church had also implemented new rules of consanguinity which could be particularly burdensome, and society as a whole had come to accept the tradition of dowry. In his call for young men to marry prostitutes and to abandon various social conventions, Henry rejected both the claims of the Church and the practice of dowry. For him, marriage was not a sacrament to be controlled by the Church; it was the simple exchange of a promise of love and faithfulness between two willing partners. Marriage was a matter of consent, not the result of priestly consecration.

Henry implemented a program in Le Mans which mixed penitence and moral reform and was rooted in the Gospels, also drawing on some of the ideals of the Gregorian movement. But in spite of his own personal example and rhetorical skill, Henry's dominant place in the city would not last long. Bishop Hildebert would soon return from Rome and confront the preacher he had held in such esteem before going to the papal city. The 'welcome' which greeted the bishop upon his return only increased his desire to confront Henry: the people of the city rejected his blessing, declaring: 'We want no knowledge of your ways! We don't want your blessing! Bless filth! Consecrate filth! We have a father, we have a pontiff, we have an advocate who surpasses your authority; he exceeds you in probity and knowledge.'[12] And they went on to denounce the clergy and to exalt Henry and his preaching in front of the bishop.

Hildebert, the chronicler tells us, bore all this patiently, expecting to debate matters with Henry. His position was strengthened when part of the city burned in a fire, which many of the people of Le Mans interpreted as God's judgment against them for following a heretic. In a public debate, Hildebert rapidly undermined Henry's support by unveiling the ignorance and lack of training of a popular preacher. So the bishop asked Henry by what special right he had come to take up his vocation; but Henry did not know the meaning of the word 'vocation.' He then asked the heretic what office he possessed, to which Henry responded that he was a deacon. The bishop went on to ask if Henry had attended mass, and, when Henry responded that he had not, he proposed that they should sing the morning hymns together. Henry was forced to admit that he did not know the order of the mass. Then, to demonstrate his rival's inadequacy even further, the bishop sang the hymns to the Mother of God. Thus Henry was exposed by the bishop, who consequently banished the heretic from the city of Le Mans. But, although much of his support had disappeared, Henry's pious example, his critique of the clergy, and his repudiation of the new definition of marriage continued to influence the people of Le Mans. He himself would emerge once again to indict the failures of the Church.

Little was heard from Henry for some twenty years to follow, until he was brought before Pope Innocent II (1130–43) and the Council of Pisa (1135); but it is likely that he was not completely inactive during this intervening period. Leaving Le Mans probably with a small band of followers, including two priests, Henry moved south and was found preaching in the towns of Bordeaux and Poitiers. Along the way, the simple anticlericalism he taught at Le Mans developed into a more intense rejection of the Church, its clergy, and its teachings. According to the chronicler of Le Mans, Henry, the 'pseudohermit,' began to spread his poison in nearby regions and 'propounded a perverted dogma which a faithful Christian ought neither recapitulate nor hear.'[13] As a result of his activity in the diocese, Henry attracted the attention of Bernard Guarin, archbishop of Arles from 1129 to 1138, who seized the wandering preacher and brought him to Pisa. Henry was condemned as a heretic at the Council, where he most likely met Bernard of Clairvaux and Peter the Venerable, his staunchest opponents, leaders, respectively, of the Cistercian and Cluniac monastic orders and great defenders of the Church against heresy. Overawed by the Council and its dignitaries, Henry abjured all the heretical doctrines he preached and was handed over to Bernard. The abbot of Clairvaux then gave Henry letters of introduction to the Cistercian monastery there, so that he could become a monk at Clairvaux. It is unlikely, however, that Henry ever reached Clairvaux; the chronicler of Le Mans explains that Henry left the province, began to preach heresy again, and made such a great impact that Christians hardly attended mass any longer and refused 'offerings to the priests, first fruits, tithes, visitation of the sick, and the usual reverences.'[14]

The chronicler of Le Mans gives a general sense of the nature of Henry's teachings, but the full extent of his dissent from the established Church became known only with the discovery, in the middle of the twentieth century, of a tract detailing a debate between Henry and a certain Monk William. The debate occurred most probably when Henry was coming to the attention of the arch-bishop of Arles; it is generally thought to have been held between 1133 and 1135. Although the name of the Catholic monk involved is not known with any certainty, he may have been William of Saint-Thierry (1085–1148), compan-ion of Bernard of Clairvaux, and author of numerous works of theology and of polemical writings against the theologians Peter Abelard (1079–1142) and Gilbert de la Porrée (1076–1154). For all the uncertainty of its attribution, the treatise remains an important source for understanding Henry's teachings and the Catholic reaction to this wandering preacher.

The treatise was clearly composed as a warning about the danger Henry posed to the established Church. In his introduction, William addresses an unnamed ecclesiastical dignitary, stating that 'by many arguments and proofs he [Henry] has been shown to be a heretic,' and advises that Henry be kept 'away from the limits of your church.'[15] William's concern to raise the alarm against Henry is reinforced in his account of the debate at a point where he refers to his opponent as a leper and insists that he, William, 'must shout unceasingly that you are a leper, a heretic and unclean, and must live outside the camp, that is to say outside the church.'[16] Along with his warning, William included extensive discussions of the Catholic faith. He felt it necessary not only to present Henry's ideas but also to provide a thorough defense of Catholic doctrine that would further demonstrate the error of Henry's ways. Aware of his anticlericalism and rejection of certain key points concerning the intermediary role of the Church and its ministers, William took great pains to defend both the clergy and the Catholic understanding of the sacraments. It should be noted, however, that at no point does William impute to Henry the rejection of Christian belief on the core matters of the person of Jesus, the godhead, or the Virgin Mary. This distinguishes Henry from Bogomils and Cathars, bringing him closer to reformers like Robert of Arbrissel. No matter how Henry's teachings are to be characterized, William's account of the debate demonstrates what a serious threat Church leaders took Henry to be. It also reveals the maturation of Henry's own ideas.

Henry's dissent was no doubt regarded as being all the more troubling in view of his source of inspiration. William opened discussion with a few questions. To whom does Henry owe obedience? Who commissioned him to preach? What scriptures does he follow? Henry's answers to these questions are indicative of the direction taken by his thought during the years which followed his appearance at Le Mans. He declared, namely, that he obeyed God and not man because all obedience is owed to God; that he was sent by Jesus Christ; and that he honored his scriptural command 'Go, teach ye all nations' (Matthew 28: 19). Furthermore, he indicated that it was Jesus's proclamation 'Thou shalt love thy neighbour as thyself' (Matthew 19: 19) that was a source of inspiration for him. Indeed, in answer to the question about the scriptures, Henry asserted his devotion to the Gospels: 'I accept the Scriptures of the New Testament, by which I verify and corroborate the aforesaid statements.'[17] Despite the vehemence of his repudiation of the Church, he was not willing to reject all tradition out of hand; he recognized the value of the writings of St. Augustine of Hippo and other Church Fathers even though he claimed that their ideas were not essential to salvation. In this way he clearly rooted himself in the evangelical tradition which the Church itself had claimed as its own, and he attempted to usurp the latter's right of interpreting the New Testament and Gospel of Christ. It may be suggested that Henry desired not so much the destruction of the established Church as the restoration of its pristine purity as originally intended.

His understanding of the Gospels, however, led him both to deny certain of the medieval Church's claims to an intermediary role between God and the believer and to reject much of what Church leaders thought to be essential to the faith. At the core of his teachings was a rejection of Catholic doctrine on the sacraments, even though he did not necessarily reject the sacraments themselves. His position on these matters, he claimed, was rooted in the truth of the scriptures; but the sacraments should not be administered without evangelical support. For this reason Henry challenged official doctrine on the sacrament of baptism. He rejected the practice of baptizing children with chrism and oil because, as William informs us, the renegade monk declared that there was no command in the Gospel to do so. Moreover, he appeared to be most skeptical of the practice of infant baptism, and he seemed to challenge Catholic doctrine on the matter of original sin. Quoting scripture again in support of his beliefs, Henry declared: 'It is a wicked thing to condemn a man for another person's sin, in accordance with the text, "The soul that sinneth, the same shall die"' (Ezekiel 18: 20). And again, 'The son shall not bear the iniquity of the father. Everyone shall bear his own burden' (see Ezekiel 18: 20 and Galatians 6: 5).[18] William accuses Henry of falling into the Pelagian heresy; and yet for Henry this is not a matter of following in the footsteps of this or that earlier heretic, but rather of following the scriptures themselves. Infant baptism is not justified in his eyes because the child has not yet reached the age of understanding and cannot freely accept the faith nor be held responsible for any sins that he or she has committed. In fact, according to some versions of the treatise, Henry argued not only that Christian children who died before the age of understanding would attain salvation but also that the children of Jews and Muslims who died before reaching the age of reason would be saved as well. Although somewhat radical in its particulars, especially in regard to Jewish and Muslim children, Henry's teachings on baptism were firmly rooted in the scriptures and reserved the practice of baptism for those able to understand the faith.

Henry's assault on the teachings of the Church concerning the sacraments extended beyond his critique of baptism, to include the rejection of Catholic doctrine on marriage. This developing doctrine had come to define the sacramental nature of marriage. Henry had already demonstrated his opposition to Catholicism on the subject when he preached in Le Mans. In his debate with William he offered further arguments against the Catholic views. For Henry, marriage needs no Church ceremony or religious rite; it does not have to be consecrated by a priest to be valid. Although rejecting the intermediary role of priest and Church, Henry recognized that marriage was a ceremony that bound two people together and stated that the agreement of the persons involved constituted legitimacy. Moreover, drawing from the scriptures, Henry argued that only fornication, or adultery in one version of the text, could dissolve a marriage. Thus Henry accepted the indissolubility of marriage as Jesus and the Church had taught it, but he denied that the Church had any place in establishing its validity.

William and Henry also debated the matter of penance and confession. Henry rejected the Catholic practice of the sacrament. William claimed in turn that it was necessary to have a mediator in order to achieve reconciliation and that, because Christ was a mediator and the priest stood in his place, confession to a priest was necessary. But Henry, drawing again from the Gospels, denied that confession to a priest was required. He argued that there is 'no Gospel command to go to a priest for penance, for the apostle James says, "Confess your sins to one another"' (James 5: 16).[19] Nonetheless, William's reply with an argument about the dangers of offering confession to peasants and to the illiterate suggests that Henry did not reject the practice of confession and penance completely; rather, he sought to return to what he was taking to be the practice of the primitive Church, as revealed in the passage from the letter of James. Indeed, rather than denying the value of confession and penance, Henry intended to restore the practice of the Apostles and to eliminate the intermediary role of the priest.

This elimination of the priest from the sacraments of baptism, marriage, and penance is also to be found in Henry's position on the sacrament of the Eucharist. As with confession, here too Henry maintained that 'Mass may be sung and Christ's body consecrated, provided anyone can be found worthy to do so.'[20] William denounces this position in most vehement terms, implying that Henry's view would make administration of the Eucharist impossible and therefore amounts to a rejection of the sacrament. But this was clearly not Henry's intent. He possessed none of the abhorrence of the material form of the eucharistic elements which the Cathars and other dualist heretics would exhibit, nor was he fundamentally opposed to the institution itself. His knowledge of the Gospels was too good for him to repudiate a practice which Christ himself had instituted – to reject it outright. Indeed, as William conceded, Henry advocated the administration of the sacrament by anyone worthy of doing so. Henry's criticism formed part of his larger critique of the clergy: it was not the sacrament itself, but those who administered it that were the problem. Henry, according to William, argued that the body of Christ 'cannot be consecrated by an unworthy minister.'[21] Although William accuses Henry of resembling the Arians – heretics in the early history of the Church – Henry was more akin to the Donatists, who deemed the sinful priests to be unworthy of the office – a position also advocated by some members of the Gregorian Reform movement. Far from rejecting the Eucharist, Henry intended to eliminate any form of corruption from the administration of the body and blood of Christ.

Writing off the role of the clergy in the sacrament of the Eucharist was part of Henry's broader criticism of priesthood. This constituted one of the centerpieces of his dissent against the Church already at Le Mans, but he seems to have elaborated on it by the time of the meeting with William. Indeed, in an assertion that reinforced his belief that the priesthood could no longer assume its intercessory role, Henry declared that 'Priests of today ... have not the power to bind or loose, for they are stripped of this power by having criminally sinned.'[22] Henry was no doubt disgusted with the behavior of the clergy of his day, which acquired wealth and power and extended the claims of the Church into ever new areas of jurisdiction. Not only did they make more and more exorbitant claims for themselves, but they were often corrupt and unworthy to stand in the place of Christ. Consequently, Henry pressed for the moral reformation of the clergy, intending them to live more truly apostolic lives, as he himself did. Although William does not quote Henry directly, he undertakes an extended defense of the various appurtenances of the bishop's office. It is most likely that Henry opposed the bishop's use of the ring, mitre, and pastoral staff as unnecessary displays of wealth and power, especially since there was no evangelical support for these things. This criticism was probably an extension of Henry's opposition to the growing worldliness and economic wealth of the priesthood. Indeed, Henry struck directly at the heart of the institutional Church as it had developed in the eleventh and twelfth centuries, by declaring that 'bishops and priests ought not to have benefices or wealth.'[23] There was none of this in the Gospels, and surely neither Jesus nor the Apostles pursued such worldly glories; in seeking them, the Church and its representatives had moved away from their call to live like Christ and to serve the poor and the weak. The pursuit of worldly wealth and power was not the proper 'obligation' of the Church and would lead to its corruption.

This rejection of clerical worldliness, which Henry saw as the root of corruption, also contributed to his denial of the need for church buildings. He declared that there was no need to build churches of stone or wood – a stunning assertion at a time when the first stirrings of the Gothic style in church-building were felt and magnificent Romanesque churches were still being built. It must be noted, however, that even Bernard of Clairvaux expressed horror at the grand style in which churches were being built, even though he did not go as far as Henry. Henry's rejection of churches of stone and wood emerged not only from his disdain for the excessive wealth and luxury of the clergy, but also from his reading of the Gospels. Jesus had declared, after all, that he would be among them whenever two or three gathered in his name; he did not stipulate that they had to be in a church or before an altar, but merely that they gathered together, in the purity of their hearts, to honor him. Henry felt it was not necessary to go to a church in order to pray; God would hear his children when they called on him wherever they were. Churches were just another external sign that had little to do with the faith as revealed in the scriptures and ran counter to Henry's understanding of the internalization of matters of faith.

Finally, William revealed one component of Henry's teaching which denied both the value of church-building – often viewed as a pious good work – and the intercessory role of the Church and its clergy. Henry asserted, namely, that 'No good work helps the dead, for as soon as men die they either are utterly damned or are saved.'[24] Henry seemed to be rejecting the doctrine of purgatory that was taking shape in the twelfth century and all the beliefs and practices associated with it. Indeed, William argued that 'certain sins are cancelled out in the next world by the gifts of friends and the prayers of the faithful,'[25] but Henry would have none of that. Contributing to the construction of a church, for Henry, would offer little to save a soul that failed to live according to the Gospels. Offering gifts to monks like William so that they might recite prayers for the living or dead would have little impact on the destiny of their souls. In this way, Henry once again undermined claims of the Church and clergy to act as mediators between God and humans.

In the debate with William, therefore, Henry's teachings, which first took shape during his appearance at Le Mans, emerged in their mature form. The simple and dramatic challenge, enunciated at Le Mans, to the behavior and authority of the clergy and to the Church's understanding of marriage evolved into a more elaborate rejection of the Church and its sacraments. Henry denied much of its traditional intercessory role, refused to accept Catholic teaching on the sacraments, and rejected the authority of the clergy, criticizing their integrity. But his program was not simply a destructive one; for he sought to create a new understanding of the faith, rooted firmly in the Gospels and the teachings of Jesus. He saw much of contemporary Church practice as an unnecessary elaboration of the original intention of its founder and envisioned instead a community of the faithful which was bound together in the faith by mutual confession and by the shared reception of baptism and of the Eucharist. Henry preached a faith which in his view was more fully in line with the Gospels – a faith based on the ideals of apostolic simplicity and individual moral responsibility, in imitation of Jesus and the Apostles.

Thus, by the time of the Council of Pisa in 1135, Henry's thought had achieved its mature form and made a profound impact on those who heard him. Hence his career was not at an end, although he was condemned as a heretic by the Council and confined to a monastery at its order. Once again, Henry would disappear from view only to resurface some years later in the Languedoc – a region to become notorious as a hotbed of heresy in the later twelfth and thirteenth centuries. Matters had become so serious at this point that a special commission was sent to Toulouse; this event foreshadowed a similar legation, involving Diego of Osma and St. Dominic, which would be sent to suppress the Cathars later in the century. This first commission included Henry's abbot, Bernard of Clairvaux, and the papal legate, Alberic of Ostia. It was sent to Languedoc in the summer of 1145, with the intention of finally putting an end to the long career of Henry the Monk.

By the time of Bernard's arrival, Henry had been preaching his fiery denunciations of the Church and its ministers and advocating his own understanding of an evangelical Christianity for some time since his condemnation in 1135. After leaving the Council at Pisa, Henry evidently refused to enter the monastery at Clairvaux and moved south, passing through Cahors and Périgeux before eventually arriving in the important town of Toulouse in the Languedoc, where he would find a receptive audience. His impact on the region was so profound that Abbot Bernard, writing to Count Alphonse of Toulouse to announce his imminent arrival in the Languedoc, declared that 'churches are without congregations, congregations are without priests, priests are without proper reverence, and finally, Christians are without Christ.'[26] Bernard denounces Henry as an apostate and a dog returned to his vomit; he condemns him further for his heretical teachings. Bernard's biographer and secretary, Geoffrey of Auxerre (died after 1188), confirms the abbot's account of Henry's teachings. Henry once again emerged as an opponent of the Church, 'irreverently disparaging the sacraments as well as the ministers of the Church.'[27] And both Bernard and Geoffrey agreed that Henry opposed Catholic baptism, prayers for the dead, pilgrimages, the invocation of the saints, the building of churches. As Geoffrey puts it, 'in a word, all the institutions of the Church were scorned' by Henry.[28]

Despite his apparent support in the region, Henry took flight upon hearing the news of Bernard's arrival. The great abbot was enthusiastically welcomed by the people of Toulouse. Bernard of Clairvaux preached in the areas where Henry's support had been strongest, in order to turn the people of the city back to the Catholic faith, so that heresy would no longer plague the region. Having reduced support for Henry in the Languedoc, Bernard returned to his monastery before his rival was captured, which happened sometime after his departure. Indeed, Henry's support melted away in the face of Bernard's preaching, combined with the effect of the heretic's own decision to flee. According to Geoffrey of Auxerre, even though Henry went into hiding, 'his ways were so obstructed and his paths so hedged that he was hardly safe anywhere afterward.'[29] Henry was finally captured, probably sometime in the autumn of 1145, by the bishop and his men and was placed in the bishop's prison, where he most probably died not long after.

Although Henry died in obscurity and only a lingering residue of his ideas may have survived, his long and dramatic career reveals a strong undercurrent of dissatisfaction with the Church and its representatives. The failures and successes of the Gregorian Reform movement were played out fully in Henry's career, and his indictment of the Church would echo in the coming generations. Even in his own time, Henry's repudiation of the Church resonated with those around him, as the episodes in Le Mans, Arles, and Toulouse indicate. Rejecting the various accretions that the Catholic Church had added to the basic practice of the faith over the centuries and especially in a few previous generations, Henry proposed a more pristine and pure expression of Christian belief and practice. Denying the way the sacraments were defined and administered, rejecting the establishment of marriage as a sacrament, and challenging the intermediary claims of the priesthood, Henry offered a viable Christian alternative to the doctrines of the established Church. In their most developed form, Henry's teachings further rejected the emerging doctrine of purgatory, the cult of the saints, and prayers for the dead. Throughout all of this, Henry remained a preacher of penitence, calling the laity and the clergy to lives of moral purity and condemning severely the corruption and worldliness of the churchmen. Henry's direct influence may not have survived his disappearance from the stage of history for long, but his call to moral reform, his denunciation of the excesses of the Church, and his rejection of central Catholic teaching would be echoed by the end of the century by new heretics responding to new social, cultural, and political conditions.

CHAPTER FOUR

VALDES OF LYONS
AND THE WALDENSES

*a*lthough outbreaks of religious dissent of varying intensity had
plagued the western Church periodically since the year 1000, the
greatest and most sustained heretic movements occurred only in
the second half of the twelfth century. The somewhat individual wandering
heresiarchs of the earlier half gave way to founders of movements which out-
lasted their progenitors. Heresy became a more integral part of the social order
and spread throughout all levels of society, including the peasantry, nobility,
and the newly forming bourgeoisie. The rapid growth of heresy at the end of
the twelfth century elicited an equally dramatic response from the Church. Just
as the earliest heretics of the medieval West suffered persecution and death, so
too did the heretics who emerged after 1150; but these religious dissidents would
face a more organized and violent opposition. Two distinct strains of heresy
took shape in the late twelfth century and somehow endured in the face of this
intense persecution. While one of them, Catharism, would fade away by the
fourteenth century, the other, Waldensianism, would survive the Middle Ages,
remaining a living 'church' to this very day.

The origins of the Waldensian church, unlike those of the Cathar heresy,
can be traced to a specific time and place: they are associated with the conversion of the merchant Valdes of Lyons, the variants of whose name include
Waldes, Valdesius, Vaudès, and Peter Waldo (this last one remained popular

until the late twentieth century). Pious legends among the Waldenses of the later Middle Ages traced the origins of the movement back to the apostolic age, which guaranteed the authenticity and integrity of their tradition. It was during the later Middle Ages, probably in the fourteenth century, that the addition of 'Peter' to the founder's name was made: this was surely intended to identify him with St. Peter the Apostle, to relate him to the primitive period of the Church, and to confirm the apostolic origins of the Waldenses. Other Waldenses maintained, however, that their church emerged later than the apostolic period, but still at an early moment in the history of the Church. Like other medieval heretics, also like the Protestant reformers of the sixteenth century and the modern critics of the Catholic Church in the twenty-first century, they identified the conversion of the Roman Emperor Constantine (ruled 305–37) as the pivotal moment in the history of the Church. The moral purity and spiritual purpose of the Church were lost when Pope Sylvester I (314–35) accepted from him the donation of authority over the western Roman Empire: Constantine had been cured of leprosy by Sylvester, then converted to Christianity, and he transformed the Church into a temporal power. This group of Waldenses claimed that Sylvester abandoned the long-standing poverty of the Church for worldly power and that only a small group retained the tradition of poverty; the Waldenses themselves were the heirs to the opponents of Sylvester's transformed Church. This account of the movement was recognized not only by the Waldenses but also by orthodox ecclesiastics, who wrote polemics attacking this story of Waldensian origins.

Despite the appeal of the Waldenses' version of their own origins, the birth of the heresy must be placed in the context of the profound social and religious transformations of the twelfth century. Indeed, Valdes's experience of conversion and the great attraction he felt for his new life – features of which in many ways prefigure the life of St. Francis of Assisi and his founding of the Franciscan order in the early thirteenth century – can be little understood without considering the broader changes in the Church and society of his day. Valdes not only tapped into the changing nature of spirituality but also reflected the new social and economic reality to which the Church had to respond.

The birth of the Waldensian movement was, in part, a reaction to these new conditions of the later twelfth century. In the earlier Middle Ages, both

Church and state had evolved in the rural-agrarian context which prevailed since the collapse of the urban world of the Roman Empire. Already in the eleventh century, however, and with greater force in the twelfth, European society changed: it became more urbanized and more commercial. As centers of trade and industry, towns and cities across Europe became hubs of growing economic vitality. Since they were the focal points of long-distance trade, a new class of international merchants assumed prominence in society, even though the established religious and social order had yet to find a place for them. The newly flourishing towns also attracted displaced peasants, or those fleeing from the burdens of rural life. They contributed to the general population growth and assumed positions in the expanding cloth industry and in other commercial ventures of the towns. They participated in the building boom which attended upon the growth of urban areas; they saw to the construction of numerous churches and cathedrals in the new, magnificent Gothic style. The new urban society also contributed to the growth of literacy, as the merchant class developed proficiency in Latin and an even greater command of the vernacular. And the merchants fostered the emergence of the money economy together with the development of banking and money-lending institutions, which ran afoul of Church doctrine on the practice of usury.

Although the Church was in many ways slow to respond to the dramatic transformation of the social and economic order, it too underwent significant change in the twelfth century. The roots of this change can be found in the previous century and more dramatically in the early twelfth century, as is already evident in the life of Henry the Monk and the other wandering preachers of his time, orthodox and heretical. Religious life and spirituality became increasingly shaped by the growing ideal of the apostolic life. This ideal was manifest in almost contradictory ways; it was identified both with the cloistered lifestyle of the Cistercian monks and with the very different one of wandering preachers like Henry and Robert of Arbrissel. In whatever fashion it appeared, however, the desire to live a life in imitation of the Apostles greatly influenced religious belief and practice during the twelfth century. Pious Christians sought to live communally, as the monks did, in imitation of the apostolic community of Jerusalem, or to adopt lives of evangelism, spreading the Gospel as the Apostles had done; by the time of Valdes's conversion, the call to preach in imitation of the Apostles was becoming particularly urgent. At the heart of both these expressions of the apostolic life was a desire for poverty; not merely economic poverty, but, as the historian and theologian Pere Chenu notes, 'the social poverty of those who for one reason or other were living on the fringes of society – feudal society based on territorial stability – and who were consequently outlaws.'[1] Paradoxically, at the same time that apostolic poverty assumed an ever greater role in religious life, the Church itself had become increasingly wealthy and powerful. The pope, partially as a result of the legislation of the Gregorian Reform, was one of the most important and influential figures in Church and society. Not only were the popes involved in political disputes, they were also leading juridical figures in society, and the papal court was becoming a court of last appeal, exercising jurisdiction over an increasingly broad range of issues. The Roman curia had developed a reputation for avarice; in order to gain access to the papal court, petitioners necessarily had to pay increasing sums to various office-holders. Indeed, the *Gospel According to the Mark of Silver* was a popular parody of Roman practice at this time. And it is against this background of changing spirituality, of ecclesiastical worldliness, and of failure to address the profound social and economic changes that the birth of the Waldensian movement can best be understood.

The history of the Waldenses begins with the conversion of Valdes, a wealthy merchant of the commercial town of Lyons, which was situated on an important route for pilgrims, crusaders, and merchants and boasted some 10,000 to 15,000 citizens.[2] The town was noted as a commercial and industrial center which had built up its economic prosperity on manufacture and trade of cloth. From all the accounts, Valdes emerges as one of the success stories of the new urban and commercial economy; he was the owner of substantial properties in and around Lyons. Along with significant moveable wealth, Valdes most likely owned a number of properties and buildings in Lyons and a wide range of properties outside the city, including fields, pastures, vineyards, woods, and other holdings, which brought him substantial revenue in the form of rents.[3] According to contemporary accounts, Valdes made a fortune in business. He most certainly invested in the cloth industry of his town, as well as buying and selling cloth. Like most merchants of his time, he must have indulged in early banking practices, including lending money at interest. This opened him to the charge of usury, which was condemned by the Church. It has also been suggested that he may have served as a financial administrator for the local bishop, but it is generally held that he was a wealthy and successful businessman, part of the rising merchant class.

Success in the world seems, however, to have affected Valdes's conscience; more likely than not, he had some reservations about the way he made his money. At any rate, although the accounts are somewhat confused, he underwent a profound religious conversion. One Sunday in early 1173, according to the Laon Anonymous, a contemporary chronicle, Valdes was attracted to a crowd surrounding a jongleur who was reciting the story of St. Alexis.[4] The story of this fourth-century saint had particular resonance for Valdes. The version he would have heard – most likely compiled as a poem, in French, in the late eleventh century – described a wealthy noble of Rome who married a wealthy noble woman. On his wedding, Alexis left his wife and fortune behind, to live a life of mendicancy in Syria, where he gave away the possessions he had with him and started collecting and distributing alms. Years later, he returned home, was not recognized by his family, and ended his life collecting alms in his father's house. The jongleur's tale so moved Valdes that he invited him back home, to discuss things with him further.

Deeply moved by the story of Alexis, Valdes visited a local theologian on the morning after his meeting with the jongleur, to get advice for the care of his soul and to learn of the best way to attain God. After receiving instruction in matters of faith, Valdes asked the theologian how to best care for his soul, and the master replied in the words of Jesus himself: 'If you wish to be perfect, go and sell everything that you possess' (Matthew 19: 21). Unlike the young man in the Gospel, Valdes did not walk away saddened, but with a new purpose. He returned home and offered his wife a choice between his moveable wealth and his property, which, as the Laon Anonymous notes, included 'lands, waters, woods, meadows, houses, rents, vineyards, mills, and ovens.'[5] She chose, perhaps most wisely, the real estate. Valdes then made restitution to all from whom he had profited unjustly, that is, from those on whom he had charged interest. Finally, he set aside yet another substantial portion for his two small daughters and placed them under the Order of Fontevrault. Having taken care of his wife and family and of those he had wronged in business, Valdes donated a substantial part of his wealth to the poor and began a life of religious poverty which was to have a lasting influence on the world around him.

Shortly after Valdes adopted this new life, a terrible famine struck parts of France and Germany, and he provided relief to his fellow citizens from May 27 to August 1. Three days a week, according to the Laon Anonymous, Valdes 'gave bountifully of bread, vegetables, and meat to all who came to him.'[6] On the feast of the Assumption of the Blessed Virgin (August 15), he distributed a large sum of money to the poor in the streets, proclaiming: 'No man can serve two masters, God and mammon' (Matthew 6: 24). At this point he attracted a large crowd from the people of Lyons, many of whom believed that he had lost his senses. Climbing to a spot where all could hear him, Valdes declared:

> My friends and fellow townsmen! Indeed, I am not, as you think, insane, but I have taken vengeance on my enemies who held me in bondage to them, so that I was always more anxious about money than about God and served the creature more than the Creator. I know that a great many find fault with me for having done this publicly. But I did it for myself and also for you; for myself, so that they who may henceforth see me in possession of money may think I am mad; in part also for you, so that you may learn to fix your hope in God and to trust not in riches.[7]

Valdes made a clear break with his former life and demonstrated, to one and all, that he would no longer pursue success and fortune as he once had. On the day after his great distribution of wealth, he asked a former associate to give him some food. The friend obliged, declaring that he would always provide for him. Valdes's wife was greatly dismayed by this and complained to the local bishop, who commanded that Valdes might not take food with anyone in the city but his wife.

His public declaration, like that of St. Francis in the next generation, was intended to reveal his dedication to the life of evangelical poverty. It was further intended, perhaps, as the first step in a life of preaching; as he had stated, his public display was meant to instruct the people of Lyons on the subject of the false hope for worldly riches. Indeed, contemporary sources indicate that the life Valdes adopted involved poverty and preaching from its very beginning, and these two ideals were at the center of the movement he inspired. In order to spread the Gospel, Valdes commissioned two priests, not long after his conversion, to translate passages from the Bible and from certain Church Fathers into the vernacular. A local grammarian, Stephen de Ansa, translated the various texts — he dictated them to the scribe Bernardus Ydros, who wrote them down. According to a later account, these texts involved passages or, as the Waldenses called them, *sententiae* ('opinions,' 'sentences') from the books of the Old and New Testaments as well as from the works of Ambrose, Augustine, Jerome, and Gregory the Great. The texts in question were frequently read by Valdes and provided the foundation for the preaching and missionary work which he undertook and which had great appeal to the people of Lyons and beyond.

Indeed, it was the Gospels themselves that provided the inspiration for Valdes's conversion, and the apostolic life he adopted inspired others to follow him. By 1177 according to the Laon Anonymous, if not even earlier, Valdes began to attract a number of disciples, including laymen and laywomen as well as priests, all of whom assumed a life of voluntary poverty and began to preach. He and his followers — the Poor of Lyons, as they came to be known — began gradually to criticize their own sins and those of others in Lyons, publicly and privately. Valdes sent his followers to teach the Gospel; they spread out from Lyons to the surrounding villages and preached in public squares, private homes, even churches, and they appeared naked as the naked Christ. Valdes himself preached what he had learned by heart from the Gospel translations he had commissioned. His preaching, together with the popularity of the evangelical life he had adopted, quickly came to the attention of the local archbishop, who must surely have frowned on this unlicensed lay preaching — especially as it criticized the faults and excesses of the local clergy and was quite popular with the townspeople. And it is possible that the archbishop, whom contemporaries mistakenly identify as Jean Bellesmains (or, in English, John of Canterbury), put a ban on the preaching of Valdes and his followers at some point before 1179. Although Jean was appointed archbishop only in 1181, hence he clearly could not have issued a prohibition before that date, subsequent events suggest that some tension existed between the movement of lay preachers and the official hierarchy.

It is equally plausible that Valdes and his followers would not easily abandon their life of evangelical poverty, since both he and his followers believed themselves to be divinely inspired. God himself, they claimed, had called upon Valdes to take up the life of apostolic poverty and to preach the message of the Gospel.

One contemporary follower observed that, when God saw 'the works of the prelates set upon cupidity, simony, pride, avarice, vainglory, concupiscence, concubinage, and other disgraces ... the Son of the Highest Father commissioned you, Valdes, choosing for the apostolic calling, so that through you and your companions He might resist the errors, since those put in charge were not able to.'[8] Moreover, writing about the origins of the Waldenses in the early thirteenth century, Stephen of Bourbon (d. 1261) noted that they openly defied the archbishop when he prohibited their preaching, citing the example of the Apostles. Valdes reacted to the archbishop's prohibition by declaring, just like the Apostle Peter had done, '"We ought to obey God, rather than men" (Acts of the Apostles 5: 29) – the God who had commanded the apostles to "Preach the gospel to every living creature" (Mark 16: 15).'[9] Reflecting what must have been Valdes's understanding of his call for preaching, Stephen observed that Valdes said this 'as though the Lord had said to them what He said to the apostles.'[10] For Valdes, the call for preaching was a divinely inspired one; besides, preaching and poverty were essential to Valdes's intention of living the life of the Apostles. Nevertheless, in spite of its scriptural basis, his dedication to poverty and preaching became a source of tensions with the Church. Strictly orthodox in many ways in their earliest days and committed to combat the Cathar heresy, he and his followers would run afoul of the Church because of their disobedience and usurpation of the clerical right to preach. As Stephen noted, the archbishop declared Valdes and his followers excommunicated and expelled them from the city.[11]

But the final break between Valdes and the Church would come only later; and even before being finally cast out and declared a heretic and a schismatic, he would still seek official approval from the highest levels of Church hierarchy. In response to the prohibition and excommunication pronounced by the archbishop, a small group of the Poor of Lyons, and possibly Valdes himself, attended the Third Lateran Council in Rome in 1179, hoping to obtain papal sanction for their life of evangelical poverty. The course of events at the Council is somewhat confused in the various sources; one of them indicates that Valdes and his followers were summoned to appear before the Council and condemned as schismatics. A first-hand account of the meeting in Rome, however, and the Council canons themselves offer a different and more plausible description of the proceedings.

The main report of the Waldenses' appearance at the Lateran Council in 1179 comes from a work entitled *De nugis curialium* ('On the Courtiers' Trifles'), by the Englishman Walter Map (*c.*1140–1208/10). Map had served King Henry II as royal justice before becoming chancellor to the bishop of Lincoln, in which capacity he attended the Council. In a somewhat mocking and derogatory account, Map, who does not identify Valdes as one of the participants, describes the appearance of the Waldenses. A group of 'simple and illiterate men,' they appeared before the Council and presented the pope 'a book written in French which contained the text and a gloss of the Psalms and many of the books of both Testaments.'[12] In this way they hoped to demonstrate their devotion to the scriptures and to prove the orthodoxy and authenticity of the life they lived. They hoped, further, that the pope would authorize them to preach, so that they could fully answer the call of the scriptures and live the life of preaching and poverty God had intended them to lead. Map notes that the Waldenses had given up all their possessions, dressed simply and, like the Apostles, were naked and followed the naked Christ. But, despite his observation that they pursued a Christ-like existence, Map denounced the group as 'nothing more than dabblers' – not 'the experienced men' they declared themselves to be – and hence little prepared to preach the word of God.

After describing the petition of the Waldenses and indulging in his diatribe against them, Map informs us that the clerics assembled at the Council chose him to interrogate the Waldenses. In this passage Map reveals his keen and sarcastic wit, taking pains to prove the ignorance of Valdes's followers. Two members of the group were given the opportunity to present their beliefs – to their interrogator and to the bishops and other clergy at the Council; they spoke, according to Map, 'not for love of seeking the truth but hoping that when I had been refuted my mouth might be stopped like one speaking wicked things.'[13] Then he asked them 'very easy questions of which no one could be ignorant.' He began with three questions concerning the Trinity, asking if they believed in God the Father, the Son, and the Holy Spirit, to which they replied: 'We do.' He then asked if they believed in the Mother of Christ, and they responded in the affirmative again, which elicited 'derisive laughter from everyone present' and forced them to withdraw in confusion.[14] Their answer to the final question implied that they put the Virgin Mary on equality with the Trinity, which demonstrated either theological ignorance or heretical beliefs concerning the Virgin. After describing the humiliation of the Waldenses before the Council, Map concludes his account with a warning about the threat that they represented for the Church.

Although the followers of Valdes seem to have been humiliated at the Council, they do not appear to have been banned or condemned, even in Map's uncomplimentary account. Indeed, the contemporary Laon Anonymous suggests a very different outcome at the Council, and one that was much more favorable to the heretics' movement. In this account, the group was led by Valdes himself and, far from being mocked and scorned, it was openly welcomed. The Council did denounce heresy but the Waldenses were not among those condemned – who included the Cathars, the Publicans, and the Patarenes. In fact the pope, Alexander III (1159–81), 'embraced Valdes, approving his vow of voluntary poverty.'[15] The saintliness of the movement's founder and his devotion to the apostolic life certainly found resonance with some leaders of the Council, who may well have recognized its value for the well-being of the Church, just as Pope Innocent III would recognize and approve of the order of St. Francis in the early thirteenth century. Alexander, however, was not ready to go as far as Innocent; he forbade Valdes and his followers to preach without the consent of the local priests. In this way Alexander saw the merits of a life of religious poverty but hoped to limit the potential for error from members of the group who lacked proper theological knowledge. For all the pope's best intentions, however, the Waldenses only observed this restriction for a short while, and their disobedience and insistence on preaching would cause problems both for their movement and for the Church.

If the Laon Anonymous is correct, after their appearance at the Council, Valdes and his followers returned to Lyons, where they quickly resumed their life of poverty and preaching. This violation of the prohibition set at the Third Lateran Council, as well as the rising tide of the Cathar heresy, which was spreading throughout the Languedoc, led to the calling of a council in Lyons by its archbishop, Guichard (the predecessor of Jean Bellesmains), in March 1180 or 1181. It was presided over by the papal legate, the cardinal and Cistercian monk Henri de Marcy, who, later on, was to lead the Church in the struggle against the Cathars in the Midi. Valdes's appearance at the council marks an important phase in his life as well as in the development of the movement; there he demonstrated both the essential orthodoxy of his teachings and the importance of poverty and preaching for his way of life.

Called before the council because of the continued preaching of his followers under the pretext of poverty, Valdes was made to issue a profession of faith.
The profession put before him is noteworthy: it indicates the real concerns of
the Church at that time. The fear was not so much about a band of itinerant
preachers dedicated to poverty, but rather about the dualism associated with
the contemporary Cathar heresy. The profession of faith issued by Valdes was
based on a text that had been used repeatedly by the Church throughout its
history, whenever it felt threatened by dualist heretics. It had been used for
the first time in the early sixth century, having developed as a defense against
the dualist Priscillianist heresy prominent then; the profession of faith was
employed as part of the rite of ordination of Gallican bishops. It was also used
by Gerbert of Aurillac, later Pope Sylvester II (999–1003), at his ordination as
archbishop of Rheims in 991; then again by Gaucelin, archbishop of Bourges
(d. 1029), at the time when heresy, under a form which some contemporaries
believed to be Manichaeanism, resurfaced in the medieval West. The profession, therefore, was intended to prevent Valdes and his followers from falling
into the Cathar heresy and from advocating dualist doctrines. Valdes's opposition to the Cathars made it easy for him to subscribe to the profession.

Although the profession was based on earlier models, it was adjusted so as to
meet contemporary needs. It surely indicates the fundamental beliefs of Valdes
and his followers, intended as it was to confirm their orthodoxy. At the heart of
this text was the confirmation of Valdes's belief in the central teachings of the
Catholic Church, together with his repudiation of the errors of the Cathars.
Valdes declared that he believed in the Gospels and that the Father, Son, and
Holy Spirit were 'coessential, consubstantial, coeternal' as is 'contained in the
creeds, the Apostles' Creed, the Nicene Creed, and the Athanasian Creed.'[16] In
direct opposition to the Cathar teaching, which maintained that the devil was
responsible for creation, Valdes further confirmed that he believed that God is
'the creator, maker, governor, and in due time and place, disposer of all things
visible and invisible, all things of the heavens, in the air, and in the waters, and
upon the earth.'[17] Unlike the dualist Christians whom the Church feared and
loathed so much, he accepted both the Old and New Testaments, as well as the
teachings of Moses and John the Baptist. Further still, the founder of the Waldenses had to testify that he believed that Jesus was 'born of the Virgin Mary
by true birth of the flesh ... [and] that He ate, drank, slept, and rested when

weary from travel.'[18] In this way he distanced himself from dualist errors and confirmed his essential orthodoxy on matters concerning the Trinity.

Valdes's profession of faith was not limited to Trinitarian issues but addressed a variety of concerns related to the teachings of the Church. It confirmed his acceptance of 'orthodox' Catholicism on sacramental and sacerdotal matters. Thus Valdes asserted his belief that all the sacraments were valid; he approved of infant baptism and expressed the belief that infants were saved if they died immediately afterward; and he recognized the validity of properly consecrated marriages. He also accepted Catholic doctrine concerning the Eucharist, affirming that 'the bread and wine after consecration is the body and blood of Jesus Christ.'[19] More importantly, he proclaimed that there is no salvation outside the one Catholic Church. He maintained that even sinful priests can legitimately confer the sacraments, as long as the Church accepts these priests; in this way Valdes confirmed his devotion to the Church by distinguishing himself from the Donatist views of other heretics, who denied that immoral priests were still valid.

Having affirmed the central teachings on matters of the faith, the priesthood and sacraments, Valdes then made profession of the life he and his followers would adopt. Although accepting that those who do not adopt poverty can be good Christians, Valdes renounced the world and its wealth, explaining that he and the other Poor of Lyons had given away all their wealth and possessions. He declared that 'we shall take no thought for the morrow, nor shall we accept gold or silver or anything of that sort from anyone beyond food and clothing sufficient for the day.'[20] Valdes showed resolution 'to follow the precepts of the Gospel as commands,' and concluded that anyone who claimed to belong to the Waldenses but did not adhere to his profession of faith should not be accepted among his followers.[21] This profession may be seen as an agreement between the Waldenses and the Church. By confirming the group's orthodoxy and acceptance of Church and priesthood, Valdes may have overcome the suspicions of churchmen and gained approval for his lifestyle of preaching and poverty; at the very least, there was no specific prohibition on preaching, and it can be assumed that, had Henri de Macy and Guichard opposed it, some official statement would have recorded that.

If some reconciliation was reached at the council in Lyons, it very quickly fell apart. The reasons for the collapse of that agreement are not altogether clear, but the death of Guichard and the appointment of Jean Bellesmains, who was apparently less receptive to the ambitions of Valdes and his sectaries, probably contributed to it. The breakdown may also have been due to the fact that Valdes or, more likely, his followers abused the privilege of preaching. Valdes himself seems to have gained approval, but other members of the Poor of Lyons may have started to preach without license from the local priests or from the archbishop; on the other hand, the priests themselves may have refused to grant such license to all of them, Valdes included. Although Valdes expressed devotion to the Church and respect for the clergy, disassociating himself from those who did not, his followers were perhaps less respectful; they may have begun to preach anticlerical sermons. Since the group lacked any formal organization or hierarchy beyond the personal leadership of Valdes, it was possible for them to adopt more radical positions than the founder – a development that would, in fact, happen soon enough. Whatever the cause, the archbishop revoked the agreement and withdrew the right of preaching from Valdes and his devotees. Yet they refused to listen and continued to preach. Indeed, rather than obey the archbishop, they declared that they should follow God rather than men. In response to their disobedience and continued preaching, Archbishop Jean took the further step of expelling Valdes and his Poor from the city of Lyons.

This was a crucial turning point for the Waldenses. Not only did they continue to preach without license, but they found popular support wherever they went, attracting even more adherents. Moving outside their traditional homeland, Valdes and his followers attacked heresy, especially that of the Cathars, and spread their message of evangelical poverty. Their movement grew in the face of opposition from the orthodox Church because Valdes and his followers personified the apostolic ideal: their simple lifestyle and poverty were a challenge even to other heretical preachers. But the movement started to take a more aggressive stance toward the opposition; some of Valdes's followers seemed to adopt heretical ideas, and these, ironically enough, were influenced by the Cathars, whom Valdes so strenuously opposed.

Continued disobedience, together with the dissemination of the Waldenses and their growth in numbers, led to a final and permanent break with the Catholic Church. At a meeting in Verona in 1184, Pope Lucius III (1181–85) issued the decree *Ad abolendam*, which signaled not only a change of relationship between the Church and Valdes and his Poor of Lyons, but also a new orientation toward heresy in general.[22] Up until that point, the prosecution of heresy was the responsibility of the local bishops; they could choose to be most forceful and aggressive in the suppression of religious dissent, but also quite restrained if they so wished. Pope Lucius's decree changed all that. It started a process of centralization in the suppression of heresy which was to culminate in the papal sponsorship of the Albigensian Crusade and in the emergence of the Inquisition. The decree sought to address the problem of heresy at a universal level. This aim was fostered through the support the *Ad abolendam* and the pope received from the emperor Frederick Barbarossa (ruled 1152–90), who had recently settled a long-standing dispute with Rome. Concerned with heresy in Lombardy, the decree was focused on that region, but also directed at other hotbeds of heresy throughout western Christendom. Although Lucius did not fully develop the apparatus necessary to put the decree into effect, he sought to enforce episcopal responsibility for the identification and suppression of religious dissent. The pope commanded in his new decree that all the bishops and archbishops, in person or through an appointed deputy, should visit, once or twice a year, every parish of their diocese where heretics were suspected to reside. In each one of these parishes three or more reliable people were to denounce, under oath, all those whom they knew or suspected to be heretics; anyone who refused to take the oath would bring himself under suspicion of heresy. All those identified as heretics were then to swear that they were not, under penalty of anathema. Lucius, however, went beyond commanding the active opposition to heresy by the episcopacy – for the suppression of heresy he recruited secular authorities. According to the *Ad abolendam*, secular office-holders – 'counts, barons, rectors, consuls of cities and other places' – were expected to take responsibility in punishing the heretics turned over to them by the Church; and any lay authority who failed in this duty would be excommunicated, deposed from office, and stripped of all legal rights.[23] Towns which sheltered heretics were to suffer commercial boycotts, and the lands of known heretics were declared forfeit. To guarantee obedience to the new decree even further, the bishops and archbishops were expected to publish it on every feast day, under penalty of suspension from office for three years if they failed to do so.

While displaying a new and more aggressive attitude toward heresy in general, the decree also denounced the order of Valdes as heretic. Lucius first condemned 'all heresy, howsoever it may be named,' and then proceeded to identify specific groups, thus: 'we lay under a perpetual anathema, the Cathari, Patarini, and those who falsely call themselves Humiliati, or Poor Men of Lyons, Passagini, Josepini, and Arnaldistae.'[24] Having listed the major heretical groups, Lucius continued with a condemnation which seems directed especially at Valdes and his followers. Turning now his attention to those who have 'assumed to themselves the office of preaching,' he pronounced perpetual anathema on 'all who shall have presumed to preach, either publicly or privately, either being forbidden, or not sent, or not having the authority of the Apostolic See, or of the bishop of the diocese.'[25] Although Lucius recognized that Valdes was not guilty of any doctrinal error, he excommunicated him and his followers on account of their disobedience: he declared their preaching to be in error because it was done without the authority of the mother Church. Without the formal sanction of the pope or archbishop, the poverty and humility of Valdes and the Waldenses could not be authentic either; it was not unlike the false piety which the earlier heretics had demonstrated.

The decree Ad abolendam repudiated the central tenets of Valdes's creed, denying the validity of his teaching and of his way of life. And thus Valdes was declared excommunicate and anathema: his refusal to follow man instead of God had led to his ejection from the Church he had hoped to restore and reform. From 1184 on, the evangelical movement founded by him would increasingly come to be seen as heretical.

Although the decree from Verona formally declared Valdes and his followers anathema, they all continued their lives of evangelical poverty. Expulsion from Lyons did little more than open the movement to broader horizons, and the pronouncements at Verona had little immediate effect on the local communities where Valdes and his followers preached the Gospel. In fact, in many places in the Languedoc, the Midi, and Lombardy, Valdes and his Poor were among the most active and successful opponents of the doctrinal heresy promoted by the dualist Cathars. As Walter Map indicated, the Waldenses went 'two by two, barefoot, clad in woolen garments, owning nothing, holding all things common like the apostles, naked, following the naked Christ.'[26] Their way of life in imitation of Jesus and the Apostles posed a stark challenge not only to the orthodox clergy but also to the preachers of the Cathar heresy, who prevailed in southern France and northern Italy. By virtue of pursuing the apostolic ideal and presenting a true model of Christian living, the Waldenses were even more of a threat to the Cathars than the official missions sent by the Church to combat heresy. Valdes's life of poverty and preaching found great favor among the populace in the areas influenced by heresy; even some members of the clergy welcomed him and the Poor of Lyons as allies in the fight against the Cathars. Indeed, the Waldenses were invited to participate in public debates, to defend their teachings, and to oppose the heretical ideas of the various enemies of the Church, especially the Cathars. Valdes's movement also attracted members of the clergy such as the learned Spanish priest Durand of Huesca, who wrote an important work, the *Liber antiheresis* (*Book Against the Heresy*, c.1191/2), a defense of Christian belief against the errors of the Cathars.

Thus, in the generation or so after his denunciation at Verona and in the closing decades of the twelfth century, Valdes witnessed a dramatic growth of his movement. While rejecting Church authority to prohibit their preaching, Valdes and his followers still taught Catholic doctrine. And there were many who ignored the declaration at Verona and saw the movement as a valid expression of Christian and Catholic life. This success demonstrates that Valdes was able to tap into the fundamental spiritual yearnings of his age and clearly reveals the importance of the apostolic life in the twelfth century. The rapid growth, however, did not come without a cost. Over the last two decades of his life, Valdes saw the movement that bore his name being plagued by schism and by the increasing adoption of clearly heretical teachings.

Until his death, probably in 1205, Valdes hoped to reconcile himself with the Church, and his own moderation in matters of doctrine and organization signals a desire to return to the fold. By all accounts, however, he continued to live in poverty and to preach, even though he and his followers had been strictly forbidden to do so by bishops, councils, and the pope. The primary focus of their preaching was the call to repentance, but they were also very much concerned with the doctrinal heresy of the Cathars. In groups of two, in sandals and simple clothing, possessing little else, they all entered the Languedoc and other regions where the Cathars flourished, with the intention of combating their errors. Nonetheless, it appears that heretical ideas crept into the teachings of the Waldenses once they were there. Adopting more extreme views than Valdes ever would, some of his Poor came to believe that swearing oaths was strictly forbidden. Some also maintained that all killing was wrong, even judicial executions, and that every lie constituted a mortal sin. Even more serious, and clearly at odds with the position of Valdes himself, was a view taken by at least one branch of the Waldenses in the Languedoc: they adopted a Donatist attitude toward the clergy and denied the validity of the baptism administered by Catholic priests. The Poor of Lyons alone were true disciples of Christ and thus they were the only ones who could legitimately bestow baptism. Denying the baptismal right not only to the Catholic priests but also to the Cathar heretics, this group performed baptisms as well as rebaptizing people, in violation of the Church. Moreover, they claimed, in contrast to the teachings of Valdes, that only those who died in a state of complete poverty would be worthy of gaining salvation. Valdes repudiated this group around 1200 and most likely distanced himself from a similar group in Metz, which adopted more extreme views than Valdes himself and expressed a more critical attitude toward the orthodox Church.

An even more dramatic schism occurred in Italy, where the Waldenses had begun their missionary work as early as 1184, under the name the Poor of Lombardy. Just as the Waldenses in the Languedoc and Metz had absorbed religious ideas and practices from the local heretical communities, so too did the Poor who preached in Lombardy. It is also possible that an apostolic or heretical movement already existed in the region and influenced the Poor. However this may be, distance from their leader and the lack of any formal organization allowed for an independent development of the Lombard Poor.

The Italian Waldenses diverged from the main group and their founder in several distinct ways. Like the group in the Languedoc, the Lombard Waldenses assumed a more aggressive stance toward the clergy, one which approached Donatism. In this matter, in particular, the influence of local conditions can be detected best, because of the long-standing anticlerical sentiment that existed in the region. The Poor of Lombardy rejected the established clergy and attacked the sacraments they performed, including marriage. What is more, they also took steps to replace the Catholic clergy with their own ministers. Unlike Valdes, who claimed the right to administer the sacraments in case of need and on an ad hoc basis, the Poor of Lombardy sought to establish a permanent ministry for the administration of the sacraments. But the creation of a permanent order to confer the Eucharist and other sacraments ran counter to Valdes's intentions and interfered with his hopes for a reconciliation with the Church. The Poor of Lombardy also recruited nuns from the local convents and proclaimed that salvation could only be found through them.

An even more serious breach between Valdes and his Italian followers involved the adoption of manual labor by the latter. Indeed, according to the *Rescriptum Heresiarcharum* (*Reply of the Leading Heretics*, written c.1218), Valdes himself is supposed to have said, just prior to his death, that the Lombard poor 'could have no peace with him unless they separated themselves from the "congregations of laborers" who were then in Italy.'[27] Under the influence of an Italian heretical group, the Humiliati, the Lombard brethren took up the practice of working for subsistence wages and did not follow the strict regimen of poverty. They also settled down in one place, abandoning the practice of itinerant preaching which was at the core of Valdes's teaching in favor of a communal life of religious devotion. Although identifying themselves as part of the movement inspired by Valdes, the Lombard Waldenses disavowed the two central features of the lifestyle established by him. Moving away from his original practices, they foreshadowed those of later Waldenses and revealed the fundamental adaptability of their doctrine. The founder himself, however, would have none of this; he insisted on strict devotion to the message of the Gospels, which included both poverty and preaching, and, as noted in the *Rescriptum*, he did not consider those who labored to be part of his order.

Valdes and the Lombards also differed on matters of organization. Valdes himself did little to provide any sort of administrative structure to the movement he founded beyond his own charismatic leadership. The Lombard Poor, however, introduced a rather elaborate organizational structure, which, like their other innovations, met with Valdes's disapproval. As part of their sedentary, almost monastic lifestyle, the Lombards divided themselves into what the *Rescriptum* termed 'brethren' and 'friends.' The brethren were members of a ministerial class of sorts, and they were fully committed to a life of preaching and poverty. The friends were lay supporters who listened to their preaching and teaching. This distinction was only one of the organizational developments opposed by Valdes. An even more serious difference emerged over the establishment of an institutionalized leadership. The Lombards elected Jean de Ronco, and after him Otto de Ramazello, as 'rector' or 'provost.' The rector's responsibility was to oversee and administer the group and to ordain ministers or brethren to preach to the lay supporters of the Waldenses. This step was unacceptable to Valdes for whom the one and only leader of the Waldenses was Jesus Christ. As already noted, the various innovations of the Lombard Poor prefigured many later developments of the Waldensian heresy, but conflicted with the original intent of Valdes, who emphasized his own vision of preaching and poverty. Valdes repudiated the Italian group shortly before his death.

By his death in 1205, Valdes of Lyons had seen his movement evolve, from a small group of preachers devoted to a life of evangelical poverty, into an international movement which had become increasingly unorthodox in its doctrinal and organizational structure. Embodying the ideal of an apostolic life, which was at the center of twelfth-century spirituality, and foreshadowing the thirteenth-century movement of St. Francis of Assisi, Valdes founded a movement which survived the Middle Ages and merged with the Protestant churches of the sixteenth century to form the modern Waldensian church. Devoted to a life of preaching and poverty, Valdes clearly hoped to reform the Church and restore it to its evangelical purity, recalling it from its worldliness and materialism to a more pristine form. Nevertheless, his refusal to abandon his life of preaching laid the ground for his own excommunication and for the increasing doctrinal heterodoxy of his followers. Although remaining true to orthodox Christian dogma and hoping for a reconciliation with the Church, Valdes witnessed the growing radicalism of his followers, many of whom he wrote off from his movement. Despite his excommunication, he remained committed to Christian teaching and to his ideal, and, together with his followers, struck out against a shared enemy, the Cathars. And it was that dualist heresy that provided the greatest challenge to the Church. The Cathars and their noble supporters would bear the greatest brunt of the Church's response to the growth of religious dissent in the late twelfth and thirteenth centuries.

CHAPTER FIVE

RAYMOND VI OF TOULOUSE: THE CATHARS AND THE ALBIGENSIAN CRUSADE

*a*ccording to the Cistercian historian Caesarius of Heisterbach (*c*.1170–*c*.1240), when the papal legate in southern France, Arnaud Amaury, was asked by the crusaders about to sack the city of Béziers, in 1209, how to tell the good Christians from the heretics, he replied, 'Kill them all. God will know his own.' There is no proof, of course, if Arnaud Amaury actually made that statement, but his alleged words reflect the attitudes involved in the most violent official response to the spread of heresy in the Middle Ages. The Albigensian Crusade, called by Pope Innocent III (1198–1216) in 1209 to suppress the growth of the Cathar heresy in southern France, was the most concentrated and destructive effort by the Church to ensure religious orthodoxy. With the support of the northern French barons, who were concerned with territorial acquisition just as much as with the suppression of Catharism, the Crusade did serious damage to culture and society in the south and caused countless deaths. The main victims of this assault were the simple peasants and villagers who had been attracted in great numbers by the preaching and behavior of the Cathars. The one who lost perhaps the most was not, however, a Cathar but one of the greatest figures of the south: Count Raymond VI of Toulouse (1156–1222), whose toleration of the heretics and tepid support for the Church helped to inspire the Crusade – and it, in turn, seriously undermined his position.

Raymond suffered on account of the dramatic growth of the Cathar heresy in his country, coupled with his failure to stem the tide. Raymond had originally shown a toleration to the preaching of the Cathars which rendered him suspect in the eyes of the Church and ultimately a victim of its ferocious backlash against the heresy; for its rise and spread were deemed to be the most serious threat to the established Church at the time. Therefore, in order to understand the life and career of Raymond best, it is necessary to examine the origins and teachings of the Cathars.

Although it was once believed that the earliest manifestation of Catharism occurred in the early eleventh century, when the outbreaks of heresy at Orléans and elsewhere in western Europe took place, it is now generally held that the first Cathars emerged in the mid-twelfth century, when foreign missionaries appeared at various places in France and in the Holy Roman Empire. Indeed, Catharism is perhaps best understood as the combination of indigenous western religious dissent and Bogomil religious dualism, and thus it may be said to have begun when Bogomil missionaries arrived in Latin Europe and their teachings were adopted by Christians in the Empire, France, and Italy. According to the Premonstratensian provost Everwin of Steinfeld, the first of the heretics who came to be called Cathars appeared in the Rhineland city of Cologne, in 1143 or 1144.[1] In his correspondence with Bernard of Clairvaux, Everwin described a group of heretics who did not drink milk or eat any food produced in some way as the result of coition. They rejected marriage and baptism in water and practiced the laying on of the hands, which was also a rite of initiation into the sect. Unlike earlier heretics of the twelfth century, notably Henry the Monk, Tanchelm, Peter of Bruys, and others, these ones were anonymous; Everwin does not identify even a heresiarch leading the group. He notes, however, that they were divided into three ranks: the auditors, the believers, and the elect, which signified degrees of progress within the group. These heretics claimed that their beliefs were not new but went back to the time of the martyrs. They also claimed to have fellow believers in Greece, most likely a reference to the Byzantine Empire, where Bogomil missionaries had spread their heresy during the eleventh and twelfth centuries. The basic outline of their creed and their claim to have coreligionists in the Greek world signal the beginnings of the Cathar movement in Latin Europe.

Reports from slightly later sources in the mid-twelfth century confirm the birth and wide diffusion of a new movement of heresy which merged indigenous religious dissent with foreign, most likely Bogomil, influence. In 1163, Eckbert, the future Benedictine abbot of Schönau, described the beliefs of these heretics in his *Thirteen Sermons Against the Cathars*. He drew his information for the sermons from a recent encounter with them at Mainz and from debates he had had with them at Bonn and Cologne during the previous fifteen years. In his sermons, Eckbert argued that the heretics were to be found everywhere throughout western Christendom and were called 'Piphles' in Flanders, 'Texerant' in France, and 'Cathars' in Germany. The last name comes from the Greek word for 'pure' (*katharos*), but Eckbert derived it from 'cat' because the heretics allegedly worshiped the devil in the form of a cat; and it is this name that has been generally used to identify Eckbert's heretics. Like Everwin, Eckbert described their beliefs in a way which suggests Bogomil influence. According to the sermons, the heretics taught a Docetic Christology, maintaining that Jesus Christ only appeared to take the flesh but in fact did not. Eckbert noted, further, that the group believed in the transmigration of souls and in the creation of the world by an evil god. Like the group at Cologne in the 1140s, Eckbert's Cathars practiced the rite of the laying on of the hands to initiate believers into the sect.

Evidence for the emergence of the Cathar heresy (or its precursor) in the south, where it was to have its greatest impact, appears in the account of a meeting in 1165 at Lombers, a castle that lies between Albi and Castres. At this meeting, local heretics known as '*bons hommes*' or 'good men,' joined in debate with various bishops of the region in the presence of important secular leaders.[2] The 'good men,' like the Bogomils, did not openly proclaim their heresy or speak falsehood, refusing to discuss baptism, marriage, or their own beliefs. They also gave rather veiled and ambiguous responses to questions concerning the Eucharist and confession and refused to swear any kind of oath. Rejecting the Old Testament, they based their arguments only on the New Testament. They spoke freely, however, of the failures of the Church, were critical of the clergy, and even called the bishops at the meeting wicked men. They were in turn declared heretics in the name of Bishop William of Alby by Gaucelin, bishop of Lodeve, who also advised the knights to stop supporting the 'good men.' The fact that the knights needed his warning suggests one of the reasons for the eventual success of the Cathars in southern France; Raymond VI was not alone in granting tolerance to these heretics.

The accounts of Everwin and Eckbert and that of the meeting in Lombers provide highly suggestive hints of the emergence of the Cathar heresy and reveal the infiltration of missionaries from the Byzantine world into Latin Europe. These missionaries most probably established the first Cathar communities and brought with them Bogomil dualism from Bulgaria – possibly following trade routes that led into the Rhineland, Lombardy, and elsewhere.

But the most unambiguous evidence of the establishment of heretical dualism in western Europe comes from the account of the so-called Council of St. Félix-de-Caraman, which is traditionally dated to 1167 but more likely took place in 1174. Although the document reporting this meeting probably conflates several such meetings and was purportedly written in 1232, it offers clear evidence of the origins and nature of Catharism in the Languedoc and southern France. The Council was a meeting of Cathar bishops from northern France, Albi, and Lombardy along with representatives of Cathar churches in Carcassonne, Agen, and Toulouse, and it was presided over by an eastern missionary, Papa Niquinta or Nicetas of Constantinople.

Nicetas introduced important administrative reforms to the emerging Cathar churches of western Europe and a fundamental change in the beliefs of the heretics. He proclaimed that the teaching of earlier Bulgarian missionaries was flawed at its heart, whereas he taught the true doctrine. He introduced his eager western disciples to the teachings of the so-called Dragovitsan church, which maintained absolute dualism. Nicetas preached the doctrine of the two principles. He asserted, namely, the existence of two equal deities, the good and the evil; these were locked in an eternal struggle and the evil god created the material world. He also organized the Cathar churches in western Europe, founding dioceses patterned after the established Catholic ones, defining geographic boundaries, and confirming the autonomy of each bishop within his diocese. He also administered the basic sacrament of the Cathar church, the *consolamentum*, a ritual that prepared the believers to step into the ranks of church elite and established them as the church's priestly order. Having redefined the basic teachings and ecclesiastical organization of the Cathar churches, Nicetas returned to Constantinople. After him, Catharism in the Languedoc and elsewhere in western Europe developed into a major threat to the Catholic Church.

The success of Catharism lies in the basic teachings and practices of its church. The Cathars offered a fully developed theology, in opposition to that of the Catholic Church — one which could provide an alternate explanation of evil in the world. Cathar dualism proclaimed that the world had been created by Satan, the evil god associated with the Old Testament; therefore all material creation was evil. Satan was a fallen angel, who had rebelled against God; he made human bodies out of clay and imprisoned other fallen angels in them. The Cathar view of creation as intrinsically evil led to the rejection of the traditional doctrine concerning the incarnation of Christ. The Cathars believed instead that Christ only appeared to take the flesh, and only appeared to suffer on the cross. He was 'born' of the Virgin Mary, according to one Cathar source, by entering her ear.

Although important as a rival to Catholic teaching, Cathar doctrine was less central to the success of the heresy than the behavior of its members. Indeed, the simple lifestyle and the religious devotion of the Cathar leaders often stood in staunch opposition to the worldliness and power of the Catholic hierarchy, which added to the ignorance of many among the parish clergy. Moreover, the Cathars erected a rival organizational structure, which could provide support for its clergy and laity alike. At the head of the Cathar churches were the bishops, who administered the consolamentum — the ritual which elevated the ordinary believer to the rank of *perfectus* ('perfect'); and it is perhaps a key to the growth of Catharism that women could become perfects no less than the men. The perfects adopted a life of poverty, celibacy (avoiding even physical contact with the opposite sex), and regular prayer. As the clerical order of the heresy, the perfects were called on to travel about, preaching the faith and taking confession from the laity. They also performed the *apparellamentum*, a confession designed to purify them of minor infractions, and the ritual of blessing of the bread at meals. Their own message, their criticism of the official Catholic clergy and sacraments, and their personal piety attracted many people to the Cathar heresy, including those who, like Count Raymond VI and other southern nobles, supported it without fully joining it, or tolerated it through animosity toward the abuses of the Catholic Church and clergy. The Cathar laity was not expected to live as strictly as the perfects but it supported them with food, lodging, and protection; it also attended their sermons. It honored the perfects with the *melioramentum* — a form of confession and request that the perfects pray for them.

The early growth and survival of Catharism was also dependent on the support of the secular nobility. True, Count Raymond V of Toulouse sought help against the preachers of the two principles, both from the pope and from his secular overlords; but many southern nobles either turned a blind eye on the heretics or supported them actively, even joined their church. Efforts by the Catholics, including missions by Cistercian preachers and special missions sent by the pope himself, proved ineffective because of the tolerance of the nobility of the Languedoc. Although there was no pronouncement of support for the heretics, the nobility as a whole showed little inclination to suppress the Cathars or support the Church's early efforts against them. Moreover, this reluctance to act against the heretics filtered down into society, where Catholics and Cathars lived side by side, often in the same household. The ease with which heretic and Catholic coexisted and the toleration granted from above allowed Catharism to spread throughout the Languedoc and to emerge as a serious rival to the authority of the Church. The failure of the greatest power in the south, that of Count Raymond VI of Toulouse, to restrict this growth led to the outbreak of the Albigensian Crusade.

Raymond, born in 1156, was the son of Count Raymond V (1130–94), who had initiated action against the first Cathars and sought aid against them from both Church and state. As son to the count of Toulouse, Raymond was related to powerful figures of the day who included King Louis VII of France and King Richard I the Lionheart of England: the latter's sister, Jeanne, was Raymond's fourth wife. Very little is known of Raymond's early years, although upon becoming count of Toulouse he would be one of the leading figures of the south. He was, apparently, a most obedient and patient son – unlike others, most notably his future brother-in-law Richard I, who chafed at waiting for power or openly rebelled against their fathers. As contemporary accounts suggest, Raymond was sent on occasion to lead a siege or a raid by his father, but otherwise there is no record of his activities; all in all, he does not seem to have gained the experience needed for good rulership. He was appointed count of Mauguio by his father, but even then many of the official duties of the office were performed by Raymond V. And it was only in 1194 that Raymond VI, at the mature age of 38, appeared fully on the stage of history, becoming count of Toulouse upon the death of his father.

Assuming authority in 1194, Raymond lacked the kinds of experience that other nobles had, and he faced the fragmentation of the lands of his predecessors. By all accounts he was a charming and attractive ruler, even though he lacked the necessary assertiveness that his more successful contemporaries possessed. He seems to have had little taste for combat, his preparation for warfare not being much during his father's lifetime; he withdrew from the battlefield without even drawing his sword on two occasions during the Albigensian Crusade. He also had a weak will and used to vacillate, often losing his nerve at times of crisis, and he could be tactless in spite of his natural charms. And yet for all his flaws Raymond remained a popular and romantic figure. He was a great lover of luxury and cultivated an extravagant court, which attracted many nobles and troubadours of the south. Raymond was a great supporter of the troubadours and promoted their works; he found them particularly useful for the art of seduction, which, according to contemporary sources, he used to great success. Raymond was notorious for his licentiousness — apart from abandoning one wife for another, he even seduced his father's mistresses and committed incest with his sister.

Although not the most morally upright figure, Raymond was a man of conventional piety. After his death in 1222, his son, Raymond VII (1197–1249), compiled a list intended to demonstrate his father's loyalty to the Church in order to secure a Christian burial for him. The document listed numerous charitable benefactions. Raymond seems to have been particularly supportive of the Cistercian order, and many of his charters reveal donations to the Cistercians and other monasteries and churches. He expressed a desire in his will to die as a member of the Order of the Hospitallers and left the order a substantial benefaction after his death.

But, even though he demonstrated support for the Church, Raymond was not above hostility toward the political ambitions of the clergy. He was putting his own interests ahead of those of the Church when they came into conflict, and he may have even held anticlerical attitudes. Unlike his father, he also exercised a certain laxness in the prosecution of heresy, as did many southern nobles. And it was widely held that Raymond was not simply being tolerant of the heretics, but he secretly supported them and may even have desired to be one of them. At the very least, he allowed Cathar perfects to preach before him, leaving them unmolested; he may very well have allowed Cathars even to reside at court. It was alleged that the count himself repudiated the Old Testament and believed that the devil had created the world. He was reported to protect the perfects and to provide them with food and money; he generally indulged them, he even married one – his second wife Matilda, daughter of King Roger of Sicily, who was sent to a Cathar convent when he repudiated her in 1193.

Many of the accusations that Raymond was himself a Cathar were made by one of his bitterest enemies and hence are suspect. It is more plausible that Raymond was a tacit supporter of the heretics, if only because this attitude was so widespread in the south of France. In fact, the general support for religious dissidents and the hostility to the clergy were firmly rooted in the region, as the success of Henry the Monk may indicate. Raymond himself was in any case limited by the political situation of his day from acting more forcefully, had he wished to. Many leaders of the towns, as well as the most prominent nobles of the region, were sympathetic to the Cathars, if not more: the sister of the powerful and influential count of Foix was herself a perfect. Hence they were unlikely to join in any effort to suppress them. Furthermore, Raymond did not have the necessary military forces, nor could he call on a feudal levy to enforce his will, and even if he had tried to suppress the heretics by force he would most probably have failed, if not through his own incompetence, then because of some terrible civil war such an enterprise may well have generated. It is not surprising that, when asked to take action against the Cathars in 1205, Raymond declared that he was a good and obedient son of the Church and would see to it that heresy was suppressed, but in fact proceeded to do absolutely nothing. Ultimately, the spread of Catharism on Raymond's domains became a matter of some urgency to the papacy. In response to his obvious lack of action, the Church adopted ever more aggressive steps against him. In 1204 and 1205, Pope Innocent III petitioned King Philip Augustus of France (1165–1223), the barons of the north, and other princes to suppress the heresy, since Raymond was reluctant to do so. Philip, however, was little interested in getting himself into a war in the south, as he was then much too involved in a dispute with John, king of England.

Pope Innocent also responded to the spread of the Cathar heresy by sending delegations of missionaries to preach to the heretics with the goal of converting them. The missionaries he sent included leading Cistercian monks, whose austere and pious lives were thought to be an important counterweight to those of the Cathar perfects. Dominic de Guzman (c.1180–1221), founder of the Dominican order in 1215 and declared a saint after his death, also preached against the heretics throughout the region. In 1207 he participated in a great debate in Montréal, along with Cathar leaders and other Catholic ecclesiastics; but no verdict was given there, due to the sensitivities of the townspeople. A subsequent debate at Pamiers was more clearly successful for the Catholics, who welcomed numerous converts from heresy. And, in the period between the two debates, a large number of Cistercian monks arrived in the area, to reinforce the evangelical mission. Yet in spite of the exemplary lives and skilled preaching of Dominic and the Cistercian monks, their efforts failed to make any significant headway against the Cathars. In fact, the Cathars in Carcassonne managed to expel the bishop in 1207 and around the same time held a great council of their own at Mirepoix, in the lands of the count of Foix. Catharism had taken deep roots and remained a significant force in the Languedoc; many of the rival preachers left after their ephemeral successes.

The most important missionary, however, was the pope's personal legate, Peter of Castelnau, a Cistercian monk, canon lawyer, and theologian. He was born just north of Montpellier and therefore had the benefit of being a man of the south. He arrived in 1203 and began the arduous task of converting the Toulousains and of persuading the bishops of Languedoc that it was their responsibility to work against the spreading of the heresy. Possessing the full authority of a papal legate, Peter deposed bishops who seemed unable or unwilling to take steps against heresy and replaced them with others, more amenable to the pope's commands. What is more, Peter sought to exploit the unsettled political situation of the lands of Raymond, the count of Toulouse, by working with his vassals. By 1207, Peter came to realize that no victory over the Cathars was possible without the count's support. But Raymond had displayed little initiative in that regard. It was two years since he had promised to suppress the heretics without doing anything in the interim. Disappointed by the Count's failure, in late April 1207 Peter forged a truce among the warring nobles of the Languedoc and organized a league aiming to bring an end to heresy on the count's lands. Raymond himself was invited to join the league but refused, indignant at the idea of joining an organization so clearly designed against him. In response, Peter of Castelnau immediately excommunicated the count. He declared him guilty of violating the truce held on feast days, of pillaging monasteries, and of other crimes, but, most importantly, of protecting the heretics instead of expelling them from his lands.

The excommunication was made all the worse for Raymond when

Innocent confirmed it on May 29, 1207. In a harsh, uncompromising letter, Innocent declared:

> Do not forget that life and death themselves are in God's hands. God may suddenly strike you down, and his anger deliver you everlasting torment. Even if you are permitted to live, do not suppose that misfortune cannot reach you. You are not made of iron. You are weak and vulnerable, like other men. Fever, leprosy, paralysis, insanity, incurable disease may attack you like any of your kind ... The hand of the Lord will no longer be stayed. It will stretch forth to crush you, for the anger which you have provoked will not lightly be evaded.[3]

The pope ordered the bishops of the region to publish the ban of excommunication in their churches until Raymond submitted. He laid an interdict over all of his lands, thereby prohibiting the holding of Church services or the administration of the Eucharist. He ordered that no one was to have any dealings with the count and released Raymond's vassals from their oaths of allegiance. In correspondence once again with King Philip Augustus, in the hope that he would take up leadership of the crusade, Innocent envisaged the possibility of the king deposing Raymond and inviting others to replace him.

Raymond's position was, clearly, most difficult, but there were certain rituals to go through that would have lifted the penalty; the king himself had been excommunicated before. But Raymond acted in a most arrogant fashion. The pope, on the other hand, had reached his limit and was little willing to compromise. As was customary, the papal legate, Peter of Castelnau, visited the count's court to inform him personally of the excommunication and to undertake any discussion that could bring an end to the impasse. The first meeting between the count and the papal legate, however, failed to resolve anything, in part because of Raymond's ill-mannered reception of the legate. The count claimed, or so it seems, that he could find numerous Cathar bishops to prove that their church was better than Peter's. The excommunication of the count and interdict over his lands remained in force, making way for an increasingly bad situation.

Following the failed meeting between Raymond and Peter, both the pope and his representative in Languedoc sought to resolve the situation. On November

12, 1207, Innocent wrote to Philip Augustus yet again, in an attempt to persuade him to invade the south in order to punish Raymond and suppress heresy. The king's response was noncommittal at best, but events would outpace both king and pope. In January 1208, Peter of Castelnau met with Count Raymond once more. Raymond himself had sent a letter to Peter in late December, indicating that he was willing to submit to his authority, provided that the excommunication and interdict were lifted. Peter and another papal legate, the bishop of Couserans, met the count at St. Gilles, where Raymond hoped to be able to outmaneuver the papal representatives and gain absolution at the cheapest possible price. An unpleasant argument ensued; at the end of the day nothing was resolved, and the excommunication and interdict remained in place. According to the pope himself, Raymond threatened the legates by declaring that he would keep a watchful eye on them. On the following day, Peter of Castelnau was assassinated by a representative of the count, who was immediately blamed for the murder. The question of his involvement is, however, open to debate; it should be said on behalf of the count that he was probably not enough of a fool to murder the pope's legate. Peter, who had created much ill will in the south, could simply have been the victim of a rash vengeful act by some angry noble.

The assassin was never identified and Raymond remained the primary suspect; his failure to express anything like sadness strengthened the belief that he was, in fact, guilty of ordering the crime. Rather than move decisively to prevent any worsening of the situation, Raymond delayed further, giving his enemies the opportunity to react first. And on March 10, 1208, Innocent III proclaimed a crusade against Raymond and his lands, addressing the king and nobles of France as follows:

> Since those who fight for liberty of the church ought to be fostered by the protection of the church, we, by our apostolic authority, have decided that our beloved, who in obedience to Christ are signed or are about to be signed against the provincial heretics, from the time that they, according to the ordinance of our legates, place on their breasts the sign of the quickening cross, to fight against the heretics, shall be under the protection of the apostolic seat and of ourselves, with their persons and lands, their possessions and men, and also all of their other property; and until full proof is obtained

of their return or death all the above shall remain as they were, free and undisturbed.[4]

Innocent thus offered a full indulgence – equal to that offered to crusaders to the Holy Land – to all those who took up arms against Raymond, a man whom the pope excommunicated for the crimes of heresy and complicity in the murder of a papal legate. The pope also promised the crusaders freedom to seize any, and all, lands belonging to Raymond; the ultimate right to those lands being of course reserved for Raymond's overlord, King Philip Augustus. The letter to the king and nobles of France was followed by similar letters to the legates in the south, who were called upon to preach for the Crusade.

Philip Augustus was, however, reluctant to involve himself in the campaign, being concerned with matters in the north and matters to do with the king of England; he even cautioned the pope against taking too precipitous an action against Raymond. Yet in the end Philip allowed a considerable number of his own vassals to participate in the Crusade.

The reaction to the pope's call for crusade was immediate and dramatic, as the French nobility enthusiastically signed up for the war in the south. According to the historian of the Crusade, William of Tudela, the response was overwhelming; an army larger than any he had ever seen came together in the spring of 1209. The response of the nobility was most understandable: what attracted them was the offer of the indulgence, which provided a much easier path to absolution than undertaking a crusade to the Holy Land. The struggle against heresy at home offered the French knights a just cause to fight against, and this was a much less difficult and expensive path to follow. But the available rewards were not only spiritual: the crusading knights could obtain material benefits, which included the acquisition of large and prosperous fiefs in the south.

The remaining papal legate in the south, the Cistercian Arnaud Amaury, recruited a number of powerful and important nobles to the cause of the Crusade, including Otto III, duke of Burgundy, and Hervé de Donzy, count of Nevers. His drive to recruit benefited from the fact that Philip granted his vassals the right to participate. Arnaud began preaching for the Crusade in the winter of 1208–9, and he encouraged his brother Cistercians to do the same.

It was the increasing success of his enemies that forced Raymond to act.

He hoped to find allies against the army of crusaders, which had been steadily growing after Innocent's proclamation of the Crusade, and he turned first to his suzerains. In the autumn of 1208, Raymond appealed to Philip for aid but found little affection there, as the king recalled a number of injuries Raymond had caused him. Whatever support Raymond could still have expected disappeared when he visited his other lord, Emperor Otto IV of Germany, one of Philip's great rivals. The emperor could only offer little help, as his own fortunes were at a low point. Finally, Raymond turned to Arnaud Amaury. He sought the legate's forgiveness and absolution, humbling himself before the Cistercian and kneeling at his feet, as a sign of contrition. Arnaud, however, did not give in; he informed the count that only the pope could lift the excommunication.

Returning home in late 1208, dismayed by the preaching of the Cistercians and the growing support they received for the Crusade, Raymond struggled to find allies against its rising tide. He forgave the citizens of Nîmes for siding with his enemies in the past and confirmed privileges for those under his authority. His most desperate gambit, however, was his effort to forge an alliance with his nephew, Raymond-Roger, viscount of Trencavel and lord of Albi and Carcassonne, who may well have been a supporter of the Cathars in the face of the common threat against them. Despite the family connection, the two nobles had been rivals for some time, and Raymond's attempt to persuade his nephew to join him against a common foe came to naught.

Practically alone, without friends or allies, by the end of the year 1208 Raymond came to realize that his only hope was to find a way of reconciling himself with the Church. At this point, Raymond made a serious and apparently sincere effort in that direction. At the same time, however, he sought to maneuver himself into a more favorable position and wrote to Innocent complaining that he could not reach any agreement with a legate as inflexible as Arnaud Amaury. He sent two ambassadors to Rome with the letter, instructing them to accept any terms Innocent would offer. He declared his devotion to the Church and admitted to his many faults, including protection of the Cathars and failure to honor the Church. Raymond also informed the pope that he was willing to surrender numerous castles and possessions as proof of good faith. The pope responded to this offer by appointing his secretary, Milo, and a canon from Genoa, Thedisius, as papal legates for the region – much to the count's pleasure. Milo was instructed, however, to obey Arnaud Amaury in all things; he was warned to treat the count with great caution and be aware of his duplicity.

As preparations for the Crusade continued apace, Raymond was restored to communion with the Church. On June 18, 1209, in front of the great abbey church in the town of St. Gilles, Raymond did penance. Stripped to the waist and before a great crowd of bishops, priests, and lay people, he agreed to obey the papal legates in all matters and admitted to a large number of offenses against God and the Church; these included favoring the heretics on his lands rather than expelling them, violating the Peace of God and the holy days of the Church, abusing the clergy and appropriating Church lands, promoting the Jews to positions of public power, employing mercenary troops, and levying unjust and excessive tolls. Curiously enough, he was not forced to confess participation in the murder of Peter of Castelnau, but only to admit that he was 'suspected' of some involvement in it. He was led into the church by Milo, who flogged him with a switch all the way to the altar, and there the papal legate pronounced his absolution.

On the following day, at Milo's request, Raymond issued a document confirming the agreement he had reached with the Church. The legates were not to be interfered with in the exercise of their duties. Seven castles, most of them in the Rhône Valley, were to be surrendered to the Church, and the garrisons of their fortresses were ordered to hold these castles at the legates' command. The various towns and nobles under Raymond's authority in the Rhône Valley were forced to promise cooperation with the legates. In this way the count demonstrated his acceptance of the terms of the agreement. The document was an act of good faith designed to prove his obedience to Pope Innocent and his legates.

After his humiliating act of submission, Raymond took one further step: he asked to be able to take the cross against the heretics. This request was granted, and he joined the crusaders at Valence on June 24. The count's reasons for joining the Crusade are not hard to discern – he was primarily motivated by a strong desire for self-preservation and for the destruction of his rivals in Occitania. The lax devotion to the Catholic faith and the relative tolerance of the Cathar heretics which he demonstrated in the past suggest that he was not moved by religious fervor; but he was very much aware that it was too late to prevent the Crusade from entering his lands. By taking the cross and undergoing the obligatory forty days of military service he would gain all the protections granted to crusaders, including the preservation of his own titles and his extensive land holdings throughout the region. Not only would he gain crusader immunity, he would also be able to assume a position of leadership in the Crusade and become privy to its plans and objectives. Moreover, he could redirect the Crusade itself, so as to make it suppress his rivals. Most importantly, he could turn it against his nephew, Viscount Raymond-Roger, who had caused him such trouble. Raymond may have hoped that the Crusade would invade his nephew's lands and defeat him, thus weakening him sufficiently for the count to be able to impose his will on this most difficult vassal. Other unruly nobles could also face the same fate and, once the Crusade had left the south, Raymond could reestablish himself as the most powerful lord of the land – indeed his position could even be stronger than ever before.

Joining the army at Valence in late June, the count took advantage of his new position and turned the Crusade's attention from his lands to focus on those of Raymond-Roger and of the Trencavel family in the area of Albi – notably the important towns of Béziers and Carcassonne. Once the army reached Montpellier, Raymond himself guided it, through the territory owned by his nephew, toward Béziers, which was well fortified and an important commercial center. The army reached the town on July 22. Its citizens had been busy preparing for the impending siege, which they felt confident they could withstand on account of the strength of the town walls and of their own determination to preserve the integrity of their home. Indeed, taking a strongly fortified town was a difficult task, and the people of Béziers believed they could outlast the forty days of service that the crusaders owed: a prolonged siege would discourage the attackers, sending the message that it could last beyond their term of service.

Expecting to face a siege of some duration, the crusaders sent the bishop of Béziers to negotiate with the townspeople. The bishop arrived with a list of names of 222 Cathar heretics resident in Béziers (a town with a population of some eight to ten thousand people) and declared that, if either the heretics were surrendered or the Catholics in town were to depart, the Crusade would spare them and their property. The people of Béziers refused; shortly after the siege began, and very quickly ended. Instead of a long, drawn-out process, the capture of Béziers took place in just a few hours. Some of the townspeople initiated hostilities, and in the confusion that followed the gates were breached and one of the worst massacres of the Middle Ages followed. According to contemporary accounts, thousands of people took refuge in the church of La Madelaine and died when the crusaders burned it to the ground. The mounted knights and foot soldiers indulged in a horrible slaughter, killing men, women, and children – Catholic and heretic alike. They plundered homes, invaded churches, burned large sections of the town, and indulged in wanton destruction and looting. Although contemporary reports of a massacre of tens of thousands are surely exaggerated, it was true that very many died, and the fall of Béziers sent shock waves throughout the region.

After Béziers, Raymond and the other crusaders moved on to the great town of Carcassonne, which they reached by August 1. Their morale was buoyed by the capture of Béziers and they hoped to repeat their success at Carcassonne. Raymond-Roger had taken command in the defense of the city, whose population swelled after the disaster at Béziers; the viscount faced the possibility of a prolonged siege during the hottest part of the summer and the prospect of food and water shortages. His overlord, Peter II, king of Aragon (1174–1213), arrived to mediate between the crusaders and his vassal. But Peter, a leader in the reconquest of Spain and a devout Catholic, had little sympathy for the Cathars and was very critical of his vassal's failure to expel them. He arrived with only a small military contingent; he could not have offered much support even if he had wanted to defend his vassal. The king tried to negotiate the surrender of the town for a guarantee of freedom of passage for Viscount Raymond-Roger and eleven companions, but the viscount rejected the offer. The siege itself lasted for about a fortnight before the viscount agreed to surrender, and on August 15 the town of Carcassonne fell to the crusaders. Its occupation took place with little of the destruction that had occurred in Béziers. The papal legate himself sought to ensure that none of that was repeated at Carcassonne, perhaps in the hope that more moderate treatment would help the crusaders to win people's hearts in the Occitan, helping to bring heresy there to an end. Raymond-Roger had agreed to surrender the town to the crusaders in exchange for his safety, but, in a clear violation of contemporary practice, he was captured and imprisoned upon leaving. He was to die of dysentery in a prison near Carcassonne, on November 10, 1209.

After the fall of Carcassonne, a successor to Raymond-Roger had to be found; the office of viscount was offered to a succession of crusade leaders ending with

Simon de Montfort, earl of Leicester, a noble of the Ile-de-France known for his personal bravery and Christian devotion. He had previously participated in the Fourth Crusade and was one of the few crusaders to have reached the Holy Land and refused to attack Zara when the rest turned on that Christian town. De Montfort used his new possessions as a base for conquering the Trencavel lands to start with, then for pursuing the Crusade against the heretics; he pursued it relentlessly until his death, even when the pope sought to limit it. Thus he came to be identified with the Crusade. He encountered great difficulties in maintaining a significant army in the field because of the limitation of service to forty days, compounded with the pope's temporary withdrawal of support; yet Simon was successful in the war and took control of much territory.

By the time this new leader of the Crusade assumed his position as viscount, Raymond VI had completed his term of service and retired from the Crusade, feeling that he had fulfilled his obligation. But both Simon de Montfort – who had continued the military campaigns in the Trencavel lands in spite of various setbacks and of the difficulty of maintaining his army – and the Church leaders, especially Arnaud Amaury, remained skeptical of the count's intentions. They complained that he had been less than zealous in his performance as a crusader and failed to discipline the heretics on his territories. In fact Arnaud Amaury and the other two papal legates, Milo and Thedisius, excommunicated the count for a second time in September 1209. In the face of this pressure from the Church and de Montfort, Count Raymond took steps to preserve his place and power. He appealed to his overlords, Philip Augustus of France and Otto IV of Germany, for aid and protection, but neither was interested in getting involved and lent him little help. Having to look elsewhere, Raymond sent an appeal to Innocent in Rome. Whatever he wrote in it, the petition seemed to have some effect on the pope; for he encouraged restraint on the part of his legates and asked them to allow Raymond an opportunity to prove his devotion to the Church.

In July 1210 Raymond met with the legates at St. Gilles. Although he arrived with the expectation that he would be reconciled with the Church and some of its members were willing to implement such reconciliation, the papal legate Thedisius declared that the count had not fulfilled the terms outlined in earlier papal bulls. Heretics still thrived on his lands, tolls were still imposed, and mercenaries still remained in his employ. Until these matters were resolved there could be no reconciliation. Raymond may have exploded in rage, but there was little he could do short of acceding to the demands of the legate.

For the remainder of the year, Raymond witnessed Simon de Montfort's campaigning in the Trencavel lands. Although de Montfort suffered some disappointments, by the end of 1210 he had secured several key towns and welcomed numerous reinforcements, including those brought by his wife, Alice of Montmorency. Raymond's military ill fortune was matched by further difficulties with the Church. The count met with the legates at a council in Montpellier in January and February of 1211. At the assembly, the legates presented him with a series of conditions which, if met, would lead to his reconciliation with the Church. The conditions themselves, however, demonstrated how little the legates desired to come to terms with the count. According to a contemporary, albeit not completely reliable, account, Raymond was to give up his tolls and mercenaries, as demanded previously, but he was also to destroy his castles and place restrictions on his vassals. He was to allow Simon de Montfort to travel without hindrance across his territories; he was to go on crusade to the Holy Land and join a military order. The count rejected these demands and left the meeting without a word to the legates. Peter II, king of Aragon, who was in attendance, was offended by the demands, a result with disastrous consequences for the future. But the count's refusal to accept the terms had the desired effect: the legates were able to renew the ban of excommunication against him and the pope subsequently confirmed their sentence.

Raymond faced increasing hostility both from the legates and from de Montfort. The latter had started a campaign to encircle the city of Toulouse, which was split between those who supported the count and those who did not. In May, de Montfort succeeded in taking the city of Lavaur. The fall of Lavaur was a turning point in the war and an example of the extreme brutality with which the Crusade was often pursued. For the first time, de Montfort approved of the execution of nobles and knights who had opposed him. The commander of the garrison and eighty of his knights were hanged, and Geralda, the lady of the castle, was thrown into a well and stoned to death. Along with them, four hundred heretics were burned – an example of terror that convinced other towns to accept de Montfort's authority. But during the summer de Montfort was unable to match this success, and his attempt to take Toulouse failed. Indeed Toulouse was a bit of a miscalculation on the part of de Montfort, whose reputation as a brilliant commander suffered accordingly. His saving grace, however, was in Raymond's being a terrible military commander and a poor strategist, who was unable to take advantage of his rival's setback.

Raymond sought to press his advantage and led a counterattack following de Montfort's failure outside the walls of Toulouse. The count organized a massive army, which included his own contingents and those of the count of Foix, of the viscount of Béarn, and of other southern nobles who had little sympathy for the invaders from the north. Simon de Montfort had taken refuge with a small force at Castelnaudary and made a stand there as Raymond began the siege. But it was a poorly designed and implemented siege. Despite significantly outnumbering his rival, Raymond failed to surround the town and refused to meet the besieged enemy in pitched battle. The camp he pitched to the north of the town faced repeated raids by de Montfort's soldiers, and it sometimes appeared that Raymond himself was under siege. As the siege dragged on, reinforcements moved southward, to support de Montfort. The count of Foix, Raymond-Roger, marched out to meet them and suffered a terrible defeat not far from Castelnaudary, at St.-Martin-la-Lande. His army, which received no help from the count of Toulouse, was driven from the field thanks to the timely arrival of Simon de Montfort with a small force of mounted knights. Raymond-Roger's men were forced into disarray; many claimed to be crusaders in the chaos and were killed by their comrades, while the crusaders themselves killed large numbers of them. This disaster was followed by the withdrawal of the siege. It was a stunning defeat for Raymond, salvaged only by the belief, spread by Raymond-Roger, that de Montfort had been defeated, which led to the defection of numerous towns loyal to him.

De Montfort responded vigorously to the defections and sought to limit the damage caused by Raymond-Roger's false rumor. He was aided by a renewed enthusiasm for crusading that burst throughout Christendom in 1212 – the Children's Crusade occurred, Christians fought successfully in Spain, and calls for aid in Constantinople were made. The Albigensian venture benefited from this; crusading against heresy was preached everywhere in Europe, and de Montfort welcomed crusaders from Germany, northern France, Normandy, and Italy during the winter and spring of 1212. This enabled him to take the offensive against Count Raymond and others who opposed his authority. De Montfort won back the important regions of the Tarn and Garonne, together with numerous towns and strongholds along the way. He took the Crusade north into the Agenais, where Raymond held lands from King John of England; it was a risky move, which might have alienated the king of England, but it ended in another success for de Montfort. He seized the territory of Raymond's supporter, the count of Comminges, and gained full control of Albi, Cahors, and much of the south. One of his most important victories, the conquest of Moissac, was also one of his most brutal. After roughly six weeks of siege, from August to early September, de Montfort agreed to a negotiated settlement that spared the city but forced the leaders of Moissac to surrender the town's defenders, who numbered more than three hundred, and also a contingent from Toulouse; the crusaders quickly killed them all. Following his military conquest of much of the south, de Montfort held a council at Pamiers in November 1212 which organized his subjugated territories around northern customs and imposed new regulations on the people of Occitania.

Although Raymond was in large measure responsible for the Crusade and failed to limit the damage caused by de Montfort, he was not without supporters, especially after the dramatic successes of the chief crusader in 1212. The pope himself began to question the intentions of de Montfort, worrying that he was more interested in acquiring territory and political power than in suppressing heresy and in protecting the interests of the Church. As early as the spring of 1212, Innocent had written to his legates, asking them to give Raymond yet another chance to clear his name and to prove his devotion to the Church. The pope also forbade his legates to seize Raymond's lands or to dispossess his heirs. Innocent's letter was prompted not only by his uncertainties about Raymond and de Montfort but also by concerns over alienating the king of France and by his desire to promote crusading in Spain against the Muslims.

Innocent took even more definite steps to restrict the actions of de Montfort in January 1213. In two separate letters, to the legates and to de Montfort, he revised his policies toward the Crusade in the lands of Raymond of Toulouse. In his letter to the legates, Innocent wrote:

> Foxes were destroying the vineyard of the Lord in Provence; they have been captured. Now we must guard against a greater danger. We hear the Saracens of Spain are preparing a new army to avenge their defeat [by Peter II of Aragon at the Battle of Las Navas de Tolosa] ... Moreover, the Holy Land needs assistance.[5]

Preaching was to be directed toward crusading to the Holy Land and against Islam, not toward the heresy in Languedoc. In the second letter, Innocent complained to Simon de Montfort that,

> not content with opposing heretics, you had led crusaders against Catholics … you have shed the blood of innocent men and have wrongfully invaded the lands of [Peter II, king of Aragon] his vassals, the counts of Foix and Comminges, Gaston of Béarn, while the king [of Aragon] was making war on the Saracens and though the people of these lands were never suspected of heresy.[6]

Innocent demanded, further, that de Montfort restore the lands seized from nobles innocent of heresy or of supporting it. He also declared that indulgences were to be offered only to those fighting the Muslims in Spain or in the Holy Lands; there was no indulgence for fighting in the lands of the count of Toulouse.

Innocent's decisions were inspired, in part, by Peter of Aragon, who had sent an embassy to Rome to discuss matters with him. Although Peter had arranged a marriage alliance with de Montfort and had recognized him as his vassal, viscount of Béziers, he had become increasingly uncomfortable with de Montfort's military successes. Peter had greater affinity with southerners like Raymond, even if his tolerance for heretics was limited. And Peter had led a successful crusade against the Muslims of Spain in 1212; the crushing victory he won at the Battle of Las Navas de Tolosa enhanced his reputation as a Christian king and crusader. As a consequence, his defense of Raymond and his complaints against de Montfort had great influence on decisions in Rome – at least until de Montfort and his supporters could reach the pope's ear.

But, even as Peter's petition was made to the pope, the legates held a council at Lavaur. Peter himself attended it to present another petition – in favor of Raymond, his son Raymond VII, and the other nobles dispossessed by the Crusade. The legates rejected the king's requests and denounced Raymond and the other Occitan nobles as heretics and enemies of the Church and crusade. They, too, sent representatives to Rome, which caused Innocent to recant and chastize Peter for misinforming him about the situation in the Occitan.

As a result of Innocent's vacillations, battle-lines were drawn between Peter and de Montfort; Raymond had now the staunch defender he had sought since the outbreak of the war. He, together with the counts of Foix and Comminges, various nobles of Gascony, and the dispossessed nobles of the Trencavel lands joined forces with Peter and the large army he brought with him as he crossed the Pyrenees. Lacking the military skill to defeat de Montfort, Raymond had now acquired an ally whose reputation as a commander and crusader was greater than that of de Montfort. Not only did Raymond have an ally of superior skill; the army commanded by Peter was at least twice, if not three times, the size of de Montfort's army. The support of that honored son of the Church and successful crusader, Peter of Aragon, further strengthened Raymond's position because it undermined de Montfort's claims that he was working to rid the land of heresy. Peter, Raymond, and their great army were therefore extremely confident – perhaps too confident – as they prepared for the battle which could bring the Crusade to a close; but de Montfort's sense of his own invincibility and deep faith that God was on his side left him equally certain of his fate.

The battle of Muret, near Toulouse, began on the morning of September 12, 1213, and by the day's end was an unmitigated disaster for Raymond and his allies. The count of Toulouse, despite his poor reputation as a soldier, offered the most sensible plan: to fortify their camp strongly and wait for de Montfort's attack from a position of strength, or else starve their enemy into submission, should de Montfort not attack. This plan, however, was scorned by Peter and the other members of the southern coalition, who desired an immediate and decisive battle. King Peter was so confident of victory that, true to his reputation, he spent the night before the battle with one of his mistresses and was so tired on the next morning that he could barely stand up during mass. He would lead his forces into battle and, unlike most commanders, take his place in the front lines wearing the armor of a common knight. The king marched out with his army and ordered his men to await the assault from de Montfort and his army. When de Montfort attacked, the poor organization of the troops and the lack of coordination between the various members of the coalition proved fatal. De Montfort's well-organized and highly disciplined troops made short work of their enemy; the army of the count of Foix was swept aside first, and then the army of Aragon was routed by de Montfort's charge. Peter himself was killed in the battle and his army quickly dispersed upon hearing the news of the king's death. Fleeing in terror, the troops of the southern coalition were quickly cut down by the crusaders or drowned in the River Garonne. The militia of Toulouse, which had launched an attack on the western wall of the town, was unaware of the massacre in the field below. The return of Simon de Montfort caused a panic; the Toulousains fled and were also killed by crusaders or drowned in the river. Contemporary accounts place the number of the dead at twenty thousand, which is unlikely, but the slaughter was significant and included Raymond's most important and powerful supporter. The battle of Muret was a great and humbling defeat for Raymond; it eliminated the Aragonese as a force in the politics of Occitania and strengthened de Montfort's position in the region even further.

Although Raymond was once again humbled on the field of battle, at least he had the hope that the pope and the king of France would not confirm de Montfort in the offices of the south. For the next two years the situation around him remained fluid, and the count saw both successes and setbacks. On the military and political front, he benefited from de Montfort's failure to follow up his victory at Muret with a conquest of Toulouse – a logical step, but one not taken because of de Montfort's inadequate number of troops. He also scored a minor triumph in the capture of his younger brother Baldwin, who had joined the Crusade in the hope of becoming count of Toulouse himself, and had fought with de Montfort at Muret. Baldwin was hanged as a traitor. Moreover, Innocent appointed a new legate, Peter of Benevento, who was instructed not to make any permanent settlement in Occitania, to preserve the political boundaries as they had existed before Muret, and to put Toulouse under the protection of Rome. This effectively restricted de Montfort's attempts to complete his conquest of the count's lands and forced him to look elsewhere in the region for military success. In April 1214, the counts of Foix, Comminges, and Toulouse, along with the people of Toulouse, appeared before the new legate, to seek absolution and restoration to the Church. Along with his submission, Raymond promised to turn over his titles to his son, Raymond VII, and to cede his territories to the Church.

Despite these minor victories, Raymond still faced major challenges. De Montfort did not rest after his triumph at Muret. In 1214 he strengthened his hold on the south, raiding the counties of Foix and Comminges, extending his control over Provence, and reducing other strongholds throughout the region. His successes were rewarded by the papal legate Robert of Courçon, who assumed the duties of Peter of Benevento during his brief absence. Robert granted to de Montfort the lands of the heretics in the Albigeois, Agenais, Quercy, and Rouergue. De Montfort earned a further diplomatic success at the Council of Montpellier in January 1215, which met under the presidency of the legate Peter of Benevento, now returned to the Occitan. The assembled bishops and archbishops unanimously agreed that the lands, titles, and rights of Raymond VI should be granted to de Montfort, and they requested that Peter invest de Montfort immediately with these honors. Peter, however, was restricted by his commission; he could only defer the final decision to the Council in Rome later that year. Although a limited victory, de Montfort nonetheless emerged in a stronger position after Montpellier. Even the crusade of Prince Louis, son of Philip Augustus, ended by benefiting de Montfort. Much delayed, the intervention of Louis in the affairs of the Occitan reinforced de Montfort's position in several ways. Louis himself was deferential to de Montfort as the chief crusader and bestowed on him the castle of Foix; he also approved of the destruction of the walls of Narbonne and Toulouse.

Raymond's great hope lay with the decisions of the pope at the Fourth Lateran Council, which took place in November 1215 in Rome. One of the greatest of all church councils, the Fourth Lateran addressed a broad range of topics, including religious reform, the definition of the Eucharist, political matters relating to France and the Empire, relations with the Jews, as well as heresy and crusading. Innocent was conflicted about the ultimate decisions concerning Raymond and his lands, and Raymond had his defenders at the Council. His old antagonist, Arnaud Amaury, the former legate and now the archbishop of Narbonne, spoke on his behalf, partly out of his animosity toward de Montfort, who had destroyed the town's walls and claimed rights over the city. Indeed, de Montfort's own ambitions in some ways played against him, supporting Innocent's suspicions that de Montfort was concerned with conquest more than with the suppression of heresy. Besides, other bishops from the south defended Raymond, and Innocent was aware of the count's acts of contrition and submission to the Church. Even if the count himself were guilty of supporting heresy and other crimes, his son, Raymond VII, was not and should not suffer for the crimes of his father. The rights of the young Raymond, furthermore, were supported at the Council by representatives of King John of England. But Raymond VI had equally powerful enemies at the Council, including the bishop of Toulouse, who spoke forcefully against him and the other southern nobles.

Because Raymond had never suppressed, nor would he ever suppress, heresy on his lands, de Montfort had assumed the territories by right of conquest and seemed a more likely candidate for the job of putting an end to heresy in the south. Innocent and the Council therefore declared that the lands of the count conquered by the crusaders were forfeited to de Montfort. Raymond was to live in exile on his wife's lands and was granted, on good behavior, a pension of four hundred marks a year. Lands of the count not conquered by the crusaders were to be given to Raymond VII once he came of age.

The Lateran Council of 1215 marked the high point for Simon de Montfort and the nadir for Raymond VI, but the wheel of fortune would turn once again, and 1216 marked the beginning of the end for de Montfort's control of the south. Indeed, the counterattack against de Montfort began not long after the Council. In April 1216, Raymond and his son returned home through the town of Marseilles, a town with no particular duties toward them but which welcomed them with cheers and oaths of loyalty. From there they traveled to Avignon, where they were again acclaimed and promised aid, and it was made quite clear that the nobility of Provence had little love for de Montfort and was willing to support the Raymonds against him. From Avignon, Raymond VI rode to Aragon to raise an army for the struggle against de Montfort, and the young Raymond rode to Beaucaire, which was held by de Montfort but declared itself in support of the Raymonds. Raymond VII took the town, but de Montfort's garrison held the citadel. Raymond VI arrived and a double siege ensued, the count attacking the citadel, de Montfort besieging the town.

Employing all his usual skill, de Montfort could neither entice the young Raymond out into the field of battle nor take the town. The young Raymond held the town, while his father drove the garrison into submission and forced de Montfort to withdraw in defeat. The victory at Beaucaire led to the defection of many other southern towns between 1216 and 1217 and undermined de Montfort's aura of invincibility.

The most important town to reject de Montfort's authority was Toulouse. Already in 1216, the town rebelled against de Montfort and drove his soldiers away from the city, but de Montfort arrived and suppressed the revolt, agreeing to spare the town in return for the payment of a fine of 30,000 marks. This burdensome fine did not sit well with the people of Toulouse, and in the summer of 1217 they offered to surrender the town to Raymond VI if he could hold it against de Montfort. In an act completely out of character, Raymond marched quickly and decisively to Toulouse with a large army from Spain, and his arrival in September, in the company of the counts of Foix and Comminges and other nobles and mercenaries, was greeted with great joy and enthusiasm. Although de Montfort's garrison had managed to retain control of the castle, Raymond secured the town as a whole, which quickly became the center for the rebellion against de Montfort. Once back in Toulouse, Raymond put its people to work, erecting a new defensive network of trenches and other barricades around the town, in preparation for the siege. And when it came, Raymond and his people were ready.

The siege of Toulouse lasted for some nine months, from late September 1217 until late June 1218, and its conclusion brought the first phase of the Albigensian Crusade to an end. It began with de Montfort arriving with what forces he could muster in his ride from Carcassonne. He saw that his only option was to take the town quickly, and he launched an all-out assault on Toulouse, which was bloodily repulsed. Having failed to take the town back, de Montfort, facing the end of the campaigning season and being short on men and money, was forced to wait until the spring. In the meantime, he encouraged the new pope, Honorious III (1216–27), to issue a call for crusade. The forces of de Montfort and Raymond engaged in modest jousting, but little was gained on either side during the winter. As the spring campaigning season began, both sides were reinforced by new troops; Raymond welcomed the arrival of his son among others. As the siege dragged on, the morale of the defenders increased, while the besiegers complained of the prolonged, difficult, and unsuccessful assault. De Montfort mounted a few direct attacks on the city, but he was driven back each time, with heavy losses on both sides. To bring the siege to a close, de Montfort ordered the construction of a great siege tower, but efforts to get it close enough to the town were met with heavy opposition from the Toulousains. In one of these struggles, on June 25, de Montfort himself was killed. His skull was crushed by stones hurled, according to tradition, by a woman operating a mangonel – a type of catapult used to throw missiles.

The war continued for a short time after de Montfort's death, but there was no one to replace him. Raymond VI had survived, and many towns returned to at least nominal allegiance to him. Following the victory at Toulouse, Raymond's son continued the reconquest of the south. The only serious challenge for him was the return of Prince Louis: in 1219 the latter took the town of Marmande, which suffered the most brutal slaughter since Béziers. Louis attempted later on to take Toulouse itself, but the town was too strong and too confident now; Louis broke off the siege and returned home. The south was once again in the hands of Raymond and his son, even though it would not stay long that way – once king, Louis would return and bring the region under his authority, making a settlement with Raymond VII in 1229.

The old count, Raymond VI, restored to his lands after long years of war, died in 1222. He was again secure in his holding, having weathered the storm of Simon de Montfort and of the Crusade, but he was never reconciled with the Church. He died in the habit of the Hospitallers but still under the ban of excommunication, and, despite repeated efforts by Raymond VII, he would remain outside the Church and was refused burial in consecrated ground. Raymond's dynasty survived thanks to the efforts of his son. The heresy that launched the Crusade also endured, but only to face a Church even more determined to extirpate it.[7]

CHAPTER SIX

PIERRE AUTIER:
THE LAST CATHARS

R aymond VI of Toulouse faced a crusade and the wrath of the papacy
on account of his lukewarm devotion to the Church and question-
able ties with the Cathars on his lands. But the Church had rapidly
lost control of the Crusade itself, and the war in the Occitan changed, from one
of religion, into one of conquest. Although claiming his rights in the south as a
result of his role as chief crusader, Simon de Montfort was seen by many not so
much as a defender of the faith as a political opportunist attempting to acquire
titles and territories for himself. Beyond that, the Crusade ultimately failed to
destroy heresy in the Occitan, or elsewhere in Christendom for that matter.
Despite the massacre of Cathars at Béziers and elsewhere, the Albigensian
Crusade did not eradicate the heresy; even after the leadership of the Crusade
was taken up by Louis VIII, king of France (1187–1226), the Cathars felt strong
enough to hold a council at Pieusse in 1225 and established a new diocese at
Razès. Throughout the remainder of the thirteenth century, the representatives
of the Catholic Church and the Cathar believers and perfects, men and women,
were involved in a prolonged struggle, which the latter would eventually lose.
They disappeared in the fourteenth century, after enjoying one final success
under the guidance of their last important missionary, the perfect or 'Good
Man,' Pierre Autier, who was executed in 1310.

The transformation which led one of the most feared sects, potential rival to the established Catholic Church, to this end was the result of both internal and external developments. Although the contention, once popular, that the life-denying aspects of the faith led to its own demise should not be exaggerated, it can be said that the heresy itself was plagued by certain contradictions and dissensions, and some of its doctrine surely alienated both the potential converts and the committed believers. Perhaps the fundamental flaw of the Cathar movement was the division between absolute and moderate dualists, which was apparent as early as the Council of St. Félix-de-Caraman (traditionally dated 1167, but more likely 1174). The split over doctrine limited the possibility for unity and led to competition between the various Cathar churches. Adding further confusion and uncertainty was the stringent moral code of the sect, which held that any perfect who suffered moral lapses and violated the rigid code of conduct lost the *consolamentum*; moreover, all those consoled by such a perfect also lost the consolamentum as a consequence of the perfect's sins. This meant, in the words of the inquisitor and former Cathar Rainier Sacconi, that 'all Cathars labor under very great doubt and danger of the soul.'[1] Although members of the community could be reconsoled, they remained in a state of uncertainty about their own salvation because of doubts concerning the moral integrity of the perfects. Moreover, the harsh attitude toward sexuality and, especially, toward the bearing of children could have negative consequences. Pregnant women were mocked at by the Cathars and told that they were carrying a demon in their belly. Female perfects were known to pray with pregnant women, asking God to free the women of the demons in them, and at least one woman with child was told that, if she died while pregnant, she could not be saved.[2] This clearly alienated many women, who might have otherwise supported the movement, and it led some into outright opposition to the Cathars. The problem was particularly difficult for the Cathars, because women played an important role in their success and also in passing on the faith within the family.

Despite various organizational and doctrinal problems, the Cathar heresy, which continued to attract followers throughout the thirteenth century, might well have endured had it not been for the increasing weight of the persecution imposed upon it by the Catholic Church, itself an increasingly centralized and efficient institution. The attack on the Cathars took two forms. First, there was the continued political and military assault on the Cathars following after the Albigensian Crusade – which, as discussed, had evolved into something closer to a political military venture than to a religious campaign and had concluded with the complete absorption of the Occitan into the kingdom of France. Although it ended as a war of conquest, the Albigensian Crusade did bring about a change in the relationship between heretics and the leaders of the south. The treaty of Paris, which settled the war in 1229, undermined the support for the Cathars throughout Occitania and limited their places of refuge. Perhaps the most important consequence of the treaty and defeat of Raymond VI and his line was the transformation of Toulouse from one of the great centers of the Cathar heresy into a Catholic city. The town itself was deprived of its walls and of the great network of defenses erected against the Crusade near the end of Raymond VI's life. Control over the city was granted to representatives of the king of France and garrisoned by royal troops, and the authority of the Catholic bishop of Toulouse was extended to include the city and numerous of its dependencies. At the same time, many other towns throughout the region suffered a similar fate; they were deprived of their defenses and placed under royal control. Moreover, Raymond VII took up the opposition to heresy, although he was slow to start and eager to retain as much control over his lands as possible. Even if, until as late as the early 1240s, Raymond had resisted the efforts to suppress heresy and had even supported the Cathars and their noble allies in revolt, in 1243 he became an aggressive enemy of the heretics. He publicly proclaimed his disavowal and his willingness to pursue the Cathars; he even offered a bounty of two marks of silver to those who helped toward arresting them and finding them guilty. He also expelled those who had supported the Cathars and fought against the Crusade, and in 1249, in Agen, he burned eighty people suspected of heresy.

The demise of the nobility's support for the Cathars was central to the decline of the heresy in the south; but just as crucial, if not more so, was the work of the inquisitors, who flooded the region following the end of the war. It was their work that helped to break the back of the movement and forced it underground. Established by Pope Gregory IX in the 1230s, the Inquisition set up a regular judicial body to root out heresy, and this body replaced the traditional episcopal tribunal. The pope turned to the Dominican order for staffing the inquisitorial tribunals; later on, Franciscans and members of other orders were included. People accused of heresy were brought before the inquisitors, who often asked leading questions which forced the accused to prove their innocence. Torture was resorted to at times, but the inquisitors' goal was to discover the heretics and to recall them to the faith. Other inquiries followed, building on the precedents and procedures established at Toulouse, and in the great inquest of 1245–46 more than five thousand people were interrogated, many of whom were found guilty of heresy and thus subject to imprisonment, exile, or loss of property. Under pressure from the inquisitors, the accused would at times denounce others, in order to prove their own commitment to the faith or to turn attention to other guilty parties.

By mid-century the machinery of repression had been effectively established on the lands of Raymond VII, but the Cathar perfects still enjoyed the respect of many throughout the south, and there was continued resentment of the northern powers. Attack against the inquisitors took place; they were sometimes murdered, expelled from various towns, or cut off from food and water. Open revolts against the authority of secular powers and of the inquisitors also occurred, but with little success. The most notorious counterattack took place in 1242, when Raymond and a collection of southern nobles participated in the revolt and a group of Cathars and their supporters attacked and killed a group of inquisitors in Avignonet. The revolt failed and Raymond finally submitted to royal authority, but the raid in Avignonet brought the death of a number of inquisitors, including the Dominican William Arnold, who had enjoyed great success since his arrival in the region in 1241. The murderers, having smashed their victims with axes and swords, seized books and various records belonging to the inquisitors; but the primary motive for the attack was to put an end to inquests in the rebels' homeland. Indeed, as one of the attackers noted later, they hoped that the attack would make it so that 'the affair of the inquisition could be extinguished, and the whole land would be freed, and there would not be another inquisition.'[3]

But, far from ending the persecutions for heresy, the murders led to the destruction of Montségur in the Pyrenees, the greatest Cathar stronghold.[4] It was in the fortress at the hilltop, which had attracted large numbers of Cathar perfects and believers, that the attack on the inquisitors had been planned. In response, the king's representative, with forces from the archbishop of Toulouse and the bishop of Carcassonne, laid siege to the fortress from the summer of 1243 to March 1244. Despite the staunch resistance of the garrison, the strength of the fortress itself, and the hope that Raymond VII would intervene, Montségur was taken. Although the defenders were spared, the heretics were not. Following the fall of the fortress, some 200 Cathar perfects, including important Cathar bishops, were burned in a great fire, which clearly signaled the beginning of the end for the heresy. Indeed, it was impossible for the Cathars to recover from the loss of so many of its leaders, and any hope of recovery was further limited by the continued vigor of the inquisitors and the final loss of support from Raymond VII and other secular leaders.

Nevertheless, it was in this environment of severe persecution from the Church and after the progressive decline of the Cathar churches in the later thirteenth century that a revival of the heresy, led by Pierre Autier, took place. The revival, lasting roughly from 1299 to 1310 under him, and, albeit greatly weakened, for nearly twenty years after his fiery death in 1310 – for the last trial of one of his followers occurred in 1329 – reveals the lingering attraction of Catharism despite its own inherent flaws and the persecution of the Church. Catharism managed to endure, and established networks between communities and their way of life set the foundation for its own resurgence under Autier. This revival extended throughout the Lauragais and as far as Toulouse and the Lower Quercy. Indeed the phenomenon was serious enough to attract the attention of three of the greatest inquisitors: Geoffrey d'Ablis, Bernard Gui, and Jacques Fournier (the future Pope Benedict XII).

Pierre Autier and his followers benefited from the developments within Catharism which had occurred in the second half of the thirteenth century, and also from certain developments involving the Church and local nobility. Despite the general collapse of the support of the nobility for the Cathars in the Occitan, a number of lesser nobles and the powerful count of Foix resumed their traditional tolerance of the heresy and hostility toward the Catholic Church. As a consequence, the leading inquisitors in the region were more concerned with the behavior of the nobility than with that of perfects like Pierre Autier. There was also lingering resentment of the northern French authority among both the secular and religious elite in the south, and this turned their attention further away from heresy. Moreover, although by Autier's time whatever organizational structure had once existed among the Cathars – bishoprics, local churches – had been destroyed for the most part, there remained a number of communities that maintained connections, if only tenuous ones. Most importantly, Cathar communities and perfects survived longer in northern Italy than they did in southern France, and were also in a better condition. The Italian Cathars would disappear during the fourteenth century, but by Autier's time they continued to be a source of instruction and encouragement to other Cathars. Indeed, this connection was exploited by the Autiers; in 1296 Pierre and his brother Guillaume went to Cuneo and other towns in Lombardy to receive the consolamentum and further initiation into the teachings of the Cathars. In southern France as well, Cathar perfects, believers, and sympathizers developed a way of life that preserved the traditional beliefs and practices despite the overwhelming burden of Catholic persecution. The perfects and their followers established safe houses throughout the countryside and secret underground networks through which messages and food were conveyed. It was in these safe houses that the perfects preached and ministered, rather than in the public square as they once had done, and they were guided from place to place by *ductores*, Cathar supporters who knew the land and its roadways well enough to lead them safely on their way in the dead of night. Believers and sympathizers not only protected and housed the perfects but also provided them with money, clothes, and a wide range of foodstuffs including fish, bread, oil, wine, apples, figs, and nuts.[5] Finally, and as an indication of the desperate situation the Cathars faced, the shedding of blood was approved in order to protect the perfects and their followers – in other words, murders and physical assaults on informers and enemies were sanctioned.

Developments within Catharism and in the broader world made conditions ripe for a committed and zealous missionary; and Pierre Autier would be that missionary. A member of a Cathar family of Ax-les-Thermes, near Foix, whose adherence to the heresy stretched back into the early thirteenth century and which included two perfects, Pierre Autier came to conversion at some point in his fifties, relatively late in life, and after a very successful professional career. Along with Guillaume, his brother and fellow 'Good Man' of the Cathar faith, Pierre was a prominent and well-to-do notary as well as a member of the nobility of the robe, with connections to the powerful. So well placed was the last great Cathar missionary that he was invited to prepare documents for an agreement between the count of Foix and the king of Aragon. He also prepared a contract between the people of Andorra and the count of Foix and an agreement between the same count and other nobles over a disputed territory. A capable businessman, Autier amassed considerable wealth, which benefited him when he took up the life of a Cathar missionary. His wealth allowed him to buy books, deposit a substantial sum with money changers in Toulouse, and cover the expenses of his wide-ranging travels as a perfect. These included the purchase of a set of fine Parma knives, which he could use to disguise himself as a wandering merchant.

Autier built not only a successful career but also a large family. His wife, Aladaycis, bore him four daughters and three sons; one of these was Jacques, who would become a perfect himself. He also had a mistress, Moneta, the sister of another notary from Autier's home town, who bore him two children: a boy, Bon Guilhem, who accompanied him on his trip to Lombardy, and a girl. His daughters seem to have married well into families at Ax and nearby towns. Raimond, another brother of Pierre, married the sister of a notary, and Guillaume married into an important family of Montaillou. Pierre's own large family and the extensive contacts between them, maintained through the brothers and their spouses, would come to play a very important role in Autier's success as a Cathar 'Good Man,' or perfect, and missionary. They secured lodging, food, and protection against informers and other threats to his mission. The extended family network also provided a ready audience to the missionary work of Pierre, Guillaume, and the other 'Good Men' associated with the Autiers.

According to one of the most important sources for the Autier revival and heresy in the early fourteenth century, namely the register of Jacques Fournier, inquisitor and bishop of Pamiers, Pierre and Guillaume took up the new life of Cathar missionaries in 1295–96. One day Pierre was reading a book, possibly a gospel or doctrinal text of the heresy, in the presence of his brother. He handed Guillaume the book and asked him to read it. After allowing his brother to read for a while, Pierre asked him what he thought about the text. Guillaume answered, 'It seems to me that we have lost our souls.' And in his turn Pierre declared, 'Let us go, my brother, let us go to find our salvation.'[6] And so the two brothers embarked on the long and arduous task of becoming 'Good Men.'

At some point in the year 1296, Pierre, Guillaume, and Bon Guilhem left for Italy to study with the Cathar perfects of Lombardy. The trip which had taken other Cathars from Languedoc to Italy took them through Provence into Nice, and from there into Italy, to the trade city of Cuneo. Disguised as merchants, the three Autiers could blend in easily with the other traders while seeking out instruction from the learned Cathars of Italy. Bon Guilhem returned home in the summer of 1297, to make sure that the place was safe for his father's eventual return. Pierre and Guillaume remained in Lombardy and made contact with senior members of the Cathar church in Italy as well as with the elder of the church of the Occitan, Bernard Audouy, who had contacts in the Lauragais. While in Italy, the two brothers obtained further instruction in the beliefs and practices of the Cathars. They also received the consolamentum, became perfects of the Cathar church, and were thus ready to preach the faith. Before their return to Ax-les-Thermes, the brothers also received training in the ways of the consoled. They learned about the proper diet of the perfects, being slowly weaned from the custom of eating meat and animal fat and introduced to the practice of eating fish, vegetables, and foods which were not produced through coition. The Autiers were also initiated into the cycle of fasting to be followed, and were taught the routine of reciting the Lord's Prayer.[7]

By late 1298 or, more likely, 1299, the two brothers had returned to the land of their birth, accompanied by a small group of perfects they had met in Lombardy, which included Pierre Raymond of Saint-Papoul, Prades Tavernier, and Amiel de Perles, formerly known as Amiel d'Auterive. Leaving the relative safety of Lombardy for Autier's homeland, this small missionary unit began preaching to the network of kin and other close connections in the Lauragais area. Once home, they took shelter in safe houses, to protect themselves from the local religious and secular authorities. They stayed for a time with Raimond Autier, who had not joined them on the trip to Italy and may not even have been informed about the purpose of the journey, but who welcomed them all the same when Bon Guilhem asked his uncle if Pierre could stay with him. They stayed at the homes of other relatives too, both shortly after their arrival and throughout their ten-year mission. Guillaume de Rodes, a nephew of the Autiers, provided shelter for them; Pierre's daughter and husband also offered advice and shelter, and other family members continued to feed the missionaries, bringing them water, wine, bread, cheese, fish, and other things. Not only did the extended Autier family provide items necessary for the missionaries' survival, but some also joined the mission: around the year 1300, Pierre's son Jacques was granted the consolamentum and adopted the life of a fugitive missionary, like his father. Connections with the local lesser nobility also proved fruitful, as the missionaries gained from them as well protection and lodging.

Although Pierre and his fellow missionaries would spread far and wide throughout the Languedoc and preach the Cathar faith to many, the need for security was most necessary because of the constant threat to their existence from the authorities and their various informers. Indeed, within a year of their return, Pierre, Guillaume, and the others faced a grave danger when the beguin (associated with the Spiritual Franciscans) Guillaume Dejean approached the Dominicans at Toulouse and offered to act as a spy for the inquisitors and to deliver the Autiers into their hands. He claimed to know the Autiers and produced more information about heresy in the region, including the allegation that Guillaume de Rodes had housed heretics. De Rodes's brother, the Dominican friar Raimond de Rodes, got wind of these accusations and sent word to his brother about the conspiracy against their uncles, the Autiers. Raimond was known to other Dominicans as a spy who acted for the heretics and protected them by sending warnings such as this one. He asked his brother Guillaume if he had housed the heretics and informed him of Guillaume Dejean's plans. Guillaume denied the allegation, declaring that Dejean was a liar. He then sent word to Raimond Autier about the conspiracy and the news spread quickly among the Cathars of Ax-les-Thermes. Shortly afterward, a Cathar sympathizer, Guillaume Delaire, met Dejean in the town square in Ax-les-Thermes and asked if Dejean wished to meet the Autiers. When he received a positive reply, Delaire offered to lead the spy to Larnat, where both Pierre and Guillaume Autier were residing. On the way there, the spy and his guide were met by other Cathar sympathizers, and possibly by Pierre Autier. Dejean was then savagely beaten and questioned about his intentions. When he finally admitted that he hoped to have the Autiers arrested, he was thrown off a cliff into a ravine, and his body was never found.

This incident demonstrates not only the importance of secrecy and the constant threat faced by Pierre Autier and his fellow missionaries, but also the importance of the network of family and sympathizers who contributed to the success of the mission. Indeed, this is not the only example of the (sometimes violent) lengths to which the missionaries and their supporters went to protect the cause. In 1304, Arnaud Lizier was found murdered in front of the castle gate in the town of Montaillou, where the Autiers enjoyed solid support and the Cathars were quite numerous. The murder followed upon a remark made by Guillaume Autier to the effect that, if it were not for Arnaud Lizier, he could preach publicly in the town square of Montaillou. Lizier's death was no doubt caused by one of the supporters of the heretics in Montaillou, who wanted to ensure that the Cathar 'Good Men' could show themselves in town without fear. The murder was clearly intended as a message of threat to those who opposed the Cathars. In fact, Pierre Autier had boasted to a fellow Cathar that the Autiers and their allies had arranged the murder because Lizier did not like their sect.[8]

Despite the constant threat to their survival, the Autiers found a ready welcome and cultivated a devoted following throughout the region. A hotbed of Catharism for a long time, the Lauragais and beyond offered a broad base of support for its mission. Even though that mission remained mostly underground and preaching took place secretly, in safe houses, beyond the watchful eye of the Catholic Church and its Inquisition, Pierre Autier and his fellows were extremely active and permanently called upon by people in the region to minister to them and to offer them the consolamentum – which some Cathars would only accept near the end of their lives. The welcome received in the region necessitated the creation of more perfects. Traditionally, the procedure was performed by a member of the hierarchy, for instance a bishop or a deacon; but Pierre, who held neither of these ranks, was intent on supplying the necessary leadership for the movement, and in about 1300 he ordained several new perfects. At a ceremony in a supporter's house Pierre consoled his son, Jacques, and Pons Baille, son of a notary of Tarascon. The two young men knelt before the older perfect and asked to be received into the church. Then they heard a sermon on the Lord's Prayer by Pierre Autier and agreed to follow a life of purity, to adhere to the dietary rules of the Cathar 'Good Men,' and never to lie or swear an oath. Pierre Autier then forgave them for their sins, put his hands on them and placed the Gospels over their heads, bestowing the Holy Spirit on them, and declared:

> Bless and forgive us. Amen. May it be done unto us, O Lord, according to Your word. May the Father and the Son and the Holy Ghost pardon and forgive you your sins. Let us pray the Father and the Son and the Holy Ghost. Let us pray the Father and the Son and the Holy Ghost! Holy Father, receive Your servant into Your justice and infuse him with Your Grace and Your Holy Spirit.[9]

The benediction was followed by a recital of the Lord's Prayer and readings from the Gospel of John. The ritual was concluded with another recitation
of the Lord's Prayer, and then Pierre kissed the two new perfects.[10] The rite
of ordination was repeated later when Pierre consoled two men who took the
names of Peter and Paul, and Pierre also sent Philippe d'Alayrac to Sicily to
be consoled. In this way, Pierre took steps to extend his influence, spread the
faith to a broader area, and respond to the needs of his flock throughout the
Languedoc.

The ordination ceremony performed by Autier demonstrates not only the
extent of the support they enjoyed in the region but also the importance of texts
to the Cathars. Indeed, the possession of books, especially Gospels, was recognized as a sign of heresy in the south. Pierre had his own personal library, which
included a book used in the consolamentum, bound in a special leather case, and
the important Cathar text *The Vision of Isaiah*. Like all Cathar perfects, Autier
traveled with the Gospels, often hiding them in his tunic to avoid suspicion. He
used the books to minister to his followers and would read from the Gospels
and other Cathar books during his services. The books themselves were often
in the vernacular – Occitan – or, as with Gospel books, included facing Latin
and Occitan versions of the text. Not only did Pierre Autier use the books when
preaching the Word; he also used some of his more elaborate ones to impress
and help convert followers. At one meeting he showed off to one of his followers, Pierre de Luzenac, a lavishly illuminated manuscript of the Gospels and
letters of St. Paul in Occitan. On another occasion Jacques Autier invited the
same Pierre de Luzenac to purchase a complete Bible for the Autiers the next
time he was in the city of Toulouse, and Luzenac delivered an Occitan version
of the letters of St. Peter and St. Paul.[11] The texts were central to the Autier
mission and contributed to their own understanding of the Cathar faith.

Traveling under cover of darkness, through back roads, and observing other
precautions, Autier preached a radical dualist form of Catharism which was
not uniformly followed by his fellow missionaries: they introduced variations
to their leader's teachings. Although historians once maintained that Autier's
Catharism was a decadent and corrupt version of the faith that emerged in the
late twelfth and early thirteenth centuries, it is now believed that he preached a
pure and traditional form of the heresy, shaped by his personal vision. Central
to Autier's beliefs was a radical dualism that posited two co-eternal principles of

good and evil. He taught that God had created all the spirits and souls in heaven and that the works of Satan brought about the fall of humankind. Standing at the gates of heaven for a thousand years, Satan entered the kingdom of heaven by trickery and seduced God's angels, who were made of body, soul, and spirit. He promised them a variety of riches, power over other creatures, knowledge of good and evil, and wives, all on condition of following him, and for nine days the angels fell from heaven to earth, where they were enclosed in earthly bodies. Finally, God noticed what was happening and put his foot on the hole in heaven through which the angels had departed. He warned the remaining ones of the consequences of following Satan and informed those who had left that they could stay out for the time being, implying that one day they might be allowed to return. [12]

Once the angels left heaven, according to Autier's cosmology, they were forced further under the devil's control. Satan ordered the fallen angels to sing, but they were unable to do so, noting that they now lived in a foreign land. They asked why Satan had tricked them, and one of them told Satan that he would never win and they would return to heaven. Satan informed them they would not, and proceeded to stuff the angels into the earthly bodies he had created, attempting to infuse them with life. But unable to give these bodies the power to move, Satan turned to God for help. The heavenly father answered that he would animate the bodies only if Satan agreed that the souls would belong to God and the bodies to Satan. The devil accepted this bargain and ruled over the bodies. Now, although the souls belonged to God and had come from heaven, once Satan had forced them into bodies of his own creation, they had no memory of having been in heaven. For Autier, bodies were thus essentially evil and the creation of the devil.

The angels would eventually obtain salvation and return to heaven, in Autier's understanding of the Cathar faith, but only after as many as seven to nine transmigrations. According to long-standing Cathar belief, which underpinned Autier's own teaching, a soul imprisoned by Satan in a human body was transferred from one body to the next until it finally reached the body of a consoled Cathar. [13] At that point the soul would be ready to return to heaven. For Autier, the bodies of the Catholic clergy contained the imprisoned souls of the leaders of the angels who followed Satan and, as such, these souls would suffer longer and go through the greatest number of transmigrations before obtaining salvation. Resurrection would be spiritual only, not bodily, because human bodies were the creation of Satan and thus evil.

Autier's dualism shaped his teachings in other ways as well, not the least of which was his belief that the present world was not only the creation of the devil but hell itself. His radical dualism naturally affected his attitude toward the Catholic Church. He rejected Catholic baptism on the grounds that it involved immersion in water, which was part of the evil creation of Satan, and that infants could not assent to the sacrament. He also rejected the Catholic practice of the Eucharist, the mass, and marriage, which was repudiated because it was the means to produce children and bring more people into an evil world. Autier also taught a unique Christology which mixed traditional Cathar teachings and his own interpretation of the nature of Jesus and Mary. As all the Christian dualists, Autier taught a Docetist Christology which denied that Christ had assumed human form or was born of the Virgin Mary, either in reality or in appearance. Christ was pure spirit who only appeared to take human form, and he had no human needs. Christ did not eat or drink, he felt no thirst or hunger, no heat or cold, and he could not die. He obtained the power to bind and set loose from God in heaven, and he bestowed it on his Apostles, who formed the true Church. Autier and the Cathars were the successors of the Apostles, and the consolamentum was the rite they had inherited from the original disciples of Christ. Beyond the traditional Docetic Christology, Autier held that Mary was not a woman at all but rather the will to do good – a teaching that diverged from earlier Cathar beliefs and was not accepted by all of Pierre Autier's fellow missionaries.

With his well-defined faith and necessary texts and assistants, Autier was most concerned to convert the people of the region and to prepare them for death. He was anxious to persuade potential converts to perform the *melioramentum* or the *melhorier*, as it was called in the local language, the ritual greeting owed to Cathar perfects. This procedure, which the inquisitors termed *adoratio*, consisted of the Cathar believers kneeling before the perfect, placing their hands on the ground, and turning their head toward their hands. The believer then asked the perfect three times for their blessing (prior to Autier's revival of Catharism there were both male and female perfects, but females faded away as a result of persecutions). The specific formula of the first two requests opened with the Latin imperative *Benedicite* and was followed by 'Lord,' 'Good Christian,' 'give us God's blessing and yours,' or 'pray to God for us.' The third time round the believer declared, 'Lord, pray to God for this sinner, that He will deliver him from an evil death and lead him to a good end.' The perfect responded to the first two requests by saying, 'Have it from God and from us,' and to the third one he said, 'May God take your prayer, may God make you a good Christian and lead you to a good end.'[14] The ritual concluded with the exchange of a kiss. There was also an abbreviated version of it, which included more limited gestures, such as the tilting of the head, and the request 'Bless us,' which was acknowledged silently by the perfect. The melioramentum was thus a means through which the believer could offer a prayer to God, since he or she was still subject to Satan and could not appeal to God in heaven except through the intermediary actions of the perfects. Performing the melioramentum was also a way for the believer to demonstrate his adherence to the Cathar faith and his acceptance of the spiritual authority of the perfect.

For Pierre Autier and earlier perfects, performance of the ritual was no mere sign of respect, as some would claim when called before the inquisitors, but an indication of commitment on the part of the believers; hence, persuading potential converts to perform the melioramentum was one of the primary goals of Autier's mission. Attempts to gain converts sometimes involved evangelism with a particular individual. One especially important conversion was that of Pierre de Luzenac, a student and future notary. Pierre and his fellow missionaries worked especially hard to convince de Luzenac to perform the melioramentum. They met with him frequently, provided loans, gifts, and money for him, and even showed him the beautiful illuminated Gospel book that Pierre Autier owned. Despite repeated attempts to get him to perform the rite, de Luzenac refused to do so, out of fear for his own safety. Ultimately, however, Pierre and his son Jacques managed to convince him to accept the Cathar faith, and de Luzenac performed the initiation rite while taking shelter from a storm in a mill, in the middle of the night. On another occasion, Pierre Autier used all his powers of persuasion to convince Pierre Maury, a shepherd of the village of Montaillou. Greeting the shepherd by the hand, the Cathar perfect offered to make him a good Christian and to put him on the path to salvation. He discussed at length the virtues of the Cathar perfects, stressing their moral superiority to the Catholic clergy, and assured Pierre Maury that the Cathar way was the true path to follow. The shepherd accepted Autier's arguments, agreed to become a

Cathar, and, after privately practicing genuflecting with Autier, performed the melioramentum.[15]

Preaching to an individual was one means that Pierre Autier used to spread the Cathar faith and convince potential followers to perform the melioramentum, but a more common means was to preach to small groups. On one occasion, such a group traveled from Arques to see Pierre Autier and met him in the house of a follower in Limoux. They all enjoyed a communal meal, which included some fish brought by the group as a gift for Autier, and afterward Autier preached a sermon. The lesson consisted primarily of various moral precepts and probably contained little instruction in the higher matters of Cathar theology. As Guillaume Escaunier, one of those in attendance, reported on his appearance before the inquisitor Geoffrey d'Ablis, Pierre explained that 'in no way should they touch the naked flesh of a woman, and that they should not return evil for evil, since God had forbidden it, and that they should not lie or kill anything except that which drags itself along on its belly across the ground, and if they were going along the road and found a purse or a money-bag, they should not touch it unless they knew it belonged to one of their believers and then they should take it and return it to them.'[16] Autier clearly had an impact on the group: before retiring for the evening, he taught Escaunier how to perform the melioramentum, which indicates that he had won a new convert.

As significant as the melioramentum was to Pierre Autier and his fellow missionaries, perhaps the most important duty of the perfects was to administer the consolamentum. Even though their followers were sometimes reluctant to perform the melioramentum or to accept the dangerous and austere life of the 'perfected' Cathar, they were most anxious to obtain final consolation before death. The consolamentum was the rite that perfected a Cathar believer and imposed upon them the life of asceticism, prayer, and preaching, which most adherents of the faith were unable to adopt. It was increasingly also administered to Cathar believers on the point of dying, because it was believed that the consolamentum would cleanse them of their sins and prepare them for entry into heaven. Indeed, belief in the power of this ritual is revealed by one of Autier's followers, who reported the occurrence of a miracle during its performance, noting that 'a great light descended from the sky upon the house and reached to the sick woman who lay upon the bed.'[17] Moreover, by the time of the Autier brothers, it had become common to perform the rite on the believer's deathbed; sometimes the Cathar perfect arrived too late.

The demand for the consolamentum by Cathar believers and sympathizers in the Lauragais area and in other parts of the Languedoc required the frequent intervention of Pierre Autier and his fellow missionaries. On one occasion, Pierre was called on to console Count Roger-Bernard III at his chateau in Tarascon. One of Pierre's fellow perfects consoled even an infant girl at her parents' request, because they feared she would die. The girl survived, and Pierre criticized the action because she was too young to understand the rite, noting that one of the errors of the Catholic Church was precisely the baptizing of infants who had not reached the age of understanding. But it was, of course, more common to console the aged or the sick unto death, and the Cathar perfects of the Autier revival were often called upon to perform the rite at a moment's notice. Although once a public process, administration of the consolamentum in the later stages of the history of the Cathars was done privately. Pierre's brother Guillaume, for example, was called to console the dying mother of Pierre de Gaillac. Guillaume, however, could not do it because of the large number of people keeping vigil by the deathbed, and so Pierre's wife, Esclarmonde, asked them to leave on the pretext that the excessive heat of the day caused undue suffering for Pierre's mother. Once the crowd had left, Guillaume secretly entered the room and performed the consolamentum.[18]

The need for secrecy and the difficulty of consoling believers yet again who had recovered from illness and taken up their former life led Pierre Autier to accept the practice of the *endura*. In this rite, a consoled believer was forbidden any food or drink other than water; in this way he or she would die without falling back into sin, and so would not need to be consoled again. Although not a new practice and not a sign of the decadence of Autier's revival, as is sometimes said, the endura came into much more widespread use in the late thirteenth and early fourteenth centuries as a result of the Cathars' persecution as well as of Pierre's desire to bring as many people to salvation as possible. Fasting to death was sometimes an easy prospect for the believer who truly was close to dying; to ease the passage, the believer was allowed to drink cold water, but was required to say Our Father after the drink. Even those near death, however, sometimes faced a prolonged endura, which could last for days. One committed believer maintained her fast for twelve weeks before dying, and another one, whose endura lasted for thirteen days, bled herself and planned even more dramatic actions to prevent herself from abandoning the fast. For some, however, the fast proved too much and they demanded food and drink, thus undoing the consolamentum and requiring consolation a second time. On other occasions, family members keeping vigil by the sick would give them food or drink, for instance some chicken soup, to ease the process. Pierre Autier himself imposed the endura on a sick woman whom he left in the care of her daughter; and after three days the daughter gave her mother some food, and she subsequently recovered.

Despite the sometimes prolonged suffering of those on fast, or their lapses into eating again, many times during his career Pierre Autier ordered his followers to undergo the endura and commanded those in charge of the dying not to give them food or drink. On at least one occasion, he even kept vigil over a dying 'consoled' – a practice once as common among the Cathars as among the Catholic clergy; but it had decreased in popularity as the practice of fasting to death became more widespread. He and his brother Guillaume consoled Huguette, the wife of Philippe de Larnat, and stayed with her until she died. At times Pierre spoke to her, encouraging her in her fast and praising her commitment. He offered kind words of praise to her family, emphasizing that she was on her way to paradise and, if she survived, she would honor her obligations as a perfected Cathar.

Even though Pierre Autier and the other perfects exercised great caution and found wide support, the Cathar revival was under constant threat, and the combination of internal betrayal and arrival of skilled and determined inquisitors such as Geoffrey d'Ablis, who was appointed inquisitor for Carcassonne in 1301, and Bernard Gui, who became inquisitor of Toulouse in 1307, would bring it to a fiery finale by the close of the first decade of the fourteenth century. Already in 1301, not long after Autier's return from Lombardy, the revival was threatened by the Dominican spy Guillaume Dejean, and threats to the safety of the Cathars continued as long as Autier and the other perfects preached.

Perhaps the first lethal blow came in 1305, when the inquisitors arrested Guillaume Peyre, a committed Cathar closely associated with the Autiers. For all his zeal, Peyre felt abandoned by Autier and the other Cathars during his time in prison. Peyre had fallen into debt paying prison guards for his food, and the Autiers refused to lend him the money to pay his debt. As a result, he betrayed them to the Inquisition and helped to set a trap for Jacques Autier.

On September 8, Jacques and his companion Prades Tavernier were arrested in Peyre's hometown of Limoux, where they had gone under the pretext that a sick woman wished to be consoled. The arrest came as a shock and would have had a disastrous effect on the movement but for the successful escape of the two Cathars while en route to the inquisitors' prison in Carcassonne. Profound damage was done, however, by Guillaume Peyre, who not only betrayed Autier but also provided substantial information to the inquisitors concerning the extent of Catharism in the region.

Pressure on the Autiers increased with the arrival of Bernard Gui, one of the greatest and most successful Inquisitors. Gui's arrival coincided with the reconciliation of the count of Foix with the Church, as well as the continued efforts of Geoffrey d'Ablis. The activities of the two inquisitors forced Pierre Autier and the others to go further underground for their safety, and the perfects still able to perform the consolamentum had to move from one hiding place to another during their final year. Already in early 1309, Jacques Autier and two other perfects, Guillaume Belibaste and Philippe of Alairac, were captured, but the latter two escaped. In the late spring or early summer of 1309, Guillaume Autier and Prades Tavernier were nearly captured in the town of Montaillou, barely managing to escape in the guise of woodcutters, and in August of that year Bernard Gui issued a call for the arrest of Pierre Autier and other leaders of the Cathar revival. Over the next several months, Autier and nearly all the perfects were captured and brought before the Inquisition, and everyone above the age of fourteen in the town of Montaillou, one of the revival's strongholds, was arrested and interrogated by the inquisitors. By the end of the year nearly all the leaders of Autier's revival with the exception of Pierre were burned at the stake for heresy. The arrests clearly had a devastating effect on the movement, and a number of Autier's followers confessed to the inquisitors after he had been taken into custody.

For a variety of reasons and mainly in order to ensure that more information on heresy in the region would be discovered, Pierre Autier himself was allowed to survive for several months after his capture. Perhaps because he felt secure in the belief that his work would long survive him despite his opponents' efforts, or, more likely, because Cathar perfects were forbidden to lie, Pierre told his interrogators a great deal about his teachings and the church he had resurrected. He offered an extensive discourse on Cathar beliefs and even performed the melioramentum on a fellow believer, before the inquisitors. He provided extensive information on his followers and may even have induced one of them to confess. But, although he may have faced torture, he did not implicate any of the Cathars in the town of Montaillou. Finally, on April 9, 1310, Bernard Gui and Geoffrey d'Ablis condemned him as a heretic and handed him over to the secular arm for execution. In the presence of a great crowd of nobles and of the inquisitors themselves, Pierre Autier was burned at the stake in Toulouse. Before he died, though, he proclaimed that, were he given the chance to preach to the crowd, he would have converted them all to his faith.

Although the last of Autier's followers would survive until 1329, the Cathar revival was essentially brought to a close with the burning of the last great missionary; Catharism itself would not survive his death for long.

CHAPTER SEVEN

FRA DOLCINO
AND THE APOSTOLICI

Tell Fra Dolcino, you who may see the sun,
If he wants not to follow soon to the same
Punishment, he had better store up grain
Against a winter siege and the snow's duress,
Or the Novarese will easily bring him down.[1]

In canto twenty-eight of the *Inferno*, the prophet Muhammad delivers this
ominous warning to Dante just as the Tuscan poet makes his way through
the ninth circle of hell, being led by his guide, the Roman poet Virgil, and
describes the torments that awaited upon Dolcino and other medieval heretics
who refused to accept the teachings of the Church. Dolcino, however, would
not have heeded the prophet's warning; he proceeded along a path of sometimes violent opposition to the Church of Rome, the clergy, and members of
the various religious orders.

A slightly earlier contemporary to Pierre Autier and the leaders of the last
Cathar revival, Dolcino assumed the leadership of the movement known as
the Apostolici, or the Apostolic Brethren, after the execution of its first leader,
Gerard Segarelli, and taught a very different heresy from that of the last great
Cathars. Dolcino's was a millenarian heresy, which vigorously challenged
the Catholic Church and its ministers and advocated a life of evangelism and

absolute poverty, even more stridently so than Valdes and other advocates of the apostolic life had done. His teachings were based on a variety of sources which included the works of the mystic Joachim of Fiore (1130/35–1201/2), the doctrines of Segarelli, the books of the Bible, and Dolcino's own prophecies – which, he believed, came straight from God above. In particular, Fra Dolcino developed a new theology of history and foretold the destruction of the established ecclesiastical order and the establishment of a new kingdom of peace under his own direction and that of his followers. His teachings and charismatic personality attracted a substantial following in Italy. The Italian movement survived its leader's death in 1307 and ultimately brought the full weight of crusade and Inquisition against Dolcino and his Apostolic Brethren.

Although perhaps the best-known member of the Apostolici, Fra Dolcino was not the founder of this movement, or its first leader. The group's founder, Gerard Segarelli, was an illiterate and humble man who turned up in Parma in 1260. This was an important year in the development of the concepts of Joachim of Fiore. According to contemporary accounts, Segarelli had sought admission to the Franciscan order but was refused. Inspired by images of the Apostles in the Franciscan church in Parma, Segarelli adopted a life of apostolic poverty and preaching which was even more rigorous than that of the Franciscans.[2] Dressed in a white robe and barefoot, in imitation of the Apostles, he wandered through the streets of Parma shouting: '*Penitenʒ agite!*' ('Do penance!'). The force of his personal example attracted a substantial number of followers out of whom he set apart two select groups, in imitation of Jesus: twelve were designated 'Apostles' and another seventy were the 'disciples.' His followers declared their conversion publicly. Initiates were first instructed in the teachings of the Apostolic Brethren and in their way of life. This was followed, according to the report of the inquisitor Bernard Gui, by a ritual – performed at a church or altar or some other public place – in which the new member removed his clothes, renounced all wealth and possessions and made a vow to God, in his heart, to follow the apostolic life. Having undergone initiation, the new brother could no longer accept money, as he was to have no possessions and to live by alms alone. After taking the vow of absolute poverty, members of the Apostolic Brethren could no longer swear oaths of obedience to any mortal; they were now subject to God alone.[3] They were so devoted to the life of absolute poverty and they despised wealth and possessions to such an extent that they called themselves not *minores* ('lesser'), as the Franciscans did, but *minimi* ('the least').[4]

Although it seems that Segarelli did not proclaim any doctrines other than the need to do penance and live a life of poverty, a collection of teachings of extreme hostility to the Roman Church sprang up among his followers by 1299 – granted, without the violence that would develop under Segarelli's successor, Fra Dolcino. The Church of Rome, they said, was the whore of Babylon from John's Book of the Apocalypse; it had turned away from the faith of Christ. The Church and its ministers had lost the power and authority bestowed on them by Jesus Christ. All that had now been transferred to the sect of the Apostles of Christ founded by Gerard Segarelli. Theirs was the only true order; all the orders associated with the Church since the time of Pope St. Sylvester I (314–35), and all their members with the exception of Pope Celestine V (July 5–December 13, 1294), were liars and seducers. The pope himself had no power to offer absolution unless he was as holy as St. Peter and lived in complete humility and piety. The laity, claimed the Brethren, should not pay the tithe to any prelate of the Roman Church whose life was not conducted in imitation of the poverty and perfection of the Apostles. The Brethren were the ones who most truly followed that teaching, and it was only to those who were called Apostles that the tithe should be given. The Brethren were not to swear oaths under any circumstances and not to reveal any of their beliefs to the inquisitors. Hence they were allowed to deny their beliefs, hide the truth, or even lie to the inquisitors; but they had to confess their beliefs openly when death was inevitable.

Segarelli's life of extreme apostolic poverty and preaching challenged the wealth and power of the Church just as his teachings rejected its worldliness. The Church, in its turn, would reject Segarelli, his teachings, and the order he founded. In 1274 the Second Council of Lyons reiterated the ban on new religious orders, first decreed by Pope Innocent III at the Fourth Lateran Council in 1215. Although Segarelli may have had no intention to found an order, he had certainly developed a sizeable following, and the ban in 1274 was aimed at groups like his. Of course, having already repudiated the Church, the Brethren and their leader paid little attention to its decree. In 1285 Pope Honorius IV (1285–87) ordered them to accept an established rule, and when they refused he condemned them outright. They were now subject to persecution and imprisonment, and in 1291, in response to their continued growth, Pope Nicholas IV (1288–92) renewed the condemnation of Honorius. Persecution of the Brethren increased thereafter, and in 1294 four members – two men and two women – were burned for heresy. Eventually Segarelli himself was arrested; he was kept in prison for a while, before being burned at the stake in 1300. Having rid itself of Segarelli, the Church now faced an even more radical and aggressive opponent, Fra Dolcino.

The illegitimate son of a priest from Novara, Dolcino was most likely raised in Vercelli in the Piemont region and had acquired a degree of learning which, along with his forceful personality, made him a most formidable opponent. He had joined the Apostolic Brethren in 1291 and was captured by the Inquisition as many as three times, recanting on each occasion. Dolcino may well have been behind the increasingly heterodox ideas that infiltrated the movement; at any rate, the Apostles became openly heretical when he assumed the leadership of the movement after the death of Segarelli. Clearly the letter he wrote in 1300, which, he claimed, was inspired by the Holy Spirit, reveals the more radical and heretical direction the movement was to take.

A gifted and original thinker, Dolcino, as his manifesto of 1300 clearly shows, was also the heir to a long tradition of unorthodox teaching and of devotion, sometimes excessive, to apostolic poverty. Like his predecessor Segarelli, Dolcino was inspired by the ideal embodied in the lives of the strict adherents to the Franciscan rule. Indeed, his movement was, in some ways, an extremist version of the Spiritual Franciscans. These rigorist advocates of the original idea of poverty, as expressed by St. Francis himself, had become increasingly uncomfortable with the direction the order had taken, especially as it had become institutionalized and had found a niche in the universities of the day. Emerging in the mid-thirteenth century, the Spiritual Franciscans rejected the various privileges the Franciscan order had received from the papacy; they were critical of the order's acceptance of property and of the establishment of Franciscan houses for the brothers. Not only did they seek to restore the original dedication to the apostolic life established by the order's founder, but they also identified Francis as the herald – the angel of the sixth seal – of a new age of radical spirituality and devotion to absolute poverty. They were inspired by the writings of Peter John Olivi (c.1248–98), who worked out a doctrine of absolute poverty and an eschatology which predicted an apocalyptic struggle and the replacement of the corrupt Church by the true spiritual church. The Spirituals adopted these ideas; they regarded themselves, together with Francis, as heroes of the new age that would follow the destruction of the established Church and its institutions. Their uncompromising devotion to poverty, however, drove a wedge between them and the main body of the order, the Conventuals. Efforts at a compromise brokered by the order's leader and one of its greatest theologians, St. Bonaventure (1221–74), failed, and the Spiritual Franciscans found themselves increasingly ostracized. They suffered outright persecution under Pope John XXII (1316–34), who ordered four of them to be burned in 1318 and declared apostolic poverty heretical in 1323.

Dolcino, like the Spiritual Franciscans and their intellectual leader Peter John Olivi, was also influenced by Joachim of Fiore, the twelfth-century Calabrian monk, theologian, and prophet whose vision of history shaped the prophetic and eschatological views of the Apostolic Brethren and others in the thirteenth century and beyond.[5] Joachim developed an eschatological philosophy of history which identified a pattern of human and sacred history associated with the persons of the Trinity. According to him, there were three ages (*status*) in history. The first age was that of the Father, initiated by Adam and associated with the Old Testament. It was the age of marriage. The second age was that of the Son, associated with the New Testament and the order of the clergy. The third age was that of the Holy Spirit; it was the age of the monks and a time of peace and spiritual perfection. The third age was to be prefigured by the appearance of a new order of monks; it would be a time of tribulations, when Antichrist would appear. Encouraged by three popes to write, Joachim, or some of his writings at least, would face censure as heretical at the Fourth Lateran Council in 1215 and at other councils in the thirteenth century. His works nonetheless remained very influential, but those influenced by them fell under the same suspicion as the works themselves.

Building on the lessons of Joachim and the Spiritual Franciscans as well as on the model of Gerard Segarelli, Fra Dolcino published his first prophetic letter in August 1300, soon after succeeding Segarelli as the leader of the movement – which by then numbered as many as three or four thousand men and women spread throughout Lombardy, Tuscany, and the surrounding regions. According to the inquisitor Bernard Gui, who included a version of the letter in his register in 1316, Dolcino taught an evil doctrine and offered his many followers not prophecy but fanaticism and insanity. In his letter, however, the new leader was offering a different perspective and demonstrating to his followers that his teachings were those of the true church. In the opening lines, Dolcino confirmed that his congregation was a spiritual one, namely the true church which accepted poverty and the apostolic life, recalling the ideas of the Spiritual Franciscans.[6] The obedience of the Brethren was an internal one, owed only to God and to no exterior power. Dolcino assured his congregation that this obedience was sent in the last days by God for the salvation of the souls of the good. He also claimed a special understanding of the Old and New Testaments; he, Dolcino himself, was sent by God with a special revelation about the future, which he would share with his devoted followers.

After declaring that he and his followers constituted the true church of God, Dolcino reinforced this idea by identifying the Church and the leaders of the social orders as enemies to the true church. For Dolcino, the members of the secular clergy were ministers of the devil. The secular clergy, the lay people and their leaders, and all the members of religious orders, especially the Dominican and Franciscan, stood in opposition to God's true church. Moreover, these groups actively persecuted the Brethren, the one true spiritual and apostolic church, and this made them even worse, according to Dolcino. Although he approved of going into hiding on account of the persecution which he, his predecessor, and his followers faced, Dolcino consoled the last by predicting that all the persecutors and prelates of the Church would be killed; the ones spared would convert, join the Apostolic Brethren, and be subject to the sect's leaders.

Having declared that he and his movement were divinely instituted and inspired, Dolcino outlined a view of history in his letter and issued prophecies concerning events to come. Drawing from Joachim of Fiore but adding his own unique interpretation, Dolcino explained that there were four ages of the world. The first age was that of the fathers of the Old Testament, the patriarchs, prophets, and just men who lived up until the time of Jesus. In that first age, marriage was a praiseworthy institution, established for the multiplication of humanity.[7] Eventually, however, the people of the world declined from the pure and honest spiritual state of their ancestors, and so Christ arrived with his Apostles, disciples, and other followers, to heal human weakness. The arrival of Christ, according to Dolcino, initiated the second age, which lasted until the age of Pope Sylvester I and Emperor Constantine. During this second age – an age of the saints – a new mode of life emerged which provided the medicine necessary to cure the ills of the first age. The saints who lived during this age displayed true faith, performed miracles, and lived humbly and patiently. They lived chastely and offered the example of the good life, in contrast to the impure life of those who lived at the end of the first age.

In the second age, the best life was that of virginity and chastity rather than of marriage, and those following the true path adopted poverty rather than wealth, having no earthly possessions.[8] The second age, too, experienced decline, and the third age began in the time of Sylvester and Constantine, when the gentiles and many others converted to the true faith. During this age, Pope Sylvester and his successors began to acquire territorial possessions and wealth for the Church.[9] At times, Dolcino continued, the love of God grew cold during this age and new orders emerged, to revive spiritual passions and restore the proper devotion to God. St. Benedict of Nursia was the first to implement a new and better way of life when he instituted his rule for the monks. The devotions of the monks and the love of God, however, grew cold again, and then St. Francis and St. Dominic revived religious life and restored the strict acceptance of poverty and Christ-like life that Benedict and his monks had once demonstrated. But, just as it happened after Benedict, religious zeal again declined following the arrival of Francis and Dominic. The friars were not the heralds of the last days, and so, according to Dolcino, God sent his last witnesses. Although they did not create a new order but only established the last of the old ones, Gerard Segarelli, the Brethren, and Dolcino himself would restore the proper mode of life. Sent by God to take up the apostolic life, the Brethren would survive and bear fruit until Judgment Day. The fourth age would then commence, and in the time following the decline of the life of St. Francis and St. Dominic, Dolcino and his followers would provide the world with the necessary medicine to cure its ills.[10]

Having outlined his theology of history, Dolcino explained further that the history of the Church itself, from the time of Christ to the end of the world, was divided into four periods. In the first period the Church suffered persecution but was good, chaste, and poor. During the second phase, beginning in the time of Sylvester and Constantine, the Church acquired wealth and prosperity but still remained good and chaste. The clergy, monks, and members of all the religious orders followed the example of the saints: Sylvester, Benedict, Francis, and Dominic. The third age, however, was one of debasement and decline, when the Church no longer sought the pure spiritual life but was eager to acquire wealth, property, and power. Dolcino insisted that this was the current state of the Church, and it would remain in that perverse condition until all the clergy were cruelly killed. This, added Dolcino, would occur in three years, after which the Church would be restored to its pure state. In fact, Dolcino claimed that the fourth age had already begun: it was initiated by Gerard Segarelli and would last until the end of the world. Although persecuted, the true church was established among the Apostolic Brethren, who lived in true poverty and goodness, and offered reform of the religious life and return to pure apostolicism.[11]

Drawing from his understanding of the writings of the prophets of the Old and New Testaments, Dolcino then announced a series of prophecies that would occur over the next three years, the period of the predicted destruction of the corrupt Church and clergy. And, indeed, his first prophecy concerns the very destruction of the Church. According to Dolcino, all the prelates and clergy, from the highest to the lowest, who belonged to the decadent Church of the third age would be destroyed by the sword of God, wielded by a new emperor and his kings. Dolcino asserted that this great destruction would include all monks and nuns, all members of the Franciscan and Dominican orders, and members of the orders of hermits. Not even the reigning pope, Boniface VIII (1294–1303), would escape destruction, and all the corrupt orders would disappear forever from the face of the earth. He continued by explaining that the agent of this destruction, which he corroborated through further reference to the scriptures, would be Frederick II (ruled 1296–1337), the king of Sicily and the son of Peter, king of Aragon (d. 1285). Frederick would be elevated to the position of emperor and would create a number of new kings, to assist him in the work of God. Having ascended to imperial power, Frederick would lead the fight against the corrupt clergy and Church and would ultimately kill Pope Boniface.

Following the death of Boniface and destruction of the clergy, Dolcino predicted that all the Christians would enjoy a period of peace in a millenarian kingdom, in anticipation of the Second Coming. During that time a new pope would miraculously take the throne; he would be sent by God from above rather than being elected by the cardinals, all of whom would have been killed in the great struggle against the false Church. The new pope and the new emperor, Frederick of Sicily, would rule together until the time of Antichrist, who would then establish his authority and rule during the last days. Under the new holy pope, the members of the order of Apostles, Dolcino and his followers, as well as the monks and clergy who had not been destroyed by the divine sword, would receive the gifts of the Holy Spirit, just as the original Apostles had. This new order of Apostles, explained Dolcino, by reference to the Holy Scriptures, had already begun to take shape, as it was founded by Gerard Segarelli and further enlarged by Fra Dolcino himself when Segarelli was killed by the corrupt Church. The order of the Apostles and the age of peace would endure and bear its fruits until the end of the world.[12]

The letter of 1300 closed with Dolcino's commentary on the seven angels and the seven churches of John's Book of the Apocalypse. The scheme he posited was intended to support his model of history and to demonstrate once again that he and his order were sent by God to minister during the last days. Just as he had associated monastic leaders and reformers in the history of the Church with its various ages and mutations, now he identified these same leaders with the churches of John's Apocalypse. St. Benedict was the angel of Ephesus, and his church was the congregation of monks. The angel of Pergamum was Pope Sylvester I, and his church was the clergy. St. Francis was the angel of Sardis and St. Dominic was the angel of Laodiciea, and their churches were the Friars Minor and the Order of Preachers respectively. These angels, in Dolcino's view, were those of the past; their existence led the way to the emergence of the final three churches, which would arise during the last days. The first of the three angels of these churches was Gerard Segarelli – the angel of Smirna. Fra Dolcino himself was the angel of Thyatira, and the pope to succeed Boniface was the angel of Philadelphia. The churches of all three of them formed the new apostolic congregation founded by Segarelli.[13]

Despite Fra Dolcino's assurances to his followers, in the letter of 1300, that his prophecies were divinely inspired, the events he foretold did not come to pass by the end of 1303. Although Boniface died, he was not killed by Frederick, as Dolcino had anticipated, and Frederick did not become emperor, nor were the clergy slaughtered by the sword of divine vengeance. In fact the death of Boniface VIII in October of that year, as a result of the rough treatment he received at the hands of the minions of the French king, Philip IV, inspired a second manifesto from Dolcino.

Although he had not seen the fulfilment of his prophecies, Dolcino remained undaunted and continued to have a devoted following. To preserve the faith of his followers and prepare them for the coming tribulations and triumph, he issued this second letter in late 1303 or 1304, offering another series of prophecies. The letter of 1303/04, which further alienated his movement from the Franciscans and other elements in the Church, reasserted that his prophecies were divinely inspired and that he and his followers played a central role in the divine plan.[14]

This new set of prophecies focused on the lives and reigns of four popes, two good ones and two bad ones. The first pair (one good, one bad) identified the popes, but the other two were unnamed. From this prophetic scheme, the opponents of the Apostolic Brethren argued that Dolcino had identified himself as the second good pope. This allegation was made in an anonymous contemporary chronicle as well as by the inquisitor Bernard Gui, who asserted that Dolcino had announced that, if he were still living at the time, he would reign as the last holy pope.[15] Although the Italian prophet had made no such claim, he had outlined events involving the popes who were to reign, as he believed, at the end of time. He had also noted in his letter that he would remain in hiding at God's command and would appear at the proper moment, which may have led to the contention that Dolcino believed himself to become the final pope.[16]

According to the letter of 1303/04, Pope Celestine V, as revealed in the scriptures, was the first of the popes whose reigns signaled the coming of the millennial kingdom. Celestine was the good pope; he was then followed by Boniface VIII, the first bad pope, who had been captured by Philip IV's men and died in late 1303. The next pope, whom Dolcino did not name, was evil too, and destined to face divine wrath at the hands of an earthly ruler. Dolcino prophesied in his second letter that Frederick, king of Sicily, would march against the perfidious newly elected pope and against his cardinals, destroying the corrupt leaders of the Church utterly and completely, as was foretold in the scriptures. Frederick would then reign as emperor and God's elect, and would be joined by the fourth and last pope. This would be a holy pope, chosen by God and not by the cardinals (all captured and destroyed by Frederick). The fourth pope would fulfill not only Dolcino's prophecies but those of Ezekiel and other biblical figures too, who had foretold the coming of the last days. Indeed, Dolcino proclaimed that the holy pope was to be the angel of Philadelphia spoken of in John's Book of the Apocalypse.[17]

Dolcino also described the role of his followers in the events of the last days. Upon the destruction of the evil pope together with his cardinals and clergy, the Apostolici would be joined by the spirituals of all the orders; they would receive the grace of the Holy Spirit and renew the Church, dedicating it to the life of apostolic poverty.[18] They would preach the imminent coming of the Antichrist and the final tribulations. When Elijah and Enoch descended to do battle with Antichrist, the Apostolici would be safely removed to paradise. Returning after the defeat of Antichrist, they would join Frederick, the last emperor on earth, and convert all the nations of the world. They would usher in an age of the Spirit and of millennial peace, and they would flourish until the end of time.[19]

Dolcino concluded the prophecy with a schedule of the events that would unfurl over the course of the next three years. In 1303, he declared, ruin would come to the king of the south (Charles II, king of Naples, ruled 1285–1309) and to Pope Boniface VIII. The next year was to bring the destruction of the cardinals and of Boniface's successor. In 1305 the desolation of the clergy would take place: priests, monks, nuns, Dominicans, Franciscans, and hermits, and all the religious prelates who had contributed to the corruption of the Church, would be destroyed. The general destruction of pope and clergy over 1304 and 1305 would be accomplished, as Dolcino saw it, by Frederick, emperor of the Romans.[20]

Having issued this second manifesto, Dolcino led his followers into hiding in the mountains between Vercelli and Novara. There he most likely produced a third manifesto, which has been lost. He intended to remain there until God revealed that it was time for him to reappear publicly. Joined by some four thousand followers, both men and women, including Margherita di Franck and his four lieutenants (Longinus of Bergamo, Frederick of Novara, Albert of Tarento, and Valderic of Brescia), Dolcino proclaimed a millennial kingdom in which all goods were to be held in common and, according to at least one contemporary account, women were regarded as 'common property and could be used without sin.'[21] Some of his followers believed that Dolcino himself would be the pope of the new age prophesied in the letter of 1303, and he continued his preaching to the effect that the pope and other leaders of the Church were not worthy of their positions. Dolcino's preaching inspired not only his own followers, who remained undaunted when Frederick did not rise up to destroy the evil pope and his cardinals, but also members of the antipapal Ghibelline party as well as the local peasants, who resented the wealth and power of the established Church.

The vehemence of his teaching and the hostility toward the Church displayed by his followers and supporters, together with the presence of the Inquisition and the increasing opposition from the Church, produced the savage violence associated with the movement. According to a contemporary anonymous chronicler from the mountains where Dolcino and the Apostolic Brethren resided, the group hanged many Christians, including a boy of ten.[22] Refusing ransoms, they hanged men in front of their wives, or starved them to death in their prisons. They cut off the lips and noses of some women, the breasts or feet of others, and even the arm of a pregnant one, whose child died shortly after birth. The brutal violence of the rebellion was not limited to individuals but extended to villages and to the Church itself. Dolcino's followers burned and destroyed a number of villages in the lower Alps in Italy, including Mosso, Trivero, Còggiola, and Fléccia.[23] They also destroyed numerous cantons in the Crevacuore and many private homes in other regions. The Church, too, suffered severe damage at the hands of the religious rebels. In the village of Trivero, the church itself was burned, and the Apostolic Brethren disfigured the sacred paintings and sculptures, stole the altar tables, ripped off the arm of a statue of the Virgin Mary, tore down the bell tower of Trivero and smashed its bells. In their raids they stole 'books, chalices, and ornaments' as well as the property of the priests and the plate of the religious confraternity serving the Church.[24] From this almost unprecedented violence against the Church and local communities, Dolcino's followers accumulated a significant quantity of goods, which they stored in their mountain hideout.

The physical violence as well as the violence of Dolcino's rhetoric inspired an equally strong response from the Church. As the inquisitor Bernard Gui recorded in his register, Dolcino was guilty of a wide range of religious offenses.[25] He was guilty of preaching numerous errors, especially that the Church of Rome was not the true church and that the true church consisted of himself and his followers. Proclaiming that he was filled with the spirit of prophesy, he declared that Frederick would become emperor, establish ten kings in Italy, and kill the pope and all the cardinals. He erred further by asserting that he himself would then assume the throne of St. Peter and rule the Church with his followers. Dolcino, Gui continued, erroneously taught that the Church had four ages that were characterized by general decline of morality. According to him, the period from the time of Pope Sylvester I to that of Pope Celestine V was one in which the representatives of the Church were liars and fornicators and made themselves guilty of the sins of pride and avarice. In sum, so Gui, Dolcino's teachings were virulently antisacerdotal, rejecting the priesthood and the sacraments of the Church and declaring that religious orders themselves were unnecessary.[26] And, finally, his teachings were a source of inspiration for the violence of his followers. For all these reasons, at the complaints of the local bishop, in 1306 Pope Clement V (1305–14) issued a bull announcing a crusade against Dolcino and the Apostolic Brethren, complete with full indulgences for the participants.

As they had struggled against the local authorities and plundered the surrounding villages, Dolcino and his followers resisted the crusaders to the death. In the face of repeated attacks directed by the bishop of Vercelli, Dolcino and some of his Apostles, including Margherita, withdrew to a mountain in Novara. They were pursued by the forces of the Church, and Dolcino and some forty followers were captured in a last stand on Holy Thursday, March 23, 1307. Both Margherita and Dolcino were held captive for some months and tortured. Finally, they were both executed in a most gruesome fashion. Margherita went first; she was dismembered alive in front of Dolcino. In his turn, Fra Dolcino had his limbs ripped from his body with red hot pincers, and then his dismembered body and that of his devoted follower, Margherita, were burned.[27]

But not even the brutal execution of Fra Dolcino and his closest adherents, or the failure of his prophecies to come true, brought the sect to an end. Although many of Dolcino's followers, men and women alike, reconverted and sought restoration to the Catholic Church, many others refused and were discovered in Tuscany and other parts of Italy. Bernard Gui warned that many of Dolcino's followers escaped the clutches of ecclesiastical and secular authorities and, under the false appearance of piety and sanctity, were secretly disseminating their teachings to the simple.[28] Gui even felt compelled to send a letter to the bishops of Spain, where the Apostolic Brethren appeared in 1315, as he was fearful of the continuation and expansion of the sect.[29] And there are numerous other records of the appearance of Dolcino's Apostles, apart from that of the great inquisitor. They were believed to have infiltrated the Order of the Franciscans. Two members of the sect were convicted in Bologna in 1311. Suspected heretics brought before the Inquisition at Toulouse claimed that Dolcino was the founder of their sect, which was known to exist in southern France in 1321 and 1322. Pope John XXII (1316–34) sent the bishop of Cracow a warning about the Apostolic Brethren.[30] And the movement apparently survived well into the fourteenth century, as adherents to the sect were found at Trentino in the early 1330s, at Padua in 1350, in Sicily in 1372, and in Narbonne in 1374 – and, even as late as 1402, in Lübeck.[31]

The sect of the Apostolic Brethren would never again achieve the size it had reached under Dolcino, nor would it be seen as the serious threat it had been during his lifetime; it would finally disappear in the fifteenth century. The dramatic rise of the movement and the impact it had on contemporaries were clearly due to its leader, Fra Dolcino. He combined an extreme apostolic poverty with a highly millenarian eschatology, in a volatile mixture which inspired large numbers of followers and was deemed a serious threat by the established Church. His teachings, which envisioned a central role for his sect in the large scheme of events at the end of time, inspired numerous followers and gave them the courage to fight against what they saw as the forces of Antichrist. A visionary and a prophet, Dolcino offered a radical path for his disciples to follow: the ideal Christian life lived at the end of time. But Fra Dolcino was not the only visionary of his day to provide an alternative to the institutional structure of the established Church. Another departure from orthodox traditions would bring about the demise of the mystic Marguerite Porete.

CHAPTER EIGHT

MARGUERITE PORETE:
MYSTICISM AND THE BEGUINES

On the first of June 1310 at the Place de Grève in Paris, Marguerite Porete was burned at the stake, enduring what the great nineteenth-century historian of the Inquisition, H. C. Lea, called the first formal auto-da-fé in Paris.[1] Condemned as a relapsed heretic, Marguerite accepted her fate calmly and without fear, and she was regarded with great admiration by those who witnessed her death, many of whom burst into tears during the execution.[2] Her condemnation came as the result of her unwillingness to discuss or denounce the teachings found in her great mystical work, the *Mirror of Simple Souls*, which she wrote in Old French. Although judged heretical, the *Mirror* was a work of great popularity and influence during the fourteenth and fifteenth centuries and beyond; it was published in the twentieth century as an orthodox text. Indeed, both the reception and the contents of Marguerite's great work raise the question of the orthodoxy of her own beliefs. Was she, like her contemporary Fra Dolcino, a heretic clearly opposed to the Church and its teachings? Or was she a devout mystic and a victim of circumstances? Her life and death, in fact, intersected with several broader historical movements of her day, so that both her fate and the extent of her heresy can be truly understood only in the context of the religious and political developments of the late thirteenth and early fourteenth centuries.

Little is known about Marguerite's life until in the mid-1290s, when she first ran afoul of the ecclesiastical authorities, and what is known comes from her writings and from the inquisitorial documents compiled at her trial. Her date of birth is not known with any certainty, nor is the exact place of her birth, although she was most likely from Hainaut, a county in the Low Countries that was under the jurisdiction of the archbishop of Cambrai, and it has been suggested that she was from the town of Valenciennes.[3] Passages from her *Mirror*, however, provide some background on her social class. Echoes of the tradition of courtly literature are found throughout her work, which suggests that she may have come from the aristocracy.[4] Other passages of the text demonstrate the author's knowledge of important mystical texts of the twelfth century and of the Bible, which indicates that Marguerite was well educated.[5] Indeed, the extent of her learning is revealed by a chronicler's claim that she even translated the Bible into the vernacular; no evidence of this, however, can be found in the trial records, and there is no surviving copy of any such Bible. Condemned and burned as a *pseudomulier* ('false woman'), Marguerite identified herself as a Beguine, as did most contemporary texts that described her. One contemporary chronicle in particular, however, noted that she wrote a book which taught that 'a soul annihilated in the love of the Creator could, and should, grant to nature all that it desires,' which raises the possibility that she was connected to another movement.[6] The antinomian and pantheistic, even autotheistic, qualities of her teachings, as described by the contemporary chronicler, led H. C. Lea to proclaim her as the first member of the German heresy of the Free Spirit to appear in France, and Robert Lerner has identified her as one of the representatives of that heresy.[7] The nature of both movements, of the Beguines and of the Free Spirit, provides important insights into the life and death of Marguerite Porete; therefore a brief survey of both is necessary in order to gain a proper understanding of Marguerite, her teachings, and her horrible fate.

The Beguines are perhaps the more important and more influential of the two groups associated with Marguerite Porete, and the movement with which she readily identified herself. This self-identification, however, is complicated by the very nature of the Beguine movement, as well as by Marguerite's understanding of it. Indeed, the lifestyle she chose to follow as a Beguine in some ways helps to explain why she was executed and reveals the difficulties that the Beguines as a whole experienced at the end of the thirteenth century and beginning of the next – a period when increasing restrictions were placed on them, and the term *beguine* came to be synonymous with 'heretic.'

Despite the difficulties the Beguines faced during Marguerite's lifetime and for much of the rest of the Middle Ages, they first emerged in Liège in the late twelfth century, and by the middle of the next they were a popular and well-received religious movement (or movements). The designation *beguine* appeared in the 1230s.[8] Although at first suspected of heresy because of their lifestyle, the Beguines were welcomed by the Church hierarchy already by the early thirteenth century; they clearly addressed the need of the Church to respond to the spiritual demands of women, notably of urban ones. The Beguines were pious religious women, who lived alone or in small communities in cities which had grown larger and more populous in the course of the twelfth century. The emergence of these religious communities was, in fact, a reaction to social changes associated with the new towns and cities as well as to the changes in spirituality generated by these social changes. Beguine communities and their way of life became necessary because the traditional outlets for women's piety no longer proved suitable in the new urban environment: these communities offered a means for pious living to the economically less well-to-do. The established monastic communities of women did not fully adapt to the changing spirituality of the twelfth century, which, among other things, emphasized the apostolic life and a more internalized form of religious piety. Moreover, those traditional communities required of their novices to bring a dowry with them. Although the size of the dowry was less demanding than in the case of arranging a good marriage, it was still large enough to bar many women. Traditionally, the established monastic communities had been the preserve of aristocratic and even royal women, and thus social status also limited that accessibility of the convents to many women. At the same time, the new orders that emerged in the twelfth century, particularly the Cistercian monastic order, were reluctant to welcome women into their ranks. Although Robert of Arbrissel and other, more progressive, thinkers implemented reforms which encouraged the involvement of women, the newly forming orders of the twelfth and thirteenth centuries tended to limit their participation.

The first of the Beguine communities appeared in the urban centers of northern Europe, spreading throughout Flanders, France, and the Rhineland. These devout women who were unable to join traditional communities because of a lack of wealth or social status first formed associations around local churches. By the early thirteenth century they had started to occupy houses where they could live according to their own lifestyle. The earliest of these houses were established by prosperous bourgeois women who also welcomed those less well off, and they were all bound by religious piety. They lived simply, supporting themselves by sewing, weaving, embroidery, and the copying of books, and they regularly attended mass and the canonical hours of the day at the local church. Beguine women seemed intent on living in voluntary poverty and chastity, and thus their movement tapped into the growing interest in the life of apostolic poverty. The Beguines were unique, however, in that they took no vows and had no formal institutional structure, local conditions often shaping the individual community or beguinage. It was this lack of formal organization and the absence of a religious vow that contributed to the great popularity and success of the movement, but also laid the foundation for its downfall.[9]

Although the Beguines would eventually face increasing suspicion from Church leaders, they found widespread support for a period during the early and mid-thirteenth century. One of their earliest and most influential advocates was the bishop Jacques de Vitry (c.1160/70–1240), confessor to one of the important early Beguines, Marie d'Oignies (c.1177–1213), and the man who convinced Pope Honorius III (1216–27) to approve the way of life of Beguines. Many other bishops came to support the communities of Beguines, as did some members of the Franciscan order, with whom the Beguines shared a certain affinity. Most notably, the great English bishop and scholar Robert Grosseteste (c.1170–1253) staunchly supported them, declaring that the life of the Beguines was superior to that of the mendicants. And in France, the Beguines found support from the king himself. By the late thirteenth and early fourteenth centuries, however, this situation had changed; various questions about the life of the Beguines and rumors of their sexual immorality had surfaced. The very lack of a rule, or vow, now reflected badly on them since no formal restraints could be imposed on the behavior of these women. Beguines could live in community or independently; and the itinerant Beguine, who often followed her own understanding of the scriptures, was deemed a particular threat to society and to the Church. As a result of this growing distrust, in 1312 the Council of Vienne issued two decrees against the women who called themselves Beguines, declaring that there was 'an abominable sect of malignant men known as beghards and faithless women known as beguines.'[10]

Marguerite clearly identified herself with the Beguines and hence suffered by this association, but she was also associated with another heresy that the Church deemed particularly widespread and threatening. During Marguerite's lifetime, the Church had become increasingly aware of, and concerned with, a mystical and antinomian sect known as the heresy of the Free Spirit. The Council of Vienna, which had condemned the Beguines, associated them and their male counterparts, the Beghards, with the Free Spirit heretics, asserting that the Beguines believed that they could become perfect in this life and, once they had achieved perfection, they were incapable of sin and thus no longer subject to the laws of Church or state.[11]

In some ways, as will be seen below, Marguerite's own work, or at least a misreading of select passages taken out of context, implied antinomian and libertine teachings. But, although the condemnation of the heresy at the Council of Vienne – where the label Free Spirit was not used – provided the 'birth certificate' for the heresy, it seems, as Robert Lerner has demonstrated in his book on the subject, that there was no such movement.[12] There were, indeed, mystics like Marguerite who expressed an autotheism, but few, if any, who taught that their union with God allowed them to pursue a life of immorality and sexual excess. The willingness of the Church to create such an image, however, reveals the concerns with heresy that existed at the time as well as the readiness of Church leaders to resort to such procedures.

It is in this context of concerns over the Beguines and fear of a widespread antinomian heresy that the life and death of Marguerite Porete can best be understood, and a partial explanation as to why Marguerite suffered the fate she did can be attempted. She first came to the attention of ecclesiastical authorities at some point during the last decade of the thirteenth century and the first decade of the fourteenth. It was sometime between 1296 and January 1306 that Marguerite wrote the *Mirror of Simple Souls* – and it must be stressed that she wrote it herself rather than having it copied by a scribe – in the everyday language of Old French. She may well have already begun disseminating her book and its teachings and she was living the life of an itinerant Beguine, when she came to the attention of Guy II, the bishop of Cambrai. At a meeting at Valenciennes, the bishop publicly condemned her teachings and cast her book into the flames, burning it in front of Marguerite. The bishop also ordered her to stop spreading her teachings and writings and threatened to turn her over to the secular authority for punishment if she failed to heed his warning.

As subsequent events proved, it is clear that she did not obey the bishop's command and continued to spread her ideas. She even sent a copy of her book – thus indicating that Guy II did not destroy all its copies – to John, bishop of Châlons-sur-Marne, for his consideration of her ideas. For this reason, and because she was accused of continuing to spread her beliefs to the simple folk of the region and to the Beghards, sometime between 1306 and 1308 she was called to appear before the new bishop of Cambrai, Philip of Marigny, who was also the inquisitor of Lorraine. Even though he had the authority of an inquisitor, Philip chose not to interrogate Marguerite, who was sent to Paris instead. There she was taken into custody, in late 1308, by William of Paris, the Dominican inquisitor and former confessor of King Philip IV the Fair, who would play a critical role in determining Marguerite's fate.

From her arrival in Paris in late 1308 until her death in June 1310, Marguerite and her confidant and self-proclaimed defender, Guiard de Cressonessart, remained subject to the authority of the inquisitor and endured confinement in William's prison. Despite his repeated entreaties, Marguerite refused to appear before the tribunal to answer questions concerning her writings and teachings. Moreover, she would not even take the oath required of those who were called before the Inquisition. William offered Marguerite absolution as an inducement to appear before the Inquisition, but she refused even this effort and remained under a ban of excommunication. Faced with similar threats and inducements, Guiard eventually yielded but Marguerite did not, and William was forced to find another method of dealing with the silent Beguine.

Failing to come to a resolution by the usual means at the inquisitor's disposal, William turned to various learned men associated with the University of Paris. In March 1310, he sought advice from several professors of law and theologians at the university concerning Marguerite and her book, as well as certain matters of jurisdiction. These scholars took a dim view of Marguerite's book and recommended that the canon lawyers be given authority over the case. Following this meeting, however, William called together a commission of twenty-one theologians, who met on April 11, 1310. The commissioners were given some fifteen excerpts from Marguerite's book, so that they could determine the orthodoxy of her teachings. One of these passages contained the damning assertion that the liberated soul should give to nature all that it ask, which, when taken out of context, was understood to show that Marguerite taught an antinomian theology which promoted libertinism and the rejection of traditional morality and virtue. The canons may have understood the passage to indicate, further, that Marguerite also rejected the established Church and denied that the soul who had received God's love needed the Church to fulfill its traditional intermediary role between God and the individual Christian.[13] She had, in fact, maintained that the liberated soul had no need for the usual good works promoted by the Church, such as fasting, attending mass, and saying prayers. The commission, having reviewed such passages, deemed Marguerite's work heretical.

Marguerite, however, offered at least some defense of her work. She declared that three other scholars had reviewed it and did not find it heretical. She had sent a copy of the *Mirror* to three authorities, including the Franciscan John of Quaregnon (Hainaut) and the Cistercian Dom Franco of the abbey of Villers, which had long supported the Beguines, and both of them approved of the work. According to John, the 'book was truly made by the Holy Spirit and ... if all the clergy of the world heard only what they understood [of it], they would not know how to contradict it in any way.'[14] And Dom Franco asserted that he had proved from scripture all that appears in the *Mirror*. Little more is known of these authorities, but the third figure, Godfrey of Fontaines, a highly respected master at the University of Paris, is much better known. He, too, approved of the work, even though he was a bit more cautious in his appraisal, noting that it was a book meant only for the strong of spirit. The support of these learned men provided little help to Marguerite, who would face a further tribunal, but it suggests that her work may not have been as unorthodox as others had claimed.

Although she had garnered endorsements of the *Mirror*, on May 19, 1310, Marguerite was called before a second commission, which was composed of canon lawyers given charge to decide her fate. The commission determined that:

> From the time Marguerite called Porete was suspected of heresy, in rebellion and insubordination, she would not respond nor swear before the inquisitor to those things pertaining to the office of inquisitor. The inquisitor set up a

case against her nevertheless, and by the deposition of many witnesses he found that the said Marguerite had composed a certain book containing heresies and errors, which had been publicly condemned and solemnly burned as such on the order of the Reverend Father Lord Guy, formerly bishop of Cambrai. The above-said bishop had ordered in a letter that if she attempted again to propagate by word or writing such things as were contained in this book, he would condemn her and give her over to the judgment of the secular court. The inquisitor learned next that she had acknowledged, once before the inquisitor of Lorraine, and once before Reverend Father Lord Philip, the next bishop of Cambrai, that she still had in her possession, even after the condemnation mentioned above, the said book and others. The inquisitor learned also that the said Marguerite, after the condemnation of the book, had sent the said book containing the same errors to the Reverend Father Lord John, by the grace of God bishop of Châlons-sur-Marne. And she had not only sent this book to this Lord, but also to many other simple persons, beghards and others, as if it were good.[15]

In sum, she was condemned on several counts, notably because she was declared a relapsed heretic having resumed her teaching of the errors she had abjured before the bishop of Cambrai at Valenciennes. She was also found guilty of obstinately holding her erroneous belief and of being contumacious in her refusal to answer the inquisitor's questions. Consequently, William of Paris announced her condemnation on May 31, 1310. She was handed to the provost of Paris and burned at the stake on the first of June, going to her death with such dignity and piety that many who witnessed the execution were in tears.

At the center of the controversy concerning Marguerite was, of course, her mystical treatise, the *Mirror of Simple Souls*. The *Mirror* caused concern for two reasons. On the one hand, the work itself seems to have been quite popular, both in Marguerite's day and after her death; it is extant in numerous editions and translations. There are three surviving copies in Marguerite's Old French, the earliest of which may date to the fourteenth century; the other two are from the fifteenth and seventeenth centuries.[16] The *Mirror* was translated from the Old French into Latin already in the fourteenth century, and four Latin versions are still in existence. The Latin translations were the source of two independent Italian translations made in the course of the same century. By the fifteenth century, some thirty-six copies of the work circulated throughout Italy. The influence of her book was not restricted to the continent; it extended also to England, where a copy of the *Mirror* may have arrived as early as 1327. That copy was probably brought to the English court by someone in Philippa of Hainaut's entourage, when she arrived to marry King Edward III.[17] If the text got in that early it left little mark, but in the fifteenth century several translations of the *Mirror* were made from Old French into Middle English. The translations were most likely made by Cistercian monks, and in 1491 the Carthusian monk Richard Methely (1451–1528) translated the text from Middle English to Latin. Popularity alone cannot explain, however, why Marguerite was executed, nor serve as a demonstration of heresy, and, as Robert Lerner has noted, the number of copies, especially those made by the monks, demonstrates that there was nothing overtly heretical about the text, even though her influence must surely have unnerved Church leaders suspicious of the existence of the heresy of the Free Spirit.[18]

The *Mirror of Simple Souls*, a book of roughly 60,000 words in some 100 folios, is both a handbook offering spiritual guidance to individual believers and a mystical treatise which explores the relationship of human and divine love and its capacity to bring the soul in union with God.[19] The *Mirror* includes an opening poem that sets the tone for the rest of the work and is divided into 140 chapters, including the prologue. Although organized as a dialogue between *Amour* ('Love') and *Raison* ('Reason') concerning the soul, the work is not uniform in structure and can be repetitive. The *Mirror* consists of extensive passages in prose, which contain dialogues and passages of great drama, but it also includes poetry and *exempla*. The prose passages themselves are often rhythmic and glide from time to time into more free-flowing and lyrical passages and then into full poetry.[20] As Peter Dronke noted, Marguerite seemed best suited to write lyrically and at times used two particular poetic forms, the canzone and the rondeau.[21] Guided by the main characters, Love and Reason, other characters burst on to the scene unannounced, to offer advice on various matters, before disappearing from the text. Marguerite incorporates chivalric and courtly ideals and refers to an aristocracy of love as well as to well-known courtly tales. Although she did not make explicit mention of earlier mystical texts, she was clearly aware of these works, including those by William of St. Thierry and St. Bernard of Clairvaux, and the text itself contains 'an extensive mystical vocabulary.'[22] There are no direct or explicit references to the scriptures in the *Mirror* but there are echoes of the Bible throughout, suggesting that she knew the good book.

In the poem which opens the *Mirror of Simple Souls*, Marguerite introduces some of the important themes to follow, including one which was a potential cause of alarm for the Church. In a verse that could perhaps be read as being anticlerical, Marguerite asserts that theologians and the clergy will not be able to understand her work unless they proceed humbly. Humility is one of the essential virtues promoted in the opening poem and the key to understanding the text to follow. It is necessary to humble the reason and to accept love and faith as a way to rise above reason in order to come to understand both the work and the will of God. Marguerite declares that it is necessary to place all faith 'in those things which are given by Love, illuminated through Faith. And thus you will understand this book which makes the Soul live by love.'[23] She thus confirms the importance of love and the acceptance of God's will as the key to spiritual fulfillment, revealing the character of the book as both a mystical treatise and a handbook for guiding other souls.

The purpose of the work is more clearly enunciated in the opening passage of the prologue or first chapter, where Marguerite declares:

> Soul, touched by God and removed from sin at the first stage of grace, is carried by divine graces to the seventh stage of grace, in which state the Soul possesses the fullness of her perfection through divine fruition in the land of life.[24]

The treatise provides a description of the soul's mystical ascent to God through seven distinct stages, 'each one of higher intellect than the former and without comparison to each other.'[25] The difference between these stages, as Marguerite wrote, is as great as that between a drop of water and the ocean.[26] And, throughout the *Mirror of Simple Souls*, Marguerite identifies the differences between the seven stages and describes the state of the soul in each one of them. The spiritual ascent through these stages or states of grace leads to ultimate union with God, annihilation of the soul in God, and total identification with God.[27]

The first four states, which are very much in line with traditional orthodox mysticism, mark the growth of the soul toward God while it remains encumbered by 'some great servitude.'[28] In the first state, the soul is touched by God's grace; in fact, only divine grace can lead the soul to perfection. Once touched by it the soul is stripped of sin and becomes intent on keeping the commandments of God for the rest of its life. The soul has been commanded by God to love God, itself and its neighbor, and so guided by grace and the desire to love it will keep adhering to the law of God 'even if she lived a thousand years.'[29]

In the second state, the soul moves beyond what God has commanded and strives to accomplish all it can to please its beloved, God. The soul abandons all self and worldly things, despising riches, honors, and earthly delights. Having no fear of losing possessions, of the words of other people, or of the weakness of the body, the soul seeks to accomplish evangelical perfection and to follow the example of Jesus Christ.[30]

In the third state, the soul moves to break the will of the spirit. Immersed in doing the good works and asceticism of the second state, the soul has come to love these works but begins now to realize that it must sacrifice them for love. In this way the soul undergoes martyrdom by giving up what it loves, and in the process it comes to destroy the will. For, as Marguerite explains, 'it is more difficult to conquer the works of the will of the spirit than it is to conquer the will of the body.'[31] Accomplishing this, the soul then enters its fourth state and is drawn by love on to the level of meditation and 'relinquishes all exterior labors.' The soul reaches a state of joy and exhilaration; it is filled with love and can only feel the touch of love. In fact at this point it is so inebriated with love that it cannot believe that God can offer it any greater gift; but, as Marguerite cautions, the soul is deceived, for there are two other stages of greater nobility beyond love.[32]

In Marguerite's plan, the soul is now about to enter the fifth and sixth states, and it is this part of the Beguine's teaching that is the most daring and original, departing from more traditional forms of mysticism in describing the movement of the soul into a mystical state on earth.

The soul takes a step toward the supernatural in its fifth state, when it is thrown, from the dizzying heights of joy experienced in the fourth, right into the abyss of nothingness – and from a feeling of youth and pride into old age and loss of desire. The soul is left to consider that God is the source of all things, whereas that the soul is nothing if not of God. God bestows free will on the soul and pours into the will the awareness that it is not of God and that it is nothing; the soul comes to realize that it must dissolve its will in order to make its will the will of God.

In the sixth state the soul is completely liberated and purified, and it sees only God. Marguerite warns that the soul is not yet glorified, for this can only come in the seventh state, when it has left the body for eternal glory in paradise. But even so, the soul 'sees neither God nor herself, but God sees Himself of Himself in her, for her, without her. God shows to her that there is nothing except Him, and so loves nothing except Him, praises nothing except Him, for there is nothing except Him.'[33] The soul is therefore united with God and there is God wherever it looks; it has reached the highest level it can in this world.

The final state in Marguerite's *Mirror*, the seventh, describes the experience of the soul after death, which consists in the Beatific Vision and the soul's eternal happiness in the sight of God. Her picture of events here is very much in line with traditional Church teaching and its understanding by other mystics.

The annihilated or liberated soul of the sixth state is no longer bound by the rules of religion and society, having transcended them through union with God. The soul, as Love declares in one of the dialogues, has six wings, like the seraphim, the highest in rank among the angels. Two wings cover the soul's face; this reveals the soul has reached understanding of divine goodness. With two other wings, the soul covers its feet, because it has understanding of why Jesus Christ suffered for us all. With the other two, the soul flies up, to dwell in being and thus in the sight of God and in the divine will. Like the seraphim, the soul has no need for intermediaries, for there is 'no mediary between their [the souls'] love and the divine love.'[34] Hence it is freed from the traditional means of approaching God, as it has already become one with Him; it no longer seeks Him through penitence, sacraments, works, or other accepted religious practices.[35] The soul is without desires, except those of God; hence it neither desires nor rejects poverty, tribulations, masses, sermons, fasting, or prayer. It gives to 'Nature all that is necessary without remorse of conscience. But such nature is so well ordered through the transformation of Love ... that nature demands nothing which is prohibited.'[36] Moreover, the annihilated soul has 'entered into the abundances and flowings of divine Love' and is 'adorned with the adornments of absolute peace in which she lives.'[37] Thus in Marguerite's understanding the annihilated soul enjoyed in this world the mystical state which most other mystics reserved for the next.[38]

For Marguerite, the annihilated soul's move beyond the need for intermediaries encompasses the Church itself, or, as she styles it, Holy-Church-Below-This-Church or Holy Church the Little. This 'Church-Below' emerges at one point so as to participate in the dialogue and to learn about the liberated souls, which have moved on and are now part of the Holy Church the Great – the real Holy Church. The lesser Church is guided by reason rather than love, which dwells in Holy Church the Great; yet it praises love and teaches love according to the holy scriptures.[39] Marguerite also notes that many members of the Church – Beguines, priests, clerics, Dominicans, Augustinians, Carmelites, and Friars Minor – claim that she has erred because of her writing about 'the one purified by Love.'[40]

Without rejecting the Holy Church the Little, the worldly Church, or what it has to offer, Marguerite does describe a higher Church: it is the annihilated or liberated souls who form the true Church. In this way, she posits a religious elite or spiritual aristocracy above and beyond the encumbered souls of the world. But, although at points Marguerite Porete pushed the boundaries of orthodoxy and was perhaps too daring for her own good, her heresy, as the historian of heresy Malcolm Lambert noted, 'if it existed at all, was of a specialized character, concerned solely with the condition of mystical adepts at an advanced stage of perfection; there was no advocacy of libertinism and disregard for the moral law for anyone; and the accusations against Porete gave an unfair picture of her views.'[41] The numerous translations and editions of her work in the fourteenth century suggest that many regarded the *Mirror* as being above suspicion, and Gordon Leff observed that her path was 'not dissimilar from that of the orthodox mystics.'[42] Robert Lerner concedes that she 'was probably a heretic,' but continues by noting that, had she entered a traditional religious community, she would have attracted little attention. Her teachings and her mysticism are in fact similar to those of important and 'orthodox' figures such as Hildegard of Bingen and Mechthild of Madgeburg. And so the question remains: why was Marguerite Porete executed as a heretic?

To answer that question, one has to consider both the broader political and religious context and Marguerite's actions and beliefs. Her personal behavior surely stood against her. Her refusals to answer the inquisitor's questions and to defend her teaching, indeed, her unwillingness even to take the necessary vow to appear before the inquisitor, revealed her as a recalcitrant, uncooperative character. In the eyes of William of Paris and other Church officials, this was surely a sign of harboring heretical thoughts. Her disobedience to the orders of the bishop of Cambrai and her own insistence on continuing to teach and disseminate her *Mirror of Simple Souls* meant to them that she was indeed a relapsed heretic. On the other hand, the great popularity and wide dissemination of the *Mirror* was also a factor against her. Then again, as a Beguine, especially an itinerant one, who did not live an acceptable cloistered life, Marguerite was even more likely to stir suspicions of heresy at a time when the Beguine lifestyle – settled or itinerant – was facing increasing disfavor. And her own writings, which admittedly were presented in brief, out of context, and in the worst possible light, seemed to implicate her in the heresy of the Free Spirit, which the Church believed to be a vast movement of immoral and antinomian heretics that could shake its own foundations. These fears of widespread heresy, along with Marguerite's own silence in front of the inquisitors and the fact that her work had gained popularity through its content, created a cluster of factors which played the decisive role in determining her fate.

Marguerite's condemnation may also have been prompted by the growing concern with heresy in France and by the willingness of secular and ecclesiastical authorities to use such fears for their own ends.[43] In the years just before and after Marguerite's condemnation, the French court of King Philip IV (ruled 1285–1314) and its ecclesiastical allies struck at two important enemies, Pope Boniface VIII and the great crusading Order of the Templars.[44] Philip and his lawyers frequently used allegations of moral turpitude against various enemies of the French crown, including the pope, French bishops, and Beguines.[45] Philip accused Boniface of a wide range of crimes, such as blasphemy, the consultation of demons, sexual immorality, and murder; indeed Philip was not above using even physical violence against the octogenarian pope. And even more dramatic perhaps was his assault on the Templars. The king's motivations remain unclear; he may have truly believed that the military order was filled with blasphemous heretics and therefore persecuted them ruthlessly. He and his allies alleged that new initiates of the order underwent a ritual in which a Templar knight kissed the new member on the base of the spine, the navel, and the mouth. The initiation ritual allegedly also involved urinating on the crucifix, and the members of the order were accused of blasphemy, heresy, and homosexuality. Such charges formed the basis on which Philip ordered the arrest of the Templars in France in 1307. Perhaps not coincidentally, these charges were also considered at the Council of Vienne, which denounced the Beguines and, possibly, some of Marguerite's teachings. Eventually, the allegations against the Templars were used to bring about the suppression of the order in 1312 and the burning of the last Grand Master Templar in 1314.

It is here that the most important connections between Marguerite and the broader persecutions can be made. William of Paris, the Dominican inquisitor who oversaw her trial, was also closely connected to Philip IV. Not only was he Philip's confessor, he had also directed Philip's campaign against the Templars in 1307.[46] William, it appears, had a central role in Philip's efforts to present himself as a most Christian king, whose realm was unquestionably orthodox. Philip may have created what James Given calls 'fantastic enemies,' whom he was able to defeat, and in so doing 'reaffirmed the kingdom's solidarity and restored the sacred moral order.'[47] Marguerite's unfortunate end is not directly connected to the fate of the Templars or Boniface VIII, but her trial emerged at a time when the religious and political authorities in France strengthened the apparatus of persecution and closed ranks against heretics, real or otherwise, who were portrayed as rejecting the teachings of the Church and indulging immoral and decadent leanings. The institutionalized Church had increasingly repudiated diversity of opinion.

Marguerite Porete followed a unique spiritual path, which led to her ultimate demise. She offered a mystical way of reaching God in her *Mirror of Simple Souls*; she may well have felt that she herself had traveled the six stages that take place in this life toward the annihilation of the soul and union with Him. Her doctrines may have been unorthodox if not truly heretical, but, unlike Fra Dolcino, she was not overtly hostile to the established Church, nor did she seek to develop an alternative one, as had the Cathars and even the Waldenses. She may also be distinguished from earlier heretics, with the possible exception of Stephen and Lisois, by her aristocratic status and her belief in the Holy Church the Great. Her heresy, such as it was, involved the promotion of a spiritual elite who were able to follow her demanding mystical path. At the same time, however, her work seems to have been disseminated widely and developed a substantial following throughout France and beyond. In this way, Marguerite is similar to the last great heretics of the Middle Ages, John Wyclif and Jan Hus, brilliant scholars whose academic teachings and sophisticated theologies were declared heretical but had the power to inspire broad popular followings.

CHAPTER NINE

JOHN WYCLIF:
ENGLAND AND THE LOLLARDS

ccording to an English chronicler writing about the year 1382, 'In those days flourished master John Wyclif, rector of the church of Lutterworth, in the county of Leicester, the most eminent doctor of theology of those times. In philosophy he was reckoned second to none, and in scholastic learning without rival. This man strove to surpass the skill of other men by subtlety of knowledge to traverse their opinions.'[1] Indeed, it was as a teacher of philosophy and theology at Oxford that Wyclif made his name and developed a loyal following among other university masters and students. He also attracted support, as a result of his teaching and theological work, from the nobility, peasantry, and parish clergy. He was a profoundly influential scholar, whose teachings had an impact on religious life and thought in England and on the continent, most notably in Bohemia and on the work of Jan Hus. A daring thinker, Wyclif came to challenge much of the traditional theology and ecclesiology of the Church, undermining Catholic doctrine on the sacraments, on the institutional Church, and on priesthood. Although he remained in communion with the Church and died hearing the mass, Wyclif faced increasing animosity from those around him even before his death; nothing reflects the changing attitudes toward Wyclif better than the case of a contemporary who changed his description of the Oxford theologian from 'venerable doctor' to 'detestable seducer.'[2] Wyclif emerged not only as England's most important heretic but also as one of its first, since the kingdom had registered very few examples of heresy before the fourteenth century. A man of deep learning, unlike any previous medieval heretical leader in this respect, Wyclif nonetheless contributed to the emergence of a popular movement in England: the Lollards. This movement lasted into the sixteenth century, when it merged with the Protestant Reformation. Indeed, in his biblical fundamentalism, in his attitudes toward the priesthood and in related matters Wyclif has sometimes been described as a forerunner of Martin Luther and the Protestant reformers of the sixteenth century; this holds especially of his doctrine of the Eucharist, which emphasized the spiritual over the physical.[3] Although this topic remains a matter for some debate, Wyclif surely offered a dramatic alternative to the doctrines of the Catholic Church and a radical reworking of Christian teaching, which inspired a large national and even international following.

The exact date of Wyclif's birth remains uncertain, but his later scholarly career offers some suggestions for a possible date.[4] The future Oxford don was probably born at some point in the 1330s, possibly as early as 1330 and most likely not later than 1335/38. Little is known of his early years and of his family, and there is little agreement over the exact place of his birth. It is likely that he came from Yorkshire, but attempts to identify him with a Wycliffe family from a village of that name near Richmond have proved inconclusive. But, even though the exact date and place of his birth remain elusive, it is certain that the intellectual, religious, and political developments in England in the mid-fourteenth century shaped Wyclif's mature outlook and influenced the personal development of his later years, which are much better known.

The record of Wyclif's life becomes much better documented after he entered the schools of Oxford, where he was to spend nearly the whole of his adult life and which shaped many of his ideas. His entry to university indicates that he had already received the basic grammar school education. He was most likely ordained a priest in 1351, then joined the Augustinian order. From here on the events of his life come into clearer focus. He was first noted at Merton College in 1356, where he was a fellow. He appeared later at Balliol College, where, in 1360, he assumed the position of master of arts. His stay at Balliol, however, was relatively short; he seems to have abandoned his post after only a year or so, to take up a curateship in Lincolnshire in 1361. This was the first in a series of ecclesiastical benefices Wyclif held, and, although he most likely took up residence in Lincolnshire after his appointment, he seems not to have lived there very much. Indeed, as with most of his pastoral appointments, he exercised the office *in absentia*, leaving his routine ministerial duties with another cleric.

Throughout the 1360s Wyclif continued his academic career while acquiring canonries and other Church offices. In 1361 he received the license to study theology at Oxford for two years, an honor he renewed for another two years in 1368, and in 1372 he became a doctor of theology. For part of that period he had lived in rented rooms at Queen's College. In late 1365 he was appointed warden at Canterbury College by Simon Islip, the archbishop of Canterbury, who had reformed the college to accept secular clergy and not just regular clergy (that is, monks). Wyclif held this position until 1367, when Islip's successor, Simon Langham, ordered him to leave. The new archbishop decided that membership of the college should be limited to Benedictine monks, as it once had been, and so Wyclif and other secular clergy were no longer welcome. His efforts to fight the ouster, which reached Rome in 1370, proved unsuccessful, and he was ultimately forced to leave the college. This development might explain the vehemence of Wyclif's later criticisms of the monks, since it caused him both personal frustration and financial loss.[5] Indeed, he would thenceforth be identified as the advocate of those in secular orders and the first university opponent of those in monastic orders.[6] Despite this setback, Wyclif had already begun to acquire a number of ecclesiastical benefices that would provide him with the resources necessary to survive and continue his studies. In 1362, the university, as it was wont to do for its more promising students, had sent a petition for a canonry and prebend in York for the young Wyclif. The request was granted only partially, and Wyclif was given a prebendary at Aust in Gloucestershire, and a canonry in the church of Westbury-on-Trym near Bristol, which he seems to have held until the end of his life, even if he was not there to fulfill his pastoral duties.[7] In 1368 he was granted a rectory in Buckinghamshire and in 1371 was promised a canonry in Lincolnshire; he held the post in Buckinghamshire until his death but seems never to have actually received the other position. In 1374 Wyclif was granted the rectory of Lutterworth in Leicestershire by the king, in recognition of his services to the crown. Wyclif retired there in 1381 but turned over the parish duties to a curate named John Horn.[8] And, even though he had accumulated a number of ecclesiastical benefices, Wyclif seems to have spent most of his time at Oxford, from 1356 to his retirement in 1381.

It was during those years that Wyclif established his reputation as the leading scholar at Oxford, and even in all of England. At Oxford he came into contact for the first time with the nominalism of William of Ockham, which he adopted in his early years, before joining in the general reaction against it. Because philosophy at Oxford was in decline and there were no real philosophers of note either at the university or in the colleges, Wyclif was particularly influenced by scholars of an earlier generation, including Richard Fitzralph and Thomas Bradwardine and the even earlier eminence, Robert Grosseteste. Along with his introduction to higher studies and to the writings of earlier scholars, Wyclif himself began to teach. He gained prominence as a philosophy teacher in the 1360s, identifying himself as a 'real philosopher' rather than a 'doctor of signs.'[9] As he came to abandon nominalism and establish himself as a philosopher, Wyclif attracted a growing following at the university, in part because his philosophy came to offer certainty. His supporters were also attracted by the depth of his learning; one of Wyclif's rivals, Thomas Netter, admitted that he was 'astounded by his [Wyclif's] sweeping assertions, by the authorities cited, and by the vehemence of his reasoning.'[10] Not content with philosophy, Wyclif began teaching theology in 1371, one year before becoming a doctor in that subject. His philosophical positions, of course, influenced the direction of his theology, and he came to examine a broad range of matters, including the institutions of the Church, the clergy, and the Eucharist.

As a scholar of growing renown, Wyclif also wrote some 132 treatises on philosophical, theological, and even legal matters, less than half of which survive in English manuscripts; only sixteen of them survive in more than one English copy. His output was significant in all areas. A sufficient number of copies of treatises apparently survived in the generation after his death, before his official condemnation, and his writings also survived outside of England. His works on theological and ecclesiastical matters are perhaps the most numerous; most of his treatises on philosophy were written before 1371, when he turned to theology. Among his works of philosophy are *De actibus animae* ('On the Actions of the Soul'), 1368–69; *De ente praedicamentali* ('On Categorical Being'), 1368–69; *Tractatus de logica* ('Treatise on Logic'), 1371–73; *De ente* ('On Being'), 1371–74; *Summa de ente libri primi tractatus primus et secundus* ('Summa on Being, Book

One, Tracts One and Two'), 1372/73; *Tractatus de universalibus* ('Treatise on Universals'), 1374. In these and other works Wyclif set out his essential philosophical positions, which influenced both his own theology and the work of contemporaries at Oxford and beyond. In terms of metaphysics, Wyclif maintained two basic principles. He believed that 'Nothing is and is not at the same time,' a position holding pure negation, and that being exists and was the first unquestionable truth.[11] For Wyclif, being is transcendent and all things participate in it, and from this he reasoned that there was a chain of being that led from God to the individual. In this way Wyclif believed that God was irrevocably connected to the world he had created and to all the creatures in it. He also maintained that all being is eternal and that all beings, at all times, are apparent to God. Along with his teachings on being, of importance to Wyclif's later thought was his understanding of universals, which were discussed in his works on being and universals. He derived his ideas on universals from Augustine and believed that all universal concepts have their own subsistence. For Wyclif, universals were a means to understand the world; for all things participate in the universal concept and share a common nature although they are distinct from the universal, and they are made intelligible through that participation.

Perhaps of greater importance than his philosophical writings were Wyclif's many theological and ecclesiastical works, which were shaped by his philosophical assumptions as well as by his own moral values and perception of the institutional Church. These works began to appear in the 1370s, and he continued to produce theological and doctrinal treatises until his death, a number of them during the last few years of his life. But one of his earliest works was a commentary on the entire Bible. At some point between 1370/71 and 1375/76, Wyclif compiled his *Postilla super totam bibliam* ('Afterthought on the Whole Bible'), the only commentary on the whole Bible from the second half of the fourteenth century.[12] The *Postilla* not only considered every book of the Bible; it also emphasized the poverty and humility of the early Church, by way of criticizing the Church of the fourteenth century.[13] The *Postilla* also illustrated Wyclif's growing focus on the Bible and his recognition of the importance of putting the Holy Scriptures at the center of Christian life. His concerns with the Bible were expressed again in 1378, in his *De veritate sacre scripture* ('On the Truth of Sacred Scripture'). In that same year he wrote *De ecclesia* ('On the Church'), which outlined Wyclif's ideas on the visible and invisible Church and criticized Pope Gregory XI (1370–78). He continued and sharpened his critique of the pope and of the institution of papacy in 1379, in *De potestate pape* ('On the Power of the Pope'). These were among several treatises he wrote in the 1370s, in which he considered civil society, the Church, and the relationship between the two. He first explored these matters in *De dominio divino* ('On Divine Dominion') and *De statu innocenciae* ('On the State of Innocence') in 1373/74, then more fully in *De civili dominio* ('On Civil Dominion') in 1375–77, and then again in *De officio regis* ('On the Office of the King') in 1379. In the last work, Wyclif stressed the authority of the king over the clergy, recognized his duty to reform the Church – one of Wyclif's greatest concerns – and repudiated some of the opinions voiced in the work on civil dominion.[14] Along with his ecclesiological works of 1379, Wyclif wrote one of his most important and controversial theological works, *De eucharistia* ('On the Eucharist'), which offered his explanation of the nature of the change taking place in the substance of the host – an explanation that was ultimately condemned as heretical. Thus these works defined his position on a wide range of topics and revealed a daring thinker, who offered sometimes radical propositions about the nature of the Church, civil society, priesthood, and the sacraments.

Along with his numerous academic treatises, Wyclif composed many sermons, but only a small number of those he delivered survive. These sermons have been collected in the *Sermones Quadraginta* ('Forty Sermons') and used to disseminate his ideas to an audience beyond that of his scholarly works, one which included simple priests. He also produced numerous sermons he did not deliver, written on behalf of other preachers. This body of sermons was designed for use throughout the Church calendar year and pointed out the scriptural readings for various Sundays. Others of his literary sermons were written for various saints' days throughout the calendar and contained comments on the scriptural passages to be used for those services.

Wyclif's activities, however, were not limited to the intellectual field but extended to the political arena, a preoccupation he would also explore in several of his treatises. As early as 1370 or 1371, in his university lectures, Wyclif may have formulated for the first time an opinion on matters of lordship and dominion.[15] In 1371, when he probably first made acquaintance with John of Gaunt, duke of Lancaster (1340–99), uncle to the future King Richard II, Wyclif was ready to involve himself in England's political life. His political activities may well have been determined by his growing reputation as a philosopher and theologian; political powers may have seen in him an effective force against the more traditional university scholars of the day.[16] Whatever the reason for his involvement in political matters, Wyclif seems to have taken his first steps in that direction when he participated in the parliament of 1371. At issue was the wealth of the clergy and the rights of the secular authority over ecclesiastical wealth. At the parliament, two Augustinian friars argued that, in times of emergency, the secular power has the right to seize ecclesiastical property and to impose taxes on the clergy. Wyclif, possibly at the suggestion of John of Gaunt, took up the controversy, arguing on the side of the Augustinian friars and against the claims of Rome to be exempt from royal taxation at all times.

His position on clerical wealth earned Wyclif the growing hostility of Church leaders but greater support from lay powers, and he would be further involved in political affairs in the coming years. In July 1374 Wyclif was sent to Bruges on a diplomatic mission, as a representative of the king, to join in negotiations with papal legates over the matter of financial payments from the English clergy to the pope. The discussions were a dismal failure for the crown and an almost complete triumph for the papacy. Wyclif was paid the handsome sum of £60 for his services but was no longer present when the negotiations were completed, and his exact role in them remains unclear.[17] It is certain, however, that he continued to develop his ideas about the relationship of Church and state, which subordinated the clergy to the king and further enhanced his reputation with the secular leaders of England.

He took part in political affairs on several other occasions in the 1370s, each time advancing the interests of the English government. In 1376, Wyclif promoted the interests of his protector, John of Gaunt, and the claims of the English monarchy against the Good Parliament and William of Wykeham, bishop of Winchester, who had emerged as an important leader during the meeting and had taken the lead in criticizing the king's advisers for corruption and incompetence. Wyclif preached against William, whom he denounced for his worldliness, wealth, excessive devotion to politics, and neglect of spiritual duties; he also spoke out against clerical abuses and the wealth of the Church and its ministers. His preaching helped to undo the efforts of the Good Parliament and of William of Wykeham, much to the pleasure of Wyclif's patron, and inspired a move toward reforming the Church and the faith. But his outspoken opposition to the

Church's claims to secular power and wealth brought Wyclif his first taste of trouble. This was from William Courtenay, the bishop of London, who had spoken in defense of Wykeham. Courtenay summoned the theologian to the episcopal court at St. Paul's. John of Gaunt's power and influence served to undermine Bishop William's efforts against Wyclif. The duke of Lancaster's appearance at the proceedings with his ally, Lord Percy, marshal of England, led them to break up in disorder; the people of London rioted in support of their bishop following a bitter exchange between Gaunt and him.[18]

Wyclif's political activities took place while he was developing his ideas on civil dominion and reflected the positions he took on behalf of the royal government and his patron. As he had done in earlier years, Wyclif spoke on behalf of the secular authority in 1377 and again in 1378. In 1377 he defended the interests of the government in a dispute over the delivery of gold bullion to the papal court at Avignon, partly as taxes and tithes owed to the papal administration and partly as revenues from benefices which a number of cardinals held in England. As all medieval rulers believed, control over gold was necessary for the strength of the government and of the economy, and so Wyclif was asked whether England

> might lawfully for its own defense in case of need, detain the wealth of the kingdom, so that it be not carried away in foreign parts, even though the pope himself demands it under pain of censure and by virtue of the obedience owing to him.[19]

As expected, Wyclif's response was fully in the government's favor, and as he had only previously expressed in a short pamphlet. He argued that the papal tax collector, who traditionally took an oath to do nothing to harm the kingdom, had in fact violated his oath. Exporting large quantities of gold, Wyclif reasoned, was so detrimental to the health of the kingdom that the tax collector was guilty of perjury. Citing natural law, the Gospels, and individual conscience, Wyclif explained that the government's position was the correct one.[20]

In October 1378, Wyclif provided support for the state in a highly controversial matter concerning the rights of the Church. He was again called upon by his patron, John of Gaunt. The duke had ordered his soldiers to enter Westminster Abbey to apprehend two prisoners who had escaped from the Tower of London and sought sanctuary at the abbey. The soldiers, violating the Church's ancient right of sanctuary, caught one of the squires and killed the other one, who was allegedly guilty of treason; they also murdered one of the abbey's servants, who attempted to prevent the arrest. The bishop excommunicated all those involved in the violation of the sanctuary, and the matter was then brought before the parliament. Wyclif defended the actions of the soldiers, asserting that the prisoner who was killed died while resisting a legal arrest. Wyclif further set out the rights of the civil authority in pursuing a suspect and entering the sanctuary, and also limited the rights of those who claimed asylum in churches. His defense of the duke and of his men before parliament also formed the basis of his treatise *De ecclesia*. Wyclif's political activities served two important ends: they allowed him to develop his own ideas on secular and religious authority and they secured for him powerful lay patrons, who were to protect him when he faced the threat of excommunication and other ecclesiastical penalties.

Lay protection would be especially important and necessary for Wyclif by the late 1370s, when his teachings had become increasingly radical and critical of the Church. Not only had Wyclif's arguments on civil dominion over the Church and clergy earned him the enmity of the Church hierarchy, but his denunciations of Church power and wealth also raised the ire of the bishops. The first attempts to censure Wyclif came in 1377, a momentous year for the Oxford theologian. His ever more strident criticisms of the papacy did fall on deaf ears, and Gregory XI, perhaps as the result of the complaints of English Benedictines or of some other enemy who sent passages from *De civili dominio*, sent a letter, denouncing Wyclif, which arrived only late in the year 1377, to the masters and chancellor of Oxford, the bishops of England and the king, Edward III. The letter included a list of some eighteen of Wyclif's teachings which were deemed offensive. According to the pope, Wyclif 'has fallen into such a detestable madness that he does not hesitate to dogmatize and publicly preach, or rather vomit forth from the recesses of his breast certain propositions and conclusions which are erroneous and false.'[21] Gregory also accused Wyclif of 'preaching heretical dogmas which strive to subvert and weaken the state of the whole Church and even secular polity.'[22] Wyclif, according to the pope, was guilty of holding opinions similar to those of such condemned thinkers as Marsilius of Padua and John of Jandun and asserted that only a righteous man may hold authority. The pope alleged further that Wyclif had led the faithful away from the true path of righteousness with his false doctrines, including the belief that only God could absolve a penitent sinner, the belief that the Church was made up of those predestined to salvation or foreknown to be damned, and his teaching that the Church, with its claims to power and wealth, had become corrupted. Therefore, reasoned the pope, Wyclif should be punished. He ordered that the university should no longer allow such opinions as those of Wyclif to be taught at Oxford, under penalty of loss of the privileges received from the Holy See. The chancellor and masters were further commanded to arrest Wyclif or have him arrested in the pope's name and delivered to the archbishop of Canterbury or to the bishop of London, where a confession could be extracted from the theologian.

Wyclif himself sent a spirited reply to this letter of condemnation to Gregory's successor, Pope Urban VI (1378–89), asserting his devotion to the faith and especially to the Gospels. He also apologized to the pope, whom he greeted as a welcome successor to Gregory, for not being able to appear in person in Rome to defend himself, and it seems most likely that Wyclif intended to remain on good terms with the new pope. An important declaration – but Wyclif was saved not so much by his personal statement to the pope as by several external developments. The force of the papal declaration was weakened significantly by the death of Gregory in March 1378 and, even more so, by the beginning of the Great Schism, which lasted from 1378 until 1417. Following Gregory's death, two claimants to the papal throne – Urban VI in Rome, Clement VII in Avignon – asserted their legitimacy at each other's expense. The Schism divided Europe and caused great difficulty for the established Church, not the least of which was the failure of the papal denunciation of John Wyclif: the attention of the popes was drawn now to matters of state and away from the teachings of an Oxford theologian. Beyond that, however, it is likely that the papal condemnation of Wyclif in 1377 would have failed even without the advent of the Schism. The authorities at Oxford, notably the master and future chancellor, Robert Rigg, a great admirer of Wyclif who would remain one of his most ardent supporters, seemed little interested in punishing their most shining star. It may be argued that, even if Wyclif had not been the leading English scholar of his day, the chancellor and masters at Oxford would have been reluctant to punish him because they resented papal interference in their affairs. Ultimately, Wyclif and the authorities at Oxford agreed that the don would be held at Black Hall until his teachings were reviewed; he was subsequently absolved by the university and his teachings were deemed to be true.

But the most important reason why Wyclif was not censured may well have been the support he received from the leading secular authorities in England. Support from figures in high places helped him to avoid an appearance at the episcopal court. When he finally did appear at the archbishop of Canterbury's chapel at Lambeth Palace to defend himself, he suffered no punishment other than a warning not to spread false doctrines. Not only had the bishops seemed reluctant to pursue the pope's case, but Wyclif's safety was guaranteed by the queen mother, Joan, widow of Edward (the Black Prince) and mother of King Richard II (1367–1400), who had sent one of her knights with the express order that no judgment should be pronounced in the case.[23] His service to the crown and its allies, as a theorist and propagandist, was, and continued to be, of vital importance; hence the members of the royal family supported him against ecclesiastical authorities. (Indeed, rather than punish him, the crown sought his advice on the matter of the export of gold.) Moreover, the temporal authority surely welcomed Wyclif's increasingly vehement critiques of the Church and of its representatives; the vigorous reforms he promoted would limit the wealth and power of the Church, to the benefit of the crown. Wyclif maintained that it was the crown that was best situated to implement the reformation of the Church, an argument that enhanced his value to his royal and aristocratic patrons. As a result of protection from the queen mother, as well as strong support from his university colleagues and the chancellor, the efforts to condemn Wyclif and his teachings failed in England in 1378, and he continued to teach and participate in the political affairs of the country.

Wyclif's troubles, however, were not at an end. Although the efforts in 1377/78 to condemn him or limit his influence failed, a new process in 1380 was more successful, in part because his own, ever more radical, views increased opposition to him and provided his enemies with more ammunition. Disappointed over the failings of Pope Urban VI and over the Schism, Wyclif took a harder line on the papacy in his writings of the late 1370s, repudiating the Church hierarchy in its entirety, and laid the foundation for even more extreme statements in his writings of the 1380s. He also produced his massive work on the Bible, which asserted the fundamental truth of the text and maintained that it should be available to all Christians, lay and religious.[24] His work on the

Eucharist, however, in which he rejected the Catholic doctrine of transubstantiation, proved to be most problematic and marked the beginning of Wyclif's transformation, from radical critic and reformer into a heretic, or, as the contemporary scholar wrote, from 'venerable doctor' into 'detestable seducer.'

In 1380, William Barton, chancellor of Oxford and fellow at Merton College, established a commission to examine Wyclif's eucharistic teachings. Barton, a doctor of divinity, had long opposed Wyclif's teachings in his own lectures and writings. Now he felt the time was right to take steps against his rival, who had begun to lose support among one of his most important constituencies – the scholars at Oxford in the mendicant orders. Barton appointed twelve doctors to the commission: six mendicant friars, four members of the secular orders, and two monks, and it appears from the composition of the commission that Barton, despite his personal opposition to Wyclif's teachings, intended to give Wyclif a fair hearing. One member of the commission was Robert Rigg, who would succeed Barton as chancellor in 1382; being a staunch supporter of Wyclif he would suffer for it in the mid-1380s.[25] The commission ultimately condemned two of Wyclif's propositions on the Eucharist, but only by the slight majority of seven to five, which reinforces the view that Barton intended a fair hearing. Wyclif's teachings that the substance of the bread and wine of the eucharistic offerings remains after consecration and that the body of Christ is figuratively and not physically present in the bread and wine were condemned as erroneous and a danger to the Church.[26] Responding to the commission's report, Barton declared that anyone holding, teaching, or defending these views would be imprisoned, stripped of any university function, and excommunicated.

Wyclif, however, remained undaunted by the report, asserting 'that neither the chancellor nor any of his accomplices could weaken his opinion.'[27] Surprised and disappointed by the decision, he made up his mind to appeal against it rather than accept it. But he would not pursue his appeal in any ecclesiastical court, as both the law of England and the Church required. Instead, Wyclif turned once again to the king, seeking from the crown protection from his ecclesiastical rivals. The king seems to have ignored Wyclif's petition, but John of Gaunt may have become involved. The duke reportedly traveled to Oxford to discuss the matter with his former client and to convince him to obey the chancellor's instructions. The duke's wishes, and the king's unwillingness to entertain the petition, reveal the growing disquiet among Wyclif's former patrons about the increasingly unorthodox tenor of his teachings. It was one thing to advocate the supremacy of the temporal power over the spiritual in political matters and to condemn the corruption and abuse of the clergy, but quite another to advocate doctrines condemned by the Church as erroneous. As Wyclif's own teachings became ever more extreme, support from his allies in the government and Church began to wane.

Wyclif, despite John of Gaunt's wishes to the contrary, undertook his own defense, publishing his *Confessions* on May 10, 1381. In this tract he defended and reasserted the positions repudiated by the commission, attempting to restore his good name after the condemnation. He railed against the opinions of the commission members and fully stated his positions on the Eucharist against what he considered to be errors of the established Church. He asserted the need for doctrinal change in order to correct the flawed teachings of the Church on the sacrament. But his vehement defense of his own ideas on the Eucharist and demand for their institution alienated the aristocratic and royal patrons who had been essential to his success and whose support would be necessary to implement any of the reforms, doctrinal and institutional, that he advocated.

Wyclif suffered even further erosion of support from his former patrons and other sympathizers as a result of the outbreak of the Peasants' Revolt in June 1381. Although it is unlikely that he backed the revolt or that his teachings were directly responsible for it, his enemies surely blamed him and his ideas for it. They were aided by the confession of one of the revolt's leaders, the priest John Ball, who reportedly declared, just before his execution after the brutal suppression of the revolt, that 'for two years he had been a disciple of Wyclif, and had learned from him the heresies he had taught.'[28] Wyclif's reaction to the revolt also undermined any support he may still have expected and added more fuel to the fire for his enemies – he condemned the murder of the archbishop of Canterbury by the rebels while admitting that the archbishop had been guilty of excessive worldliness; and he denounced the revolt in general, but he argued that the rebels' biggest error was their failure to get support from parliament. He also expressed some sympathy for the rebels, even arguing that they had a legitimate complaint about excessive taxation, for which Wyclif blamed the clergy.[29]

Following the condemnation of his teachings and the Peasants' Revolt,

Wyclif left Oxford, retiring to his rectory at Lutterworth. There he continued to write at a feverish pace, completing treatises he had begun at Oxford and preparing numerous pamphlets and sermons in attack of the friars, whom he blamed for his exile from Oxford. In his last years, Wyclif completed three volumes on different kinds of heresy: *De simonia* ('On Simony'), *De apostasia* ('On Apostasy'), and *De blasphemia* ('On Blasphemy'). In these works, composed in 1381 and 1382, Wyclif offered some words of moderation, in a half-hearted attempt to regain support from his former allies, but mainly criticized the clergy forcefully and endorsed his position on the Eucharist. In his work on simony – the sin of the buying and selling of Church offices or spiritual preferment – Wyclif denounced as simony any form of clerical worldliness and corruption. And apostasy, for him, included the failure of members of the clergy to live up to the demands of their vocation and the support of the Church's teaching on the Eucharist. In *De apostasia*, Wyclif offered an impassioned defense of his own teachings on the Eucharist as well as denouncing the errors of others. *De blasphemia* is a long and somewhat disorganized catalogue of the sins and abuses of the clergy at all levels, with particular bile reserved for the cardinals and the friars. These works were followed by the *Trialogus* ('Trialogue') in 1382 – a discussion between Truth, Falsehood, and Wisdom, which offers a summation and restatement of many positions Wyclif took in earlier works, including a commentary on the Eucharist and further attacks on the friars. Of all his works, this was one of the most popular; it was printed at Basel in 1525, offering a possible link with the Reformers of the sixteenth century.[30] At the time of his death, in 1384, Wyclif was working on the *Opus evangelicum* ('Opus on the Gospel'), which revealed its author's respect for the Bible and for Augustine. In the first volume of the *Opus*, Wyclif provided a commentary on the Sermon on the Mount, and in the second volume, subtitled *De antichristi* ('On Antichrist'), he discussed the Gospel of Matthew.

Although free to write during his last years, Wyclif was troubled by two major events in his life: further persecution from his enemies and ill health. The hand of his critics was strengthened by the murder of the archbishop of Canterbury during the Peasants' Revolt, because the new archbishop, William Courtenay, had long led the opposition to Wyclif. As the leading primate in England, he took the initiative to stamp out heresies taking root in the kingdom.

He was motivated not only by Wyclif himself but also by Wyclif's supporters at Oxford. Ironically, the atmosphere at Oxford had improved following Wyclif's departure. The new chancellor, Robert Rigg, had supported Wyclif at the commission that condemned the theologian and would as chancellor support Wyclifite scholars. In particular, Rigg was an advocate of Nicholas of Hereford and Philip Repton when both took clear Wyclifite positions. When Hereford preached a sermon arguing that clergy in orders, meaning monks and friars, should not be allowed to take a degree at Oxford, Rigg invited him to deliver the second sermon on Ascension Day, at which point Hereford defended Wyclif's teachings.[31] Similarly, Repton received the enthusiastic approbation of the chancellor when he defended Wyclif's teachings on the Eucharist and the clergy in a sermon he delivered.

Courtenay, shortly after assuming the see at Canterbury, called a council to condemn the teachings of Wyclif and his followers on May 17, 1382. Known as the Earthquake Council because an earthquake shook London during the meeting – an event seen as an omen both by Wyclif and by his opponents – the meeting was held at the house of the Black Friars in London and would formally condemn a number of Wyclif's teachings. The new archbishop called together nine bishops, thirty-six theologians and canon lawyers, and a number of lesser clergy to debate twenty-four propositions from Wyclif's writings. After four days of discussion and debate, the members of the council declared ten of Wyclif's teachings heretical; the other fourteen were deemed erroneous. Wyclif's views on the Eucharist, the sacramental powers of the clergy, clerical wealth, and papal power were among those declared heretical. Although Wyclif himself was not excommunicated, his followers were to be punished, and the archbishop submitted a petition to the government, subsequently approved, which called for the arrest and imprisonment of unlicensed preachers. Courtenay also sent a friar to Oxford, to implement the decrees and enforce the will of the council and of the archbishop at the university. Despite their efforts on Wyclif's behalf and vocal support of his ideas, the chancellor and Wyclif's allies buckled under the pressure from the archbishop. Rigg accepted the condemnation of Wyclif's teachings and published it at Oxford, thus forbidding the dissemination of Wyclifite doctrines there. He also forbade Wyclif and his supporters to teach at Oxford, and both Hereford and Repton were excommunicated for their views.

Along with the condemnation of the Earthquake Council, Wyclif was plagued by strokes, which makes his substantial literary production all the more remarkable. In November 1382 Wyclif suffered his first stroke, a debilitating attack that left him partially paralyzed. Despite continued poor health, Wyclif did not stop writing his sermons and treatises. His pastoral duties, however, were undertaken by his curate John Horn, as they had been since his return to Lutterworth. And it is Horn who offers moving testimony on Wyclif's last days and death following a massive stroke on December 28, 1384:

> On Holy Innocents' Day, as Wyclif was hearing mass in his church at Lutterworth, just as the Host was elevated, he fell smitten by an acute paralysis, especially in the tongue so that neither then nor afterwards could he speak.[32]

He lingered for three days after that and then died on December 31, 1384. Despite the condemnation of several of his propositions, Wyclif had remained in communion with the Church and was therefore buried in consecrated ground, in the graveyard at the church of Lutterworth.

Wyclif's story, however, does not end on the last day of 1384, but continues into the fifteenth century, in England and on the continent. The Lollards and various continental theologians and churchmen were influenced by Wyclif's teachings on different matters, and these opinions form Wyclif's greatest legacy. Disseminated by his direct and indirect followers, Wyclif's views on civil dominion, the Bible, the Church and its priesthood, and the Eucharist constitute a powerful body of ideas which in some ways foreshadowed the doctrines of Martin Luther and other Protestant reformers. The Reformation did not arrive in Wyclif's day, of course, but his ideas must be considered in order to understand his importance in the history of the late medieval church.

Among Wyclif's important teachings – although it is not given now the weight it was once believed to have in his thought, and it should not be considered to be part of his broader theological program – was his opinion on civil dominion.[33] His theoretical preoccupation with matters concerning the state may have attracted his attention to contemporary politics and drawn to him figures such as John of Gaunt. After his publication of the work on civil dominion in 1375–77, Gaunt called Wyclif to London to preach against the bishops, who came to a very critical opinion of the work, different from the stand taken by the duke of Lancaster.[34] Whatever the immediate impact, Wyclif himself would ultimately leave this work behind as he developed his ideas about the Church, but it remains of note nonetheless, and it helped in bringing him to the attention of the great powers of his day.

Underlying his conception of civil dominion was the belief that all earthly power derives from God's grace. His understanding of dominion drew from such earlier thinkers as Richard Fitzralph, Giles of Rome (through Fitzralph), and Marsilius of Padua.[35] He argued that the secular power represented by kings and lords was empowered by God himself and that, as proved by scripture, they had the authority to rule over the Church. Kings and lords must, however, follow the dictates of the pope so long as they adhere to the teachings of the Gospels, which are the central source of authority for Wyclif in both spiritual and secular matters. On the other hand, Wyclif rejects the authority of the pope to excommunicate anyone, claiming that only the individual can excommunicate himself through sin. Driving Wyclif's thought on dominion was not only his recognition that the power exercised by kings was scripturally sanctioned, but also his thought that true lordship was characterized by justice, so that, without it, there was no lordship. He did accept that tyrants could rule and were sent to punish sin and establish civil dominion, but a tyrant would not exercise true dominion. Civil law, Wyclif held, was established for the benefit of the community and in order to ensure the safety and necessities of life, but true dominion was exercised only by the righteous; the true lord followed the teachings of the Gospel and had received God's grace.

More important and developed than his expressed views on civil dominion was his understanding of the Church, which had a more lasting and profound impact on his thought than his understanding of grace and dominion had. Worked out in several treatises, including those on the Church, on the king's office, and on the powers of the pope, his conception of the Church drew from Augustine's *De civitate Dei* ('On the City of God'), but pushed to the extreme Augustine's identification of two cities – the earthly one and the heavenly one.[36] Although Wyclif recognized three distinct meanings of the term 'church,' he stressed that the true meaning, or the true Church, was that which is made up of the elect. Only those who were predestined to salvation are part of it, and the Church itself is comprised of three parts: 'one triumphing in heaven, one sleeping in purgatory, and one battling on earth.'[37] The saved are bound together by God's grace and constitute the true Church under Christ, just as those not among the elect are bound together for all eternity under the authority of Antichrist.[38] The two groups are strictly divided and no one, in Wyclif's view, knows to which group he or she belongs, nor can anyone claim to know or assert that they belong to the true Church, or claim to be its head.[39]

Wyclif's understanding of the 'true Church' had clear implications for his attitude toward the Church militant and its representatives, the pope and the clergy. As he declared in *De potestate papae*:

> The Catholic truth which I have often repeated consists of this: that no pope, bishop, abbot, or any spiritual prelate is to be believed or obeyed except in so far as he says or commands the law of Christ.[40]

For Wyclif, it was not necessary to follow the dictates of the pope or other cleric unless that dictate itself followed the law of the Gospel. Many of the institutions and sacraments of the Church were called into question by Wyclif's view on the visible Church; the intercessory role of the clergy was also denied, even though he never explicitly said so. Because it is uncertain whether any member of the clergy, including the pope himself, can be identified as belonging to the true Church, then, reasoned Wyclif, it was not necessary for the hierarchy to exist – which he often denounced for its avarice, worldliness, and corruption. The pope and other members of the hierarchy, because of their failure to live according to the Gospels, had demonstrated their very uselessness and, even worse, their identification with Antichrist. The Church and its leaders had become more concerned with worldly power and possessions than with the care of souls, and, like many of his contemporaries, Wyclif identified the moment of fall of the visible Church with the endowment of this institution by the Roman Emperor Constantine, in the fourth century. Wyclif believed that it was better to return to a time before the establishment of the imperial Church by Constantine and to disendow the Church, so as to make it possible for it to return to its apostolic purity.

Wyclif's repudiation of the visible Church on account of its failure to live according to the teachings of the Gospels demonstrates the fundamental importance of the Bible to him. Known as *Doctor Evangelicus* ('the Evangelical Doctor'), Wyclif placed an emphasis on the scriptures which links him not only to earlier medieval heretics like Valdes but also to the Protestants of the sixteenth century like Martin Luther. Yet Wyclif did not adopt the notion of *sola Scriptura*, as did Luther and the Protestant Reformers, but he recognized the value of the writings of Augustine and other exegetes and theologians on the Bible. Moreover, his emphasis on the scripture itself was nothing new, but part of a long tradition going back for centuries; his own commentary on the Bible borrowed from the Franciscan scholar Nicholas of Lyra, among others. But in spite of his debt to other exegetes and acceptance of the work of earlier theologians, Wyclif asserted the absolute truth of the scripture and the absolute centrality of the Bible to Christian life. So important was the Bible to Wyclif that he declared that 'all Christians, and lay lords in particular, ought to know holy writ and defend it,' and, again, 'no man is so rude a scholar but that he may learn the words of the Gospel according to his simplicity.'[41] Indeed, his rejection of the visible Church was the result of his belief that the Church and its ministers were not necessary intermediaries for understanding the Holy Writ. Although it is perhaps anachronistic to speak of the 'priesthood of all believers', it is certain that Wyclif hoped that all could read the Bible, and his sentiments concerning its importance inspired the first English translation of the text. Wyclif himself was most probably not involved in any such enterprise, even though an attribution to him was made as early as 1390; but he can certainly be seen as the guiding light behind the translation.[42]

Wyclif's stress on the importance of the Bible for all Christians stems from his understanding of it as the absolute and unchanging word of God. For him, those who raised questions about the scriptures or pointed out inconsistencies in the text were the real heretics, because the Bible was the truth – it was God's word. As he declared in his work on the sacred scripture:

> For since the whole of sacred scripture is the word of God, there could not be a superior, safer, or more effective testimony than this: if God who cannot lie says this in his scripture, which is the mirror of his will, then it is true.[43]

As the word of God, then, the Bible is the absolute and ultimate authority in all matters. But it must be noted that Wyclif was not a biblical literalist; rather, it was the underlying sense of the words of the Bible that was true. As he argued in *De veritate sacrae scripturae*, the Bible is the combination of the written word in the book and the meaning derived from the symbol in the text. Moreover, Wyclif asserted that there were five levels of truth in the Bible: the truth of life, the truths of life in their ideal being, the truths in their existence, the truths written on man's soul, and the truth of sounds or books. The Bible was, therefore, the source of all truth for Wyclif. It was the mirror of God's will and the mirror of right conduct for all Christians. It was also the voice of the Son of God and, as such, it was the law of the Church and the source of all true doctrines.[44] The Bible was, therefore, the final authority and the absolute truth, and the failure of the visible Church to adhere fully to its teachings rendered it unworthy of any authority it might claim.

Although Wyclif's political philosophy, which rejected the established Church and asserted temporal authority over it as well as biblical extremism, brought him to the limits of orthodoxy, it was his position on the Eucharist that was clearly heterodox and caused the greatest difficulties both during his lifetime and after. Wyclif did not come easily or early to his controversial understanding of the nature of the Eucharist; as late as 1378 he still accepted the Church's teaching on transubstantiation, before his own study and application of philosophical realism to the question led him to reject Catholic doctrine as in error.[45] And even then, he did not reject the sacrament as instituted by Jesus, but only denied a teaching of the Church which, as he explained, had been formalized during the reign of Pope Innocent III (1198–1216) and no earlier. It should be noted that Wyclif's concern was also motivated by his understanding of the Church and its clergy; eucharistic doctrine as taught in his day maintained the sacerdotal authority of these institutions, about which Wyclif had serious doubts.

But Wyclif came to reject the Catholic teaching on the sacrament for philosophical and theological reasons. He could not accept the standard explanations for the transformation of the Eucharist into the body and blood of Christ that were given in his day. These held that the bread and wine were completely replaced by the body and blood of Christ after consecration; only the appearance of bread and wine remained, while the substance was that of the flesh and blood of Christ. For Wyclif, this could not stand from a philosophical perspective because the bread and wine had to preserve their substance even if they were – in philosophical terms – only accidents. Moreover, Wyclif could find no scriptural justification for the doctrine of transubstantiation, a potentially more troubling problem than the philosophical difficulties of accepting Church teaching. He was, however, convinced that the rite was a sacrament instituted by Jesus at the Last Supper, when he said to the Apostles: 'This is my body' (Matthew 26: 26). This passage led Wyclif to the belief that, at the moment of that declaration, the body and bread existed together, and thus when the bread and wine are consecrated on the altar they exist with the body and blood of Christ, although not the literal body born of the Virgin Mary. Wyclif's teachings on the Eucharist, therefore, approached the Lutheran doctrine of consubstantiality. For him, the so-called miracle of the mass was not that the bread and wine were transformed into the body and blood of Christ, but that the two substances coexisted. The eucharistic offerings underwent a spiritual transformation whereby they were 'naturally bread and wine and sacramentally Christ's body.'[46]

These teachings laid the foundation for the continued growth and development of movements in England and on the continent into the fifteenth century, despite the condemnations faced by Wyclif before his death. As is evident from the activities of Robert Rigg, Nicholas of Hereford, and Philip Repton, Wyclif found support at Oxford even after he had been condemned by Church authorities in 1380, and even, for a brief moment, after the Earthquake Council. It was among Wyclif's Oxford supporters that the movement which came to be known as Lollardy first emerged. These university Lollards — a term of derision meaning 'mumblers,' first applied to one of Wyclif's followers in 1382 — adopted the Oxford don's teaching on the Eucharist, his ardent antisacerdotalism and criticism of ecclesiastical corruption, his views on the subordination of spiritual to temporal authority, as well as his belief in the necessity of moral reform.[47] They had supported him throughout the 1370s, attracted by his daring and radical solutions to various philosophical and theological questions, and preached on his behalf after the condemnations of 1380 and 1382. They were unable, however, to withstand Archbishop Courtenay's onslaught and were excommunicated and suspended from teaching. Some of them recanted their support for Wyclif and were brought back into the Church and university, but in 1382 a major step was taken in the suppression of Lollardy.

Wyclif's supporters were not completely eradicated by Courtenay, and over the next few decades they provided leadership and composed key works for the Lollard movement. During the late fourteenth century a Wyclifite English Bible was produced, numerous sermons were written, a gloss of the Gospels and a separate commentary on the Book of the Apocalypse were composed, and a theological dictionary of some 509 entries drawing, in part, from Wyclif's pastoral work was compiled at Oxford between 1384 and 1396, for the use of preachers without access to a good library.[48] Among those who continued to preach Wyclifite doctrines was Richard Wyche, a priest of Hereford who was active from the late fourteenth century until his burning in 1440. Another figure was William James, an Oxford scholar who was finally captured near Oxford in 1395. Along with those associated with Oxford, there was a number of lesser clergy and parish priests who promoted Wyclif's teachings. That group included, among others, William, a priest in Thaxted, John Brettenham of Colchester, William Sawtry, a chaplain of Norfolk who was the first Lollard to be burned (February 23, 1401, or shortly thereafter), and William Ramsbury of the diocese of Salisbury.[49] Perhaps the most important of the lesser clergy was William Swinderby, an orthodox preacher before his conversion to Lollardy and a speaker of great skill who attracted a significant number of followers to the movement, including John Oldcastle, a Lollard leader of the early fifteenth century. Swinderby naturally attracted the attention of the authorities, who pursued and condemned him, but he disappeared into Wales in 1391 before he could be captured and most likely continued to preach for some time to come.[50]

Wyclif's impact was felt well beyond his original Oxford circle and the lesser clergy that taught variations of his propositions and reached all levels of the laity. His strident denunciations of the clergy and of their worldliness and wealth certainly resonated with the laity responsible for paying tithes and taxes to support the Church. The Lollards included artisans and skilled craftsmen, townsfolk in Leicester, London, Northampton, and elsewhere, and even some gentry. Those attracted to the group included the poor, but also the more prosperous; some may have come from the highest levels of society. Perhaps the most important sub-group was that of the so-called Lollard knights, ten of whom were identified by name in the pages of contemporary chronicles. The knights – and it seems that there were well more than ten – played a key role in the growth and development of the movement, and their status and sympathetic attitude offered to the Lollard preachers and scholars a degree of protection which allowed them to continue their work of developing and disseminating Wyclifite ideas. The most prominent of the Lollard knights was Sir John Oldcastle, a secular leader of the movement who raised rebellion in 1414 after his conviction for heresy. Intended to prevent his own punishment and institute a Lollard reform of the Church, Oldcastle's revolt failed and demonstrated the dangers of Wyclifite teachings. In consequence, the king ordered the suppression of Lollardy, and many of the leaders were hunted down and massacred. Lollardy, however, somehow survived and remained a viable, albeit underground, movement throughout the fifteenth century.

The final chapter of Wyclif's story involves his official denunciation and completes his change, from theologian and radical critic of the Church, into a heretic. This chapter opens just prior to Oldcastle's defeat and the persecution of the Lollards, and it reveals the hardening of attitudes toward heresy and heretics in England. In 1407, William Courtenay's successor as archbishop of Canterbury, Thomas Arundel, ordered the heads of the Oxford colleges to hold regular examinations of the college members, to ensure that Wyclif's teachings were not being taught and that all members were strictly orthodox. The archbishop also established yet another commission to examine the works of Wyclif. Four years later, the commission condemned some 267 propositions of Wyclif as heretical or unsound, and then sent the list to Rome for further consideration and condemnation by the pope. At the Lateran Council of 1413, a number of Wyclif's works, but not all of them, were burned. A moment of perhaps even greater consequence for Wyclif's teachings occurred at the Council of Constance in 1415, which also condemned Wyclif's Bohemian disciple, Jan Hus, and resolved the Great Schism. At this meeting, one of the most important in Church history, forty-five of Wyclif's doctrines, which had previously been condemned at Prague in 1403, were condemned again, including his teachings on the Eucharist, the clergy, the papacy, the tithes, and others.[51] This condemnation by one of the highest authorities of the Church confirmed that Wyclif had been a heretic unworthy to remain buried in consecrated ground. The order was given that his body was to be exhumed; but the local bishop at that time was the old Wyclifite sympathizer, Philip Repton, who did nothing. Wyclif's body was, however, exhumed by Repton's successor, Richard Fleming.[52] In the spring of 1428, the body was dug up and burned, and the ashes were thrown into a stream running through Lutterworth. Despite this ignominious end, Wyclif's legacy had a marked impact on further developments – in England and especially in Bohemia.

CHAPTER TEN

JAN HUS:
REFORM AND HERESY IN BOHEMIA

lthough Wyclif made an important impact on the Church and (especially) on the Lollards in England, he may have left his deepest mark on developments on the continent, where his teachings found ardent supporters in Bohemia. Adopted by a number of reform-minded ecclesiastics there, Wyclif's teachings helped shape the direction of Church reform – a process which itself formed part of broader social, political, and religious developments in the later fourteenth and early fifteenth centuries. The complicated interconnection between political and religious trends further shaped the nature of Church reform in Bohemia and contributed to the transformation of reform ideals into heresy. The increasingly hostile relationship between German scholars and theologians on the one hand and Czech reformers and nationalists on the other, as well as the negative consequences of the Great Schism that had broken out in 1378, also affected events in Bohemia. Wyclif's teachings found increasing resonance with many Czech leaders and seemed to offer a solution to the many problems facing the Church in Bohemia; the most important of these reformers was Jan Hus, a leading scholar and theologian whose writings and, especially, whose execution at the Council of Constance in 1415 contributed to reform and revolution in his native land. And, beyond that, according to a modern biographer, Hus's ideas 'may be regarded as a transitional stage from the earlier medieval period to the Reformation.'[1]

Although Jan Hus gave his name to the reform movement in Bohemia, emerging as its most outstanding figure, and his tragic end at Constance inspired the Hussite Revolution and the birth of the Czech national Church, he was not the only reform leader in his country's Church. The movement for reform reached deep into the fourteenth century. It was initiated by the Holy Roman emperor and king of Bohemia Charles IV (1316–78) and determined by a number of factors, both religious and non-religious. Its roots can be found in the very nature of the Bohemian kingdom and of its larger overlord, the Holy Roman Empire. The region had become part of the Empire and was colonized by Germans, who were at first welcomed and respected but eventually came to be regarded less favorably by the native Czech population. Not only had the immigrants carved out a prominent socio-economic position, but they had also acquired the leading ecclesiastical offices and educational positions. German domination of the Church and of the University of Prague (founded in 1348) alienated the Czechs, who had become increasingly self-aware as their culture blossomed during the fourteenth century. Rising Czech nationalism easily merged with a growing desire for reform stimulated by the relationship between the hierarchy and the Germans. The Church in Bohemia, as in other parts of Europe, faced problems of corruption and clerical abuse. The Church was regarded as worldly and too concerned with land and wealth, a problem exacerbated in Bohemia by the fact that the Church was the greatest landowner in the kingdom – greater than the king himself.[2] The clergy were scorned for their immorality and lack of religious devotion. Hus himself would later denounce 'priests who shamefully squander pay for requiem masses in fornication, in adorning their concubines, priestesses, or prostitutes more sumptuously than the church altars and pictures, purchasing for them skirts, capes, and fur coats from their tithes and offerings of the poor.'[3] The wealthy Church and the corrupt clergy stood in stark contrast to the simple, poor Czech clergy – which only reinforced demands for reform and for the rejection of the German clergy.

In the last quarter of the fourteenth century, the situation in Bohemia and much of Europe worsened. One challenge that the universal Church faced was the Great Schism, which divided the Christian nations of Europe between those who supported the pope in Rome and those who supported the pope in Avignon. This division, and the excommunications each pope laid on the other, reinforced the need for a far-reaching reform of the Church. The Schism also weakened the power of the two popes, who were less able to impose order and discipline on the Church. At the same time when the Great Schism broke out, Bohemia's golden age came to an end with the death of Charles IV in 1378. He was succeeded by his son Wenceslas IV (1361–1419), a relatively ineffective ruler who never secured imperial coronation and found himself constantly at odds with members of the ruling family as well as with the nobility. His difficulties were not limited to opposition from the secular hierarchy, and in 1393 a conflict erupted between Wenceslas and the archbishop of Prague, which was ultimately resolved in favor of the king and forced the archbishop's resignation. Wenceslas also sought to play one side of the Schism against the other, and his involvement in papal politics left him little time or opportunity to monitor religious affairs in his kingdom.[4]

It was against this background that the first steps at reform had been taken by Charles IV. Owner of one of the great relic collections which contributed to Prague becoming an important center of the cult of the saints, he was a devout and religious ruler, whose piety in many ways was very traditional. He issued harsh legislation against heresy and the Beguines, but also sought to limit worldliness and excessive materialism both at his court and in the Church. Moreover, he was sincerely concerned about the well-being of the Church; he was among the leaders of Europe who encouraged the popes at Avignon to return the papacy to Rome. He was equally committed to the reformation of religious life and practice in his kingdom and forged an agreement with the pope in Avignon concerning the appointment of bishops in Bohemia. In other hands this might have led to corruption and abuse, but Charles's appointments were generally good and wise. The king also founded the University of Prague, which he hoped to make a leading intellectual center. To further guarantee both the health of the university and reformation of the clergy in his realm, Charles invited reform-minded Augustinian canons to the university, most notably Conrad of Waldhauser (also spelled Waldhausen).

The arrival of Conrad of Waldhauser (d. 1369) in Prague in 1360 set the stage for more dramatic reform efforts and initiated a line of reformist preachers who advocated the ideas of John Wyclif and paved the way for Jan Hus. Conrad began to preach against clerical abuses and corruption and was particularly critical of the monks and mendicant friars. He preached against false prophets and denounced simony and the cult of relics. His denunciations of moral laxity attracted the support of both clergy and laity, including women who abandoned their finery, usurers who paid back excessive interest, and the youth who gave up affected manners.[5] But his harsh critique of the Church and clergy endowed his enemies with the tools necessary to force him to answer before the pope. He was acquitted, but died in December 1369, on his way back to Prague from the papal court. He nonetheless attracted a sizeable following, including a number of prominent reformers who were active throughout the rest of the century. Among these reformers was Jan Milič of Kroměříž (c.1325–74), the father of Czech reform. Milič, an imperial notary from Bohemia, underwent a religious conversion after witnessing clerical corruption and hearing Waldhauser preach. He was ordained a priest, then granted a canonry by Charles IV in 1363, only to give up his offices and take up a life of poverty and preaching in Latin, German, and, most importantly, Czech. He preached penitence and Church reform, denouncing the sins of the clergy, and even, for a time, identified Charles IV as Antichrist – of whom Milič predicted that he would come in 1368. He founded a hospice, which he called Jerusalem, for reformed prostitutes, which was viewed critically by his enemies. Along with his harsh condemnations of the clergy, he advocated frequent communion and reform of the clergy and Church. Despite being called to the papal court, Milič inspired a number of followers who furthered the cause of reform.

Milič had numerous disciples, most notable Matthew, or Matthias, of Janov (c.1355–93), the great theorist of Czech reform who studied at the University of Paris and brought scholarly weight to the effort at reformation in Bohemia. Returning from Paris after the university's decision to accept the pope at Avignon – Janov was a supporter of the Roman pope – he became a canon at the cathedral in Prague in 1379. He later acquired further ecclesiastical benefices, but nothing that would lift him far beyond poverty, which he came to accept as the true Christian lifestyle. Devoted to the study of the scriptures, Janov carried the Bible with him at all times and found the answer to all his questions in its pages. Central to his own beliefs and one of the reasons why he took up Milič's reform, the Bible was so important to Janov that he advocated its translation, so as to make it accessible to those unlettered in Latin; he was also involved in the first translation of the Bible into Czech. Janov was deeply concerned about the imminence of Antichrist, whom he saw operating in his day. Antichrist stood for all that was contrary to the true faith and to Christ, and, as such, the pope at Avignon, a false pope, embodied Antichrist according to Janov. He also criticized, as did his mentor, the corruption of the Church. He opposed too much devotion to images, ritualism, and ceremonialism, and excessive concern with pilgrimage, indulgences, and the miraculous.[6] He demanded the return to the simple purity of the Bible and of the apostolic Church, which he praised over the elaborate and worldly Church of his day. To cure the ills of the latter, Janov prescribed frequent, even daily participation in the Eucharist. His calls for reform and frequent communion were met with stern opposition by the Church, which forced him to recant and forbade him to preach or hear confessions for some eighteen months. He put this time to good use, however, writing the great treatise of Czech reform, *Regulae veteris et novi testamenti* (1392; 'Rules of the Old and New Testaments').

Although Janov died in the year following the completion of his great work, the Czech reformation movement continued to grow and was further shaped by the influence of the teachings of John Wyclif. His works arrived in Bohemia because of the close connection between Oxford and the University of Prague, brought about by the marriage of Anne of Bohemia and King Richard II of England. Even as Wyclif's works were being condemned in England, Czech scholars were copying them and returning to Bohemia with them.[7] Wyclif's philosophy had a profound effect on thinkers in Bohemia, but perhaps even more influential were his attacks on the corruption of the Church and his ecclesiology and theology; they resonated within Czech reformation circles, which had begun to make similar criticisms. His virulent denunciations of the papacy as of 1378, together with the Great Schism, and his increasing disdain for the visible Church, to which he had denied any connection with the true Church, influenced the way Czech reformers regarded both Church and papacy. Czech reformers like Waldhauser and Janov shared with Wyclif an understanding of the centrality of the Bible and of its character as the truth because it was the word of God.[8] Wyclif also found greater support among the Czech masters and students at the University of Prague than among the German contingent, which on the whole opposed his ideas. This response to Wyclif drove a further wedge, reinforcing the social and political tension that already existed between Czechs and Germans.[9] Although an official attempt was made to suppress Wyclif's teachings in Bohemia, it failed, and his writings continued to shape the Czech reformation movement into the fifteenth century.

It was in this environment of failed political leadership, a growing religious reform movement, nationalistic animosities, Czech nationalism, and the arrival of the writings of John Wyclif that the great Czech reformer, Jan Hus, emerged. Of peasant origin, Hus was born in 1372 or 1373, or perhaps earlier (1369) – the date is uncertain – in the small village of Husinec on the River Blanice in southern Bohemia; little is known of his early life or family. He seems to have had a brother who predeceased him, as Hus asked a friend to look after his nephews shortly before his own death. All that is known of Hus's father is his name, Michael, and he seems to have had little influence on the direction of his son's life. Although the father may have receded from Jan's memory, his mother seems to have had lasting influence on him, as he revealed in one of his treatises. It was she, he recalled, who taught him to say: 'Amen, may God grant it.' It seems that she was behind his decision to become a priest, concerned as she was for her son to find a respectable profession, which would provide the financial security she apparently did not enjoy.[10] There is also a story from the late fifteenth century confirming the important role of Hus's mother in his life. According to this account, Hus was accompanied by her when he entered the grammar school in the nearby town of Prachatice in 1385. His mother brought a loaf of bread as a gift for the schoolmaster and, during the trip to the school, she knelt seven times to pray for her son.[11] Although the story may be apocryphal, it demonstrates the central role Hus's mother played in his first steps along the path to a clerical career. Beyond her lasting impact, though, little can be said of Hus's early life.

Events in the life of Jan Hus come into sharper focus once he began his education and entered the priesthood. His first step, of course, was taken when he entered the school at Prachatice, where he learned Latin, an essential skill for those wishing to become priests. During his years at Prachatice, Hus supported himself by singing in church choirs and participated in a blasphemous Christmas ritual, the 'Feast of the Ass,' in which a choir boy dressed as a bishop, rode a donkey, and led the other boys of the choir into a mock mass.[12] He also was introduced to the basic elements of medieval education: grammar, rhetoric, dialectic. He would study these subjects more fully at university, along with the other four liberal arts: arithmetic, astronomy, geometry, and music. In 1390, or perhaps as early as 1386, at the age of 18, Hus entered the University of Prague, enrolling under the name Jan of Husinec, which later on was shortened to Hus (the Czech word for 'goose'). He was most likely introduced to the city and university by a friend from his village, Christian of Prachatice.

Hus's university years were successful and enjoyable. He continued to support himself as a singer and developed a reputation for good humor, eloquence, and wit. He seems to have been intent upon pursuing a clerical career, hoping to ascend into the ranks of the ecclesiastical hierarchy. As he wrote later, 'When I was a young student, I confess to have entertained an evil desire, for I thought to become a priest quickly in order to secure a good livelihood and dress well and to be held in esteem of man.'[13] A university education was the best way for a poor young man like Hus to accomplish this end, and he undertook his studies most diligently. At the University of Prague he was introduced to Aristotle, who was known as 'the Philosopher' in the Middle Ages and whose system laid the foundation for all the higher disciplines, including philosophy and theology. He continued his study of Latin and he learned German, which he may have started at Prachatice; he worked toward becoming a bachelor of arts. Following the traditional three-year course of study, Hus was awarded his bachelor's degree in 1393, the first time that his name appears in an official document.

After receiving his degree, Hus immediately registered for study toward the master's degree, which would open numerous doors for him as a teacher and scholar. He spent the next three years studying at the university under its Czech, and not German, masters. His situation was eased somewhat by his appointment to a position in one of the colleges as servant; he was responsible for keeping the masters' rooms in order and for helping out in the kitchen, and he was given room and board for his labors. With less concern about financial matters, Hus was able to dedicate himself fully to his studies. Although it is uncertain whom he took as his primary master, Hus benefited from the possibility of studying at the university and living at its center. During his time there he was probably introduced to the works of Thomas Aquinas, whom he held in high regard, as well as to the philosophical and theological trends current at the time. He was exposed to Nominalism and came to know the works of St. Bonaventure, John Duns Scotus, William of Ockham, and others. It was also at this time that Hus was first introduced to the ideas of John Wyclif, which had become popular with Czech scholars at just about the time when Hus had arrived at the university.

His first contact was with Wyclif's philosophical works, which Hus found to be of great worth. Later on he came to know Wyclif's theological works and even copied four of his treatises for his own use.

Completing his course of study in 1396, Hus was awarded the master of arts degree and began his teaching career. From 1396 to 1398, he devoted his lectures to the works of Aristotle, offered tutorials and presided over student disputations, and after 1398 he lectured on the works of John Wyclif. He seems to have been a popular and successful teacher, attracting many students to his lectures, where his natural eloquence enabled him to give consistently interesting and informative lessons. His talents as a professor were recognized by his colleagues in the faculty of the university and by his former masters, who helped advance Hus's career. In 1398 he was given responsibility for the promotion of students to the rank of bachelor, and later he was granted the duty of promoting students to the level of master. His speeches at the promotion ceremonies reveal him as a man of good humor and kindliness and as a teacher able to establish close and warm relationships with his students.[14] In 1401, he was named dean of the Faculty of Arts and served in that position until the following year, when he became rector and preacher of Bethlehem Chapel, having been ordained a priest in June 1400. At that time, Hus also enrolled in the university's Faculty of Theology in pursuit of a doctorate in that field, which he never completed; yet he advanced toward his doctorate by earning lower degrees.

His ordination and interest in a theology degree signal a profound change in Hus's personal and professional life. It was at some point prior to ordination that he seems to have undergone a religious conversion which led to his committing fully to the religious life and turning away from the life of the careerist ecclesiastic, who sought ecclesiastical benefices and other privileges. Up to that point, as Hus himself freely admitted, he indulged in 'youthful follies,' playing chess and taking pride in his academic position and dress. He often wore elaborate university gowns, decorated with white fur. He willingly participated in the banquets of the university masters and generally enjoyed his life as a student and teacher, while ambitiously seeking advancement. All that ended sometime before 1400, but Hus provides no clear answer concerning the precise moment when this happened or the reason for such sudden and profound change. Near the end of his life, however, he noted that, when he was young, he had belonged to a 'foolish sect,' but God had shown him the way through the scriptures and thereafter he abandoned the life of frivolity. As with his predecessors in the Czech reformation movement, Hus seems to have come to personal reform and to the religious life through the serious study of the Bible.[15]

For twelve years following his appointment on March 14, 1402, Hus continued to hold his position as rector and as preacher of Bethlehem Chapel, which had been founded in 1391 by a wealthy Prague merchant. Thus he combined both popular and university reform traditions and made that chapel the center of the Czech reformation movement. During his tenure as rector, he delivered some three thousand sermons; many of them were originally composed or preserved in Latin.[16] His sermons attracted to the chapel large and enthusiastic crowds, including many noble women and even the queen. Unlike earlier rectors, Hus preached only in Czech and not in Czech and German, demonstrating his own Czech nationalism and proclaiming the important role of Bohemia in God's plan. He also identified himself more fully with the Czech reformation and its ideals, and his preaching was an essential stimulus to the growth and expansion of that movement. Its goals moved beyond the academic and ecclesiastical circle and were adopted by Czech artisans and the Czech middle class. Indeed, as one historian has noted, through his sermons at the Bethlehem Chapel, Hus created the concerns of the reformers and the ecumenical agenda, transforming himself into a 'national religious leader.'[17]

The sermons Hus delivered at Bethlehem Chapel covered a wide range of topics concerned with the moral and institutional reform of the Church. In some of his early sermons, he exhorted his listeners to take up a life of repentance and holiness and to follow Christ. He challenged the laity, including nobles and kings, as well as his fellow clerics, to renounce corruption and immorality and to live a virtuous life without avarice, pride, or other sins, and he taught that the highest goal of the religious life was to love God.[18] In sermons delivered between 1405 and 1407, however, he moved beyond moral exhortation – of laity, clergy, and university masters and students – to address the problems facing the clergy and the Church. From this period on, his sermons became more aggressive and critical. He ferociously attacked the failings of the clergy, denouncing the corruption of the priestly office and demanding reform. In his sermons he proclaimed that corrupt and immoral priests were really the devil's own, and he attacked priests who had concubines or committed adultery. Also of concern to Hus was simony, which, in his treatise on this topic, he defined in traditional terms, as 'an evil consent to an exchange of spiritual goods for nonspiritual.' It is a 'trafficking in holy things,' and 'both he who buys and he who sell [sic] is a merchant, a simoniac is both he who buys and he who sells holy things.'[19] He criticized the clergy for accepting money or gifts in exchange for performing the sacraments and he virulently attacked both the priests and the monks for various financial exactions. In these sermons Hus addressed the hierarchy of the Church as well, and criticized excessive claims to papal power and authority, raising questions, in particular, over indulgences and matters of excommunication. The Church itself was defined as the body of the elect, all those who had been predestined to salvation. Although both the predestined and the foreknown existed together in the Church militant, only the predestined were part of the true Church.

During his tenure as rector at Bethlehem Chapel, Hus continued his scholarly career and worked toward his doctorate in theology. He earned his bachelor's degree in divinity in 1404, and from 1404 to 1406 he gave lectures on the Bible. In 1407 he earned the degree that would allow him to lecture on Peter Lombard's *Book of Sentences*, which he did from 1407 to 1409. He also engaged in academic disputations with other scholars as he prepared for the doctoral degree, and he wrote a commentary on Lombard's *Sentences*, even though other duties prevented him from taking the doctoral degree. It was at this time that Hus also became better acquainted with Wyclif's views, some of which he accepted, others not. Wyclif's teachings would seem to have influenced Hus even though the Czech scholar was never a thoroughgoing disciple of the Oxford theologian. He would, however, defend Wyclif's teachings against the increasingly hostile and irrational attacks on them by the German masters at Prague.

Hus's career at Bethlehem Chapel and at the University of Prague overlapped with broader changes in Czech society and culture, which included increasing tensions between the German and Czech populations. These changes were manifest in the reaction against Wyclif's teachings, led by the Dominican John Hübner and by the German masters at the University of Prague, which broke out in 1403. Hübner petitioned Rome about some forty-five of Wyclif's propositions as well as on the matter of the realism currently taught by the Czech masters of the university. Some twenty-four of the propositions listed by Hübner had previously been condemned at the Blackfriars' Council in England in 1382, and the remaining twenty-one were compiled by Hübner himself. The

Wyclifite teachings included positions on the papacy, on the pope as Antichrist, and on the monastic orders, among other things. Hübner argued that, since some of these propositions had already been condemned, they should be condemned in Bohemia as well. The repudiation of Wyclif's teachings was also sent to the archbishop of Prague, who, in turn, asked the university for an opinion. When the university masters took up the debate, the underlying tensions between the German and Czech masters exploded into the open, since the German scholars had rejected Wyclif's ideas and the Czechs had adopted them as central to their reform program. The Czechs strongly opposed Hübner's condemnation and accused the Dominican of misquoting or taking passages out of context. They asserted that Wyclif's teachings were not in error and declared that they would continue to support these teachings. Despite the vehemence of their opposition to Hübner, the Czech masters lost the university debate when the vote was tallied. The three German nations at the university voted in favor of Hübner's condemnation, whereas the Czech nation voted against it. (A 'nation' was a basic organizational structure of the medieval university, made up of students from the same country or religion.)

The dispute, however, did not put an end to the general interest in Wyclif's ideas. The university did not forbid the study of Wyclif's books but only of the specific articles listed in the condemnation. The archbishop, a well-respected former soldier and noble, Zbyněk, was ill-equipped to render a decision but sympathetic to reform, and he hesitated to make a pronouncement on the matter. The Czech masters, especially Hus, pursued their study of Wyclif more eagerly than before, and some of them went so far as to declare publicly their endorsement of the most controversial of Wyclif's ideas. Although Hus was not among them, he would defend Wyclif and approved of many of the Oxford theologian's positions. In debate with Hübner in 1404, Hus rejected the Dominican's denunciations of Wyclif and accused Hübner of distorting Wyclif's positions. Moreover, Hus ardently maintained that the forty-five articles had been taken out of context and that Wyclif himself was not a heretic. Despite this show of support by Hus and others, the acceptance of Wyclif's teachings faced serious setbacks. In 1407, two of the most active Czech supporters of Wyclif's ideas, Stanislav of Znojmo and Jan Páleč, were called before the pope and forced to recant their teachings. Under papal pressure, they rejected their former advocacy, and when they returned to Prague they were among the staunchest critics of Wyclif. And in 1408, the archbishop prohibited the teaching of the forty-five articles condemned by Hübner, while the Czech masters agreed not to defend the articles 'in their heretical, erroneous, and objectionable sense' – a most ambiguous acquiescence.[20]

Another development of major significance for Jan Hus was King Wenceslas's change of allegiance during the papal schism, which enhanced Hus's standing but also contributed to the estrangement between him and Archbishop Zbyněk. Wenceslas and the university and clergy had supported the popes in Rome, most recently Gregory XII (1406–15), as the legitimate popes against those in Avignon. In an effort to end the schism, however, a number of cardinals withdrew their allegiance to their respective popes and, with the support of the French king and of the University of Paris, agreed to hold a general council to depose the reigning popes and to elect a new one. Meeting at the poorly attended Council of Pisa in 1409, the cardinals elected Peter of Candia, who took the name of Alexander V. Wenceslas, who received promise of support from the French if he backed the Council and the new pope, saw his opportunity to undermine the authority of his brother, Emperor Rupert, and to gain greater power in the Empire. In order to switch his allegiance, the king needed the support of the University of Prague, but he faced the difficult proposition of persuading the German nations, which remained united in their support of Rome. To resolve that dilemma, Wenceslas issued the decree of Kutná Hora on January 18, 1409, which reorganized the nations at the university. The German nations had been divided into three voting blocks, but the decree merged them into one, and the Bohemian block was divided into three blocks from one. The Czech reformers, who made up the majority of the Bohemian nation, hoped to find backing from the conciliar pope, and so they were supportive of the king's move to endorse the Council and the pope it chose, and voted in approval of the conciliar movement. The German nations abandoned the university, returning to new or established universities in other parts of the Empire, where they continued their opposition to Wyclif and to the Czechs at the University of Prague.

Changes of papal affiliation affected Hus and the Czech reformation movement directly, in ways they had surely not anticipated. Rather than support the king and the new conciliar pope, Archbishop Zbyněk refused, as any good soldier would, to break his oath to the Roman pope, Gregory. This enraged Wenceslas, who took steps against the archbishop. Zbyněk was forced to renounce his allegiance to Gregory and declared Alexander to be the legitimate pope; he was also ordered to proclaim that Prague and its university were free from heresy. These humiliations drove Zbyněk away from the reform camp and led to his request that Alexander should issue a bull condemning Wyclif's teachings and prohibiting any preaching outside the cathedral church or monasteries. Issued on December 20, 1409, this bull clearly drove a wedge between the archbishop and Hus, who was obviously the target – if not in the bull, at least as far as Zbyněk was concerned. Hus continued preaching and gained popular support against the archbishop, whose high-handedness alienated not only the people of Prague but also the king. Zbyněk was not going to back down, and on July 16, 1410, he gathered together copies of Wyclif's books and had them burned. Although surrendering his own volumes, Hus protested Zbyněk's actions as unwarranted and arbitrary, especially since Wyclif had not yet been declared a heretic. The archbishop excommunicated Hus and reported the case to the papal curia, which then examined the matter to Hus's disadvantage. Refusing to report to Rome to answer questions concerning his case, Hus was excommunicated in 1411 by the cardinal in charge of his case and by Zbyněk for a second time. The archbishop also placed the city of Prague under an interdict, but the king declared it should not be obeyed. Efforts to resolve the crisis were made by all parties and nearly reached a successful conclusion. Zbyněk was charged with lifting both the interdict and the excommunication of Hus in exchange for concessions from the king, and Hus was to make a full confession of faith, declaring his adherence to orthodox teaching, which he sent to the pope. The archbishop, however, decided to flee Prague for territories of Wenceslas's brother Sigismund, king of Hungary, before fulfilling his end of the agreement and died on the way there, in September 1411.

Hus assumed such a pivotal role in the dispute with Zbyněk in large measure because he, a charismatic preacher, had emerged as the leader of the Czech reformation movement by 1407. Earlier leaders, including some of his own teachers, had begun to pass away, while others, closer in age to Hus, notably Stanislav of Znojmo and Jan Páleč, had defected from the reform camp and turned into harsh critics of the reform and of Wyclif. Preaching from the pulpit at Bethlehem Chapel attracted a large following for Hus from outside the university, but, more importantly still, it allowed him to give voice to his own criticisms of the Church, which coincided with broader reform goals. And since he was

also guardedly sympathetic of Wyclifite teachings and open to Czech national-
ist ideas, he seemed to be the natural leader of the movement, even though he
was not the most radical theologian of his day. His stature was most clearly
recognized when the masters at the university chose him as rector on October
17, 1409, an office he held throughout the rest of that year and the next. The
election was one of the results of the Kutná Hora decree, which put control of
university policy into the hands of the Czech nation.

As leader of the popular reform movement in his capacity at Bethlehem
Chapel and as rector of the university, Hus held a unique position at the time
of his controversy with Archbishop Zbyněk. Speaking out on behalf of his
fellow university scholars, Hus attacked the actions of the archbishop, and
found further popular support due to his position at the chapel. Although the
compromise brokered between Hus and the archbishop broke down because of
Zbyněk's flight and death, and Hus's status at the papal curia remained uncertain at best, he surely emerged in an even stronger position in Bohemia than he
had before, and his support among the Czech reformers was enhanced when
he challenged the anti-Wyclifite John Stokes to a debate over Wyclif's teachings – which Stokes declined on the grounds that anyone who read Wyclif was
a heretic. Attempts to have the agreement declared valid after the death of
Zbyněk failed, but that too seemed to have little impact on Hus's standing. But,
having survived the struggle with the archbishop, in the years to come Hus was
to face an ever greater challenge over the matter of papal indulgences, which
led to an irrevocable break with both pope and king, and over the excesses of
the reformation movement he was heading.

On September 9, 1411, the antipope John XXIII issued a bull of indulgences on behalf of his crusade against King Ladislas of Naples, a supporter of
Gregory XII, who had been deposed at the Council of Pisa. Ladislas had aided
Gregory to take control of Rome and to force John to flee from the papal city; in
response, John sought to raise a crusade. He also ordered all bishops and priests
to declare Ladislas 'excommunicated, perjured, a schismatic, a blasphemer, a
relapsed heretic, protector of heretics, guilty of the crime of lèse majesté, a
conspirator against us and the Church,' and called on all the princes, clergy,
and laity to take up the sword in defense of the Church against the heretic
Ladislas.[21] In a second bull issued on December 2 of that year, John appointed
commissioners to preach indulgences, restated their terms, and proclaimed a

crusade against Gregory XII and Ladislas as enemies of the Church. John's call to crusade and offer of indulgences were not enthusiastically supported throughout the Church, and in some quarters they were opposed. They found, however, a ready supporter in Wenceslas, who most likely was guaranteed a part of the proceeds from the sale of the indulgences.

Although the king of Bohemia supported the papal bulls, the Czech reformers did not, and some spoke out quite vociferously against the sale of indulgences. Among the loudest opponents to John XXIII's actions were some reformers who had recently arrived in Prague. One of them, most likely, was Nicholas of Dresden, who published a highly critical treatise on the Church and papacy later on. He and other newcomers were associated with public demonstrations and provocations against the Church. They joined many of those, already living in Prague, who opposed the antipope's proclamation; these included members of the university and even the more conservative masters. The more reform-minded masters and students also rejected the indulgence bull, even though the authorities of the university would not allow protests against it. Despite this restriction, reformers came out against the bull and stimulated popular protest against it. This stoked the king's anger and led to a reaction against the protest. In July, three opponents were beheaded at the order of the magistrates of Prague. Buried at Bethlehem Chapel, they were the first martyrs of the Hussite reform.

It was not just the more extreme wing of the reformation movement that opposed the sale of indulgences and would suffer the king's wrath, but also its more moderate leader, Jan Hus. Indeed, it had been Hus's preaching as much as anything that stimulated the dramatic and sometimes violent popular opposition to the indulgence bull. Although Hus did not deny indulgences in principle – he had, in fact, purchased one when they were offered for sale in 1393 – he denounced the gross and sacrilegious sale of the indulgences for the most unholy cause of war.[22] He was particularly outspoken on this matter and harshly critical of John XXIII's offer of an indulgence to any Christian who would go to war against fellow Christians. In fact, Hus argued that it was not the pope's duty to wage war – nor the duty of any cleric for that matter – because that responsibility was held by the secular power: the temporal sword held by the king was to enter battle, but not the spiritual sword held by the pope.[23] It may also be that Hus, like Wyclif, was distrustful of the crass sale of spiritual gifts;

he clearly believed that forgiveness comes only from God and only to a truly penitent sinner, whereas in the purchaser of an indulgence there was no guarantee of a pure heart. In other words, Hus maintained that God alone can offer an indulgence, through an act of grace to a sinner who repents and confesses his or her sins. And, just as Martin Luther did later during his controversy over indulgences, Hus asked why the pope would not save all Christians.

This daring critique of the papal indulgence proved central to Hus's undoing: it was not just that he lost many friends – his position, after all, was quite popular with the laity and with many of the students at the University of Prague – but he also ran afoul of university administrators and, even more seriously, of King Wenceslas, who stood to benefit materially from the sale of indulgences and also hoped to preserve good relations with John XXIII.[24] Along with his treatise against the papal indulgence, Hus made his position known publicly on a number of occasions, and his sermons against indulgences further inspired the reformers and the people of Prague. He spoke out against the bull in a disputation in January 1412 and again in June 1412, and his second debate was in open violation of the dean's prohibition to discuss the matter. Hus's outspoken views led to popular agitation and to the arrest of the three leaders of the opposition; Hus volunteered to change places with the three, but the magistrate in charge assured him that nothing serious would happen to them – just before he ordered their beheading.

As desperate as the situation seemed at that point, matters worsened still for Hus, who found himself clearly opposed on this matter by the king himself. This left him without the necessary protection from his enemies, who scored repeated successes against him. Various Bohemian bishops and the inquisitor of Prague formally denounced Wyclif's opinions and forbade their teaching. But Hus, who had been away at the time, was unaware of this and openly discussed the ideas of the Oxford theologian. In July, Hus faced further problems when one of the cardinals in Rome excommunicated him; this was the result of an examination of his case by a commission established by the pope in April. Moreover, the ban of excommunication forbade anyone to offer him food, drink, hospitality, or indeed any contact of any kind whatsoever. The town of Prague itself was threatened by an interdict for harboring Hus, once the verdict against him was announced in October 1412. Having lost the support of king, university, and now pope, Hus had little recourse but to appeal to Christ himself, and, while awaiting that verdict, he left Prague, to spare the city and its people of the penalty of the interdict. His departure, possibly orchestrated by the king himself, took place at the same time that the peace treaty concluded between John XXIII and Ladislas was announced in Prague.[25]

Even though Hus was forced to leave the city, he remained in contact with friends there, including Christian of Prachatice, now rector of the university, who consoled him and encouraged him not to lose hope. Hus, as his letters from the time indicate, did not seem to have been overly discouraged by the turn of events and even hoped to regain the good graces of the king. Hoping to overturn the decision rendered against him at Rome, Hus appealed to the royal couple, who accepted his petition and ordered the new archbishop, Conrad of Vechta, to hold a Council at Český Brod in January 1413 to eliminate heresy in the kingdom. The king also invited members of the faculty of the University of Prague to attend, which only served to undermine any chance of success the meeting might have had. Although some of Hus's university colleagues spoke on his behalf at the meeting and defended his teachings, the members of the faculty of theology worked toward a very different outcome. They drew up a *consilium* which outlined the essential terms for resolving the conflict. The document asserted that all good Christians must believe as the Roman Church does, obey the clergy, and recognize the legitimate authority of the pope and cardinals. The masters of theology also declared that Wyclif's forty-five articles must be acknowledged as either heretical or erroneous. When presented with this *consilium*, Hus replied with a strongly worded letter which denounced its terms and the faculty members who authored it, especially Stanislav of Znojmo and Jan Páleč. Hus declared that he would rather die than accept the terms of the document; it would be 'better to die well than to live evilly.'[26] The breakdown of the Council revealed the complete failure of a negotiated settlement, even though one further attempt was made.

The commission's failure to find an equitable solution and Hus's refusal to accept any reconciliation with his rivals left him little option but to defend himself as best he could. He spent much of the two years of exile, before his departure for the Council at Constance, writing various responses to the charges and teachings of his enemies. Among his works in Czech and Latin were sermons designed to appeal to the people of Bohemia and denounce the errors of his rivals and the corruptions of the Church. On occasion, he returned to

Prague; he certainly remained in touch with reformers in the city and preached before its people several times. Each time, however, the authorities imposed the interdict and forbade his preaching. Hus noted in one of his letters that, 'when I preached once, they immediately stopped the services, for it was hard for them to hear the Word of God.'[27]

Suppression by the authorities did not silence Hus, however. While in exile, he had recourse to the composition of a number of treatises, which, among other things, attacked the views of his most ardent foes, Stanislav of Znojmo and Jan Páleč, although they, too, had been sent into exile by the king – who was angry over their involvement in the failure to find a peaceful solution at the Council. The three of them indulged in something of a pamphlet war during Hus's absence from Prague; Hus seemed most intent on demolishing their arguments in his written works. It was during this period that he wrote his two most important treatises, the Latin *De ecclesia* ('On the Church') and the Czech *O svatokupectví* ('On Simony').

Published in May 1413, *De ecclesia* offers Hus's mature thinking on the nature of the Church and on the state of the clergy and ecclesiastical hierarchy. Drawing on great Church Fathers such as St. Augustine and Gregory the Great, Hus attacked the views of his rivals and the tenets of the *consilium* compiled by the theology faculty. In *De ecclesia* Hus described his understanding of the true Church, which drew, although not uncritically, on the teachings of Wyclif. For Hus held that the true Church was composed of all the predestined, who included the living, the dead, and those yet to be born. The true Church was invisible, as Wyclif had argued; Hus explained that it consisted in the mystical body of Christ, and Christ himself was the sole head of the Church. All the predestined were bound together in the one true Church and bound to Christ. Hus held, like Wyclif, that the foreknown are excluded from the true Church, even though they are not predestined to damnation but through their own free will turn from God. The foreknown and the elect, however, are joined together in the Church militant, in the Church in the world, and it is not possible to discern the saved from the foreknown. Hus argued further that, even though members of the clergy and laity of the Catholic Church are surely among the predestined, the Catholic Church itself is not to be identified with the true Church of Christ.

In developing his concept of the Church, Hus was clearly influenced by

Wyclif; but he departed from the Oxford theologian on various practical matters concerning the earthly Church and the clergy. Attention to these practical details is the second major theme of his work *De ecclesia* and reveals that Hus was more in the tradition of the Czech reformers than in the line of the more radical Wyclif and his Lollard followers. In one respect, though, Hus did follow Wyclif, albeit in a more moderate form. Like Wyclif, Hus was critical of the claims to papal primacy and authority over the Church and rejected papal claims to a fullness of power over all Christians. Unlike Wyclif, however, Hus did not deny that the pope and the cardinals were the most esteemed and respected figures in the Church. He denied that the pope was the direct successor to Peter, maintaining that the papacy was a human and not a divine institution and that the pope was fallible and could sin.[28] Commenting on Matthew 16: 18–19, which was the traditional foundation of claims to papal primacy and descent from St. Peter, Hus declared that the words 'You are Peter, and on this rock I shall build my church' refer, not to Peter, but to Peter's recognition that Jesus was the Son of God. Peter did not become Christ's vicar but could claim to be the prince of the Apostles because of his virtues and understanding of who Christ was. It was Christ who was the foundation of the Church and remained its head and to claim otherwise, according to Hus, was to deny the ultimate authority of scripture. Indeed, for Hus scripture was the supreme authority in the Church because it was the infallible word of God and not the opinion of flawed humans.

In *De ecclesia*, Hus also touched on other matters concerning the clergy and the Church. Once again asserting the necessity of clerical morality, Hus declared that only those priests who live in accordance with the teachings of Jesus Christ are worthy of the office. They must eschew worldliness and pride and follow the laws of God over the laws of humankind. A true priest is also defined by his devotion to preaching and by a life of apostolic poverty and devotion. Hus also examined the nature and powers of the priesthood, restricting the authority of the priest to spiritual matters and denying him any temporal power, which belongs only to nobles and kings. He noted that no priest, no matter how high in the Church hierarchy, could forgive sins on his own power. It was God alone who could forgive sins for the truly penitent, and the priest was merely God's minister in this matter. Furthermore, like Wyclif, Hus denied that any cleric has the power to bind and loose, to excommunicate or to grant indulgences, because only God may do so and only the sinner can separate himself or herself from God. The priest is responsible for administering the sacraments, but their efficacy is the result of God's grace rather than of any spiritual power possessed by the priest. Hus held, further, that it is better for a sinful priest not to administer the sacraments, but, even if a priest does so in the state of sin, the sacrament is still efficacious because of God's grace. In this, he confirmed his earlier position on the Eucharist. For in his treatise on the Lord's Supper Hus had written that it was not the priest who transformed the bread and wine into the body and blood, but Christ himself was the originator of this miracle. On this matter, Hus clearly turned away from Wyclif's teachings on remanence. But, although rejecting Wyclif's view, Hus used his language to explain what happened to the bread after it had been transformed into the body of Christ, differentiating between the form of the bread and the substance of Christ within it.[29]

Hus's other major work during his exile was focused on the matter of simony, which he had already declared in *De ecclesia* to be one of the worst sins that any member of the clergy could commit. A popular treatise written in Czech between the end of 1412 and February 1413, 'On Simony' attacked one of the most serious problems facing the Church in Hus's day. As he observed, 'there are but few priests who have secured their ordination without simony ... And since simony is heresy, if anyone observe carefully he must perceive that there are many heretics.'[30] Drawing from Gregory the Great and other Church Fathers, Hus, as noted above, defined simony as the 'exchange of spiritual goods for nonspiritual.' It was the buying and selling of holy things as well as the tacit approval of such exchanges, and the source of simony was corruption of the will, that is, an evil will.[31] According to Hus, all ranks of society, both clerical and lay, were guilty of simony. Popes and bishops committed it whenever they strove for office or appointed someone to clerical rank for payment or offered it to the highest bidder. The sale of indulgences by the pope (or priests or bishops) was among the acts of simony described by Hus. It was not only those who sold offices that were guilty of it, argued Hus, but also those who bought them. Any monk who paid to gain entrance to monastic orders or any priest who paid for his ordination was guilty of the crime. Priests also committed simony when they accepted payment for performing their sacramental duties, or when they demanded payment for burying the dead. The laity too committed simony when they paid the clergy for bestowing the sacraments or other spiritual gifts on the laity; kings and emperors were guilty when they appointed clerics to ecclesiastical benefices or offices. Although thoroughly consistent in his denunciations of simony in both clergy and laity, Hus further alienated the king by his attack on royal appointments.

In these late works, just as in sermons and treatises throughout his career as a preacher, university master, and popular leader, Hus provided a sometimes daring reforming program which sought to improve the life and structure of the Church. Although sometimes extreme, in most cases Hus's positions were not altogether unorthodox. Indeed, in many ways he was a very conventional churchman of his day. Critical of numerous aspects of Church life and belief, Hus nonetheless accepted many of the teachings of the Church. He accepted, albeit in a somewhat unique form, the doctrine of transubstantiation as well as the authority of the Bible, of the councils and of the Church Fathers. He approved of the veneration of the saints, especially the Virgin Mary. He believed in purgatory, masses for the dead, sacraments, and other conventional beliefs and practices of the Church of his day. But his teachings on the nature of the Church and on the powers of the pope and clergy set him somewhat apart from the mainstream of orthodoxy. Even more damning was his qualified support for, and public defense of, a number of Wyclif's teachings. His continued preaching while under the ban of excommunication and his sometimes strident criticisms of clerical abuse and corruption also contributed to his identification as a heretic. And his attack on papal indulgences and royal privileges in the Church lost him the support not only of the Church but also of his royal patron and protector. This was indeed a fatal blow.

The last phase of Jan Hus's life coincided with the resolution of the Great Schism at the Council of Constance.[32] Efforts to end the Schism by conciliar decree had not only failed at the earlier meeting in Pisa but worsened the situation by leading to the election of a pope that very few recognized. The meeting at Constance, however, had gained the support of King Sigismund, the younger brother and sometime rival of Wenceslas; this support would be critical to its ultimate success. There was also a great popular support for the Council, which was much better attended than its predecessor. As a consequence, Constance succeeded where Pisa failed. The reigning popes abdicated; they were to be deposed or stripped of any authority if they refused abdication or deposition.

A new pope, Martin V (1417–31), was elected and numerous reforms were implemented to improve the health of the Church. It was also agreed that universal Church councils would be held on a regular basis in the future. And the fate of Jan Hus was finally and tragically determined.

Although anxious about his own fate to the point of writing his will before departing for Constance, Hus welcomed the opportunity presented by the Council hoping that his positions and the Czech reformation movement would gain conciliar sanction. He was granted safe passage by Sigismund himself, and was joined by some thirty companions when he departed for Constance on October 11, 1414. Shortly after his arrival on November 3, John XXIII lifted the interdict against him and granted him the freedom to come and go as he pleased and to participate in the various discussions that were going on at the meeting. But things very quickly turned against Hus, as his enemies worked to his detriment, bringing new charges against him, and, perhaps most ominously, the Council issued its first denunciation of Wyclif's teachings on November 11. Later on, when given the opportunity to reject the forty-five articles, Hus rejected nearly all of them, but enemies such as Jan Páleč undermined his credibility by painting him as one who had been known to disobey the pope and to accept heresy in the past.

Despite promising overtures at the Council, Hus's situation worsened progressively, although his supporters defended him as best they could; they even wrote to Sigismund, making him consider seriously the claim that a decision against Hus would be an insult to the whole of Bohemia. Hus was arrested and imprisoned on November 28, and at times he was kept chained to a wall in the evenings. A commission was formed to examine him and his teachings; this commission included his old and new rivals, such as the noted Parisian theologians Pierre d'Ailly and Jean Gerson, whose theological and philosophical views opposed those of Hus and who arrived at the Council convinced of his guilt and hereticism. A trial was opened against Hus on June 5, 1415, but the judges had already made up their minds against him. Hus was given little opportunity to explain his positions and was routinely forced to give yes or no answers; the first session ended without a decision being reached. Hus's friends had obtained an agreement from Sigismund that no decision could be made against Hus without the king's presence at the session, and on June 7 Sigismund attended the proceedings. As during the previous meeting, Hus was given little opportunity to defend his own teachings and, even worse, he was now forced to defend himself in regard to Wyclif's errors. He was also accused of supporting various teachings of Wyclif and of inspiring unrest in Prague and dissension between the German and Bohemian nations.

At the final session of the trial, on June 8, Hus was presented with a list of errors drawn from his writings. These errors focused on his attitude toward the Church and the clergy; no mention was made of his support of Wyclif, his errors concerning the Eucharist, or his alleged Donatism. As Matthew Spinka notes, Hus's heresy was his conception of the true Church as the association of the elect, and the errors listed in the condemnation were related to this central conception.[33] Those various errors included his understanding of the place of the predestined and of the foreknown in the true Church; his placing of Christ, but not of the pope, at the head of the Church; his conception of the various duties and powers of priesthood; his attitude to matters of excommunication and interdict; and his position on the forty-five articles of Wyclif. By this point it was clear that not only his judges believed him to be guilty of heresy, but Sigismund too, and Hus was commanded to abjure his own teachings. Hus appealed to be allowed to defend himself but, again, was given no opportunity to speak, and it was clear to all that he was to be condemned as a heretic. On June 9 Sigismund allowed the Council to proceed along this line, and on June 18 the final list of charges against Hus and his condemnation were issued.[34]

Although further efforts to convince Hus to accept the decisions of the Council and to abjure his alleged errors were made by his friends, Hus insisted that he must follow his conscience. On July 6 Jan Hus was publicly degraded of his clerical rank and defrocked. One last time he was offered the chance to recant, but according to an eyewitness account he refused, declaring:

> God is my witness that those things that are falsely ascribed to me and of which the false witnesses accuse me, I have never taught or preached. But that the principal intention of my preaching and of all my other acts or writings was solely that I might turn men from sin. And in that truth of the Gospel that I wrote, taught, and preached in accordance with the sayings and expositions of the holy doctors, I am willing gladly to die today.[35]

Hus was then led to the pyre, which was set ablaze as he sang the Credo. He died while offering his last prayers to God.

His executioners broke his bones, so that they would burn completely, and they ensured that his organs were turned completely to ashes, so that the Czechs would not have relics to venerate and so that Hus's movement ended on that day. Despite these efforts, Hus's execution enraged the people of Bohemia; the Hussite reform carried on and eventually led to revolution.[36] Reformers continued his program and introduced new demands, such as for receiving both the chalice and the bread at communion (Utraquism), and the radicals became more outspoken. In 1419, Wenceslas sought to suppress the Hussites. This led to open warfare and the pope himself, at Sigismund's suggestion, called what was to be the first of five crusades against the Hussites and their radical wing, the Taborites. The long struggle finally ended with the defeat of the Taborites in 1436, but concessions were made to the Utraquists that laid the foundation for the emergence of an independent church in Bohemia, foreshadowing events of the next century.

The life and tragic death of Jan Hus brings to a close the history of medieval heresy. Hus may be seen as the last of the great heretics of the Middle Ages, echoing as he did the thoughts of earlier religious dissidents. His teachings addressed some of the most serious problems of the medieval Church; but, as harsh as his attacks may have been, he seems not to have rejected the structure of the Church, even if he advocated its reform and the limitation of papal power. His reforms, however, were not as radical as those of John Wyclif, whose influence on Hus cannot be dismissed; they keep him fully in the tradition of medieval dissent. Moreover, his burning at the stake echoes the common fate of many medieval heretics. But Hus and the movement he inspired foreshadowed the more dramatic events of the sixteenth century and the Protestant Reformation. Like Wyclif before him, Hus set out propositions which would be repeated by Martin Luther and the other reformers of the sixteenth century. Moreover, the establishment of an independent national church in Bohemia after the Hussite wars clearly prefigured the national and sectarian divisions which emerged in the wake of Luther's protest. And so Hus was the last of the great medieval heretics and a forerunner of the reformers of the sixteenth century.

FIVE CENTURIES OF
RELIGIOUS DISSENT

*t*he lives of the medieval heretics, as we have seen, had a profound and lasting impact on the development of Church and society in the Middle Ages, and their teachings, at times, foreshadowed the Protestant Reformation of the sixteenth century. Throughout the Middle Ages pious Christians inspired by the Bible, the saints' lives, learned theological treatises, contemporary religious reform movements, or, as they claimed, God above, sought to live the true Christian life as they understood it and rejected the authority of the established Church. At times, these Christians struck at the Church militant, denouncing the abuses and worldliness of the clergy, and at other times, they simply rejected the Church and its ministers in order to follow the apostolic life. Whatever the case, throughout the Middle Ages heretics appeared to offer a distinct understanding of the Christian life, and their emergence was both a response to the changing conditions of their day and an influence on those developments.

From the beginnings of medieval heresy, religious dissidents expressed their discontent with the structure and organization of the Church in the hope that they could restore it to its original purity. Shaped by influences from as far away as Bulgaria and the Byzantine world, heresy in western Europe was also determined by local political, social, cultural, and religious factors. And the rise of heresy in France and other places in Latin Christendom around the year

1000 influenced, in its turn, events which were to develop over the next five centuries: the Crusades, the movement of apostolic poverty, the unification of medieval France, the growth of mysticism, and other important developments in the Middle Ages. The influence of the heretical leaders can be seen in such great events as the Gregorian Reform. Even the absence of outbreaks of heresy in the second half of the eleventh century is often attributed to the Church's adoption of some of the ideas of the heretics of the year 1000.

In the first half of the twelfth century, Henry the Monk and other itinerant preachers embodied the spirit of religious reform and adopted the apostolic life. Henry and other heretical preachers who promoted the emerging ideal of the *vita apostolica* often were virtually indistinguishable from their orthodox and saintly contemporaries, who also adopted the evangelical life and criticized the worldliness of the Church. One of the greatest of the medieval heretics, Valdes of Lyons perhaps best exemplified the apostolic ideal and actively led a life of poverty and preaching despite opposition from the pope himself. Just as earlier orthodox reformers may have adopted some of the ideas of the heretics, so too would the far-sighted leaders of the twelfth and thirteenth centuries; recognizing the appeal of the religious life of poverty and preaching, Pope Innocent III approved the Order of St. Francis of Assisi, whose life was in many ways similar to that of Valdes.

Innocent also called a crusade against the heretics of southern France, thereby redefining one of the great movements of the Middle Ages as a war not only against Muslims in the Holy Land but also against all the enemies of the Church everywhere. His crusade undermined the strength of the Cathar churches in southern France, but may be said to have had a greater impact on the unification of medieval France as a result of the invasion of the northern barons and later participation of the French king. The Cathars also contributed to the formation of the Inquisition as the central tool in fighting heresy; and this fight was itself a part of what the historian R. I. Moore has termed the formation of a persecuting society. Although ultimately suppressed by the Church through sword and fire, heresy repeatedly shaped developments in medieval society between the tenth and the fifteenth centuries.

Heresy also reflected broader developments in the medieval world. The movement of Gerard Segarelli and, especially, his successor Fra Dolcino provides a classic illustration of the peasant movements and uprisings that broke out throughout the Middle Ages. Preaching a radical version of apostolic poverty, motivated by an aggressive apocalypticism, Fra Dolcino attracted a sizeable following, which wreaked havoc in the mountains of northern Italy. Hostile to the Church, which he and his followers identified as false, and to its worldly wealth and power, Dolcino led his peasant followers into open rebellion both against the Church and against its secular allies. This mixture of religious zeal and social and political discontent in his movement echoes that of similar peasant uprisings – in France in 1251 and 1320, in England in 1381, and even in Germany in 1524–25. Dolcino's preaching of a millennial kingdom in this world and his call to establish it can be seen as one of the repeated expressions of the revolutionary and mystical pursuit of the millennium described by Norman Cohn.

Whether or not we can accept this interpretation, Fra Dolcino clearly inspired an important following as a result of his apocalypticism and reputation as a prophet. Another visionary and prophet, who is perhaps more characteristic of medieval developments, is Marguerite Porete. Although addressed to all Christians, her great work, *Mirror of Simple Souls*, reveals a more learned and elitist heresy. In most dramatic fashion, she turned away from the established hierarchy, which she nevertheless accepted as important and necessary, to seek God directly and personally. Her work was an attempt to describe this journey to God and to offer instruction for others to follow. Although it led to her condemnation as a heretic and burning at the stake, the mystical approach was not unheard of throughout the Middle Ages and was advocated by many others who were deemed orthodox, including Hildegard of Bingen, Bernard of Clairvaux and, to a lesser extent, Meister Eckhart. Medieval heretics, therefore, influenced numerous movements and were important examples of the great developments of the Middle Ages.

Indeed, the lives of the heretics provide important insights into the great cultural, political, and especially religious developments of the Middle Ages, but their activities also foreshadowed dramatic events to come. The last of the great medieval heretics, John Wyclif and Jan Hus, offered both a look back to the earlier traditions of medieval heresy and also forward, to Martin Luther's Reformation and to the Protestants of the sixteenth century. Like many of the great leaders of heresy, Wyclif and Hus exercised an important influence on the development of medieval religion and society. Indeed, these great university heretics influenced movements which emerged after their deaths: Wyclif's teachings were of central importance to the Lollard movement in England and Hus's ideas shaped the movement of the Hussites, with their radical wing of the Taborites. In a sense, both of them unleashed wider movements, although neither of them had intended to do more than reform the Church. Their views on the nature of the Church, the role of the clergy, and the definition of the Eucharist were all designed to reform Church doctrine and to return the Church to its apostolic origins. The very nature of these teachings, however, led to their rejection by the Church and prefigured the doctrines of Martin Luther and other Protestant Reformers. The views of Wyclif and Hus on the powers of the papacy in some ways prefigured Luther's more forceful and dramatic criticism of the office of the pope, and Wyclif's theories on the sacrament and on questions of transubstantiation and related matters have frequently been compared to those of Luther. The emergence of a national church in Bohemia after the Hussite wars heralded the emergence of later churches during the Protestant Reformation.

The lives of the heretics, from Bogomil to Hus, therefore are an essential guide to the history of medieval society and the Church, and their devotion to the Christian life stands as testimony to the power of faith in the face of suffering and persecution.

CHRONOLOGY

864	Boris I of Bulgaria converts to Christianity
889	Boris I retires to a monastery and dies
910	*Foundation of the monastery of Cluny*
911	Death of Louis the Child, last of East Frankish Carolingian kings. Charles the Simple grants Normandy to the Viking Rollo
918	Henry the Fowler elected German king
936	Otto I becomes German king
940/50	*Theophylact Lecapenus, patriarch of Constantinople, notes appearance of heresy in Bulgaria*
955	Otto I defeats Magyars at the Battle of Lech
962	Otto I crowned emperor
967	*Gerbert of Aurillac begins study in Spain*
970	*Heresy of Vilgard of Ravenna; Cosmas the priest writes sermon denouncing the Bogomils*
972	Otto II marries the Byzantine princess Theophanu; John I Tzimisces, Byzantine emperor, conquers Bulgaria; Majolus, abbot of Cluny, captured by Muslims
975	Magyar leader Géza converts to Christianity
976	Basil II the Bulgar Slayer becomes Byzantine emperor
983	Otto II defeated by Muslims in southern Italy; he dies December 983
987	Fall of the Carolingian line, Hugh I establishes Capetian dynasty; Bulgaria regains independence
989	Council of Charroux, beginning of Peace of God movement
994	Peace council held at Limoges; plague of firesickness (ergotism) strikes Aquitaine
999	*Otto III appoints Gerbert as Pope Sylvester II*
1000	Stephen crowned king of Hungary
1000	*Heresy of Leutard of Vertus*
1002	Death of Otto III; Conrad II elected king
1003	*Death of Pope Sylvester II*
1009	Fatimid ruler al-Hakim orders attack on the Holy Sepulchre and other shrines
1010	Attacks on Jews in Aquitaine and other parts of Europe
1014	Basil II defeats Bulgarian army, ends Bulgarian resistance to Byzantine authority
1018	*"Manichaean" heretics appear in Aquitaine*
1022	*Heresy of Stephen and Lisois exposed at Orléans*
1025	Death of Basil II
1025	*Heresy in Arras*
1028	*Heresy discovered at Montfort in northern Italy*
1031	Peace Councils of Bourges and Limoges
1033	*Mass pilgrimage to Jerusalem*

1043	*Heretics appear at Chalons-sur-Marne*
1045	*Euthymius of Periblepton notes appearance of Bogomils in Constantinople*
1046	*Synod of Sutri and deposition of popes Gregory VI, Benedict IX, and Sylvester III*
1049	*Council of Rheims; beginning of the Gregorian Reform movement; Hugh becomes abbot of Cluny*
1050	*Berengar of Tours excommunicated for his views on the Eucharist*
1051	*Execution of purported heretics at Goslar, Germany*
1053	Papal forces defeated by Normans at Civitate
1054	*Humbert of Silva Candida and Michael Kerularios declare mutual excommunications initiating the schism between the Roman Catholic and Greek Orthodox Churches*
1056	Death of Emperor Henry III; Henry IV becomes king
1058	*Emergence of the Patarines in Milan*
1059	*Pope Nicholas I publishes papal election decree; Berengar of Tours forced to recant his views*
1064	Death of Edward the Confessor; Harold Godwinson becomes king of England
1064	*Mass pilgrimage to Jerusalem*
1066	Battle of Hastings; William the Conqueror becomes king of England
1071	Byzantine armies defeated at Battle of Manzikert
1075	*Beginning of the Investiture Controversy; Pope Gregory VII compiles the* Dictatus Papae
1077	Henry IV appeals to Pope Gregory VII for forgiveness at Canossa
1077	*Gregory VII officially prohibits lay investiture*
1080	Rudolf of Rheinfelden, antiking, killed in battle; German rebellion ended
1080	*Wibert of Ravenna becomes (anti)Pope Clement III*
1081	Henry IV invades Italy and forces Gregory VII into exile; Alexius I Comnenus becomes Byzantine emperor
1084	*St. Bruno of Cologne founds Carthusian order*
1085	Alfonso IV of Castile captures Toledo
1085	*Death of Gregory VII*
1086	Domesday Book; the Almoravids invade Spain
1087	*Relics of St. Nicholas of Bari stolen from Myra and deposited in Bari*
1088	*Urban II becomes pope*
1091	Norman conquest of Sicily completed
1094	El Cid, Rodrigo Diaz, conquers Valencia
1095	Pope Urban II proclaims First Crusade at the Council of Clermont
1096	Crusaders massacre Jews in the Rhineland; Peasants' Crusade
1098	*Stephen Harding founds monastery at Citeaux and establishes the Cistercian order*
1099	Sack of Jerusalem by crusading armies
1099	*St. Anselm completes* Cur Deus Homo
1100	*Chanson de Roland appears in written form*
1101	*Robert of Arbrissel founds Fontevraux*

1104	Rebellion of future Henry V in the Empire
1111	*Paschal II concedes regalia to secular rulers*
1112	*Bernard of Clairvaux joins the Cistercian order*
1114	*Guibert of Nogent reports heretics at Soissons*
1115	*The heretic Tanchelm preaches in Antwerp*
1116	*First appearance of Henry the Monk*
1120	Sinking of the White Ship
1120	*Peter Abelard compiles the* Sic et Non; *Norbert of Xanten establishes Premonstratensian order*
1121	*Peter Abelard condemned at the Council of Soissons*
1122	Concordat of Worms
1123	*First Lateran Council*
1130	Roger II crowned king of Sicily and Palermo
1135	Civil war in England between Mathilda and Stephen (ends 1154)
1135	*Henry the Monk brought before the Council of Pisa*
1137	Aragon and Catalonia united under Ramón Berenguer IV
1139	*Second Lateran Council; Henry the Monk begins preaching in the Languedoc*
1140	*Publication of Gratian's* Decretum; *Peter Abelard condemned at the Council of Sens; death of the popular heretic Peter of Bruis*
1142	*Abbot Suger completes construction of church at St. Denis outside Paris, the first Gothic church; Abbot Peter the Venerable of Cluny commissions translation of the Qur'an into Latin*
1143	Revolution in Rome and establishment of republic
1143	*Arrival of heretics in Cologne*
1144	Zengi captures Edessa
1145	*Henry the Monk imprisoned, dies a short while later*
1147	Crusaders depart on Second Crusade
1151	*Peter Lombard completes his* Four Books of Sentences
1152	Henry of Anjou (the future King Henry II) and Eleanor of Aquitaine marry
1154	Henry II becomes king of England; Nur al-Din captures Damascus
1154	*Adrian IV becomes pope (the only English pope) and reigns until 1159*
1155	*Execution of Arnold of Brescia*
1157	Incident at Besançon; dispute between Emperor Frederick Barbarossa and Pope Adrian IV
1158	Frederick Barbarossa issues the Roncaglia decrees
1159	*Papal schism between Alexander III and (anti)Pope Victor IV*
1163	*Cathars recorded to be still in Cologne*
1164	King Henry II of England issues the Constitutions of Clarendon
1165	*Cathars appear in Lombers*
1167	Lombard League forms
1169	Saladin rises to power

1170   Thomas Becket murdered
1171   Saladin ends Fatimid Caliphate of Egypt
1173   Valdes takes up the apostolic life after hearing the story of St. Alexis
1174   Frederick Barbarossa defeated at Battle of Legnano
1174   Cathar Council of St. Félix de Caraman held
1177   Valdes attracts disciples
1177   Peace of Venice
1179   Third Lateran Council; Valdes seeks papal approval for his life at the Council
1180   Frederick Barbarossa defeats Duke Henry the Lion of Saxony
1180/1   Valdes declares profession of faith
1184   Pope Lucius III issues Ad abolendam; Valdes and his followers are condemned in the bull
1187   Crusaders' defeat at Battle of Hattin; Saladin captures Jerusalem
1189   Death of Henry II of England; Richard I becomes king; Frederick Barbarossa departs on Third Crusade
1190   Attacks on Jews in England; Richard I and Philip Augustus of France depart on Third Crusade; Frederick Barbarossa drowns in the River Saleph
1191   Saladin defeated at Arsul
1192   Treaty of Jaffa
1193   Death of Saladin; beginning of Baltic Crusades (end 1230)
1194   Emperor Henry IV conquers Sicily; Raymond VI becomes count of Toulouse
1198   Frederick crowned king of Sicily
1199   Death of Richard I the Lionheart
1201   Fourth Crusade begins
1204   Crusaders sack Constantinople, establish Latin Kingdom; Philip Augustus completes conquest of Normandy
1205   Death of Valdes of Lyon
1207   St. Dominic debates Cathars at Montréal; Durand of Huesca abandons the Waldensians and joins the Catholic Church
1208   Peter of Castelnau murdered; Pope Innocent III proclaims Albigensian Crusade
1209   Pope Innocent III approves the order of St. Francis; sack of Béziers during the Albigensian Crusade
1212   Spanish forces defeat the Almohads at the Battle of Las Navas de Tolosa; Children's Crusade
1213   Battle of Muret; death of Peter II of Aragon; King John of England surrenders the kingdom to the papacy and receives it back as a vassal
1214   Battle of Bouvines
1215   King John signs Magna Carta at Runnymede
1215   Fourth Lateran Council; Innocent III approves the order of St. Dominic
1218   Beginning of Fifth Crusade (ends 1221); *death of Simon de Montfort at the siege of Toulouse*
1220   Frederick II Hohenstaufen crowned emperor

1221	*Death of St. Dominic*
1223	*St. Francis issues final rule*
1225	*Cathar Council of Pieusse*
1226	King Louis VIII of France invades Occitania
1226	*Death of St. Francis*
1229	Treaty of Paris
1230	*The Beguines first appear during this decade*
1231	*Establishment of the Inquisition*
1242	Alexander Nevsky defeats Teutonic Knights at the Battle of Lake Chud
1242	*Cathars attack and kill a group of inquisitors at Avignonet*
1244	*Cathar fortress at Montségur falls to Catholic forces and 200 Cathars are burned*
1245	Frederick II Hohenstaufen deposed at the Council of Lyon
1245	*Great Inquisition held in Toulouse; Rainerius Sacconi converts from heresy and enters the Dominican order*
1248	Crusade of Louis IX (ends 1254)
1249	*80 suspected Cathars burned at Agen*
1250	Death of Frederick II
1250	*Sacconi writes* Summa on the Cathars and Poor of Lyon
1251	*First Shepherds' Crusade (Pastoureaux)*
1254	Interregnum in the Empire
1258	King Henry III of England accepts Provisions of Oxford
1260	*Gerard Segarelli begins preaching in Parma*
1261	Byzantines retake Constantinople and expel Western knights
1264	Rebellion of Simon de Monfort in England (ends 1265)
1264	*Feast of Corpus Christi instituted*
1267	Louis IX departs on crusade a second time
1270	Louis IX dies on crusade in Tunis
1273	Reign of Rudolf of Habsburg begins in the Empire
1274	*Death of Thomas Aquinas*
1277	*Condemnation of various philosophical and theological theses by Stephen Tempier, bishop of Paris*
1282	Sicilian Vespers
1283	Edward I completes conquest of Wales; the Teutonic Knights complete conquest of Prussia
1285	*Segarelli and his movement, the Apostolic Brethren, are condemned by Pope Honorius IV*
1289	Fall of Tripoli
1290	Jews expelled from England
1290s	*Marguerite Porete begins preaching*
1291	Fall of Acre, last Crusader outpost in the Holy Land
1294	*Pope Celestine V abdicates the papal throne*

1296	King Edward I of England deposed and imprisoned; John de Balliol, king of Scotland
1296	*Pierre and Guilaume Autier enter Italy to begin study to become Cathar perfects*
1299	*Cathar revival under Autier begins*
1300	*Gerard Segarelli burned as a heretic; Fra Dolcino becomes leader of the Apostolic Brethren and issues first prophecy*
1302	*Boniface VIII issues the bull* Unam Sanctam
1303	*Humiliation at Agnani; Boniface VIII captured by King Philip IV's men, is rescued and dies shortly after*
1304	*Fra Dolcino issues his second prophecy; Apostolic Brethren withdraw to mountains and begin attacks on the Church*
1306	Robert the Bruce declared king of Scotland and leads rebellion; Jews expelled from France
1307	Philip IV of France begins persecution of the Knights Templar
1307	*Bernard Gui commissioned as inquisitor in Toulouse; Fra Dolcino and followers captured and executed*
1309	*Papacy moves to Avignon—beginning of Babylonian Captivity of the papacy*
1310	*Marguerite Porete burned at the stake; Pierre Autier condemned as a heretic and burned at the stake*
1311	*Pope Clement V calls the Council of Vienne (lasts until 1312)*
1314	Great Famine; final destruction of the Knights Templar and burning of the last grand master, Jacques de Molay; Robert the Bruce wins the Battle of Bannockburn
1320	*Second Shepherds' Crusade*
1321	Dante completes the *Divine Comedy*
1323	*Pope John XXII condemns Spiritual Franciscan view of poverty; Bernard Gui completes his handbook for inquisitors*
1327	*A copy of Marguerite Porete's* Mirror of Simple Souls *arrives in England*
1328	End of Capetian dynasty in France; Scotland gains independence
1329	*Trial of last follower of Pierre Autier*
1330s	*Birth of John Wyclif*
1331	*Death of Bernard Gui*
1334	*Jacques Fournier, former bishop and inquisitor, becomes Pope Benedict XII (reigns until 1342)*
1337	Beginning of the Hundred Years' War
1346	Battle of Crécy between England and France
1348	Black Death strikes Europe
1354	Ottomans invade the Balkans
1356	Golden Bull issued; Battle of Poitiers between France and England
1358	Jacquerie Rebellion
1372	*John Wyclif becomes doctor of theology*
1378	*Beginning of Great Schism (lasts until 1417)*

1379	*John Wyclif writes* De eucharistia
1381	English Peasants' Revolt; Richard II, king of England, marries Anne of Bohemia
1382	*Blackfriars' Council in England*
1384	*Death of John Wyclif*
1387	*First official use of the term "Lollard"*
1398	*Jan Hus lectures on the writings of John Wyclif*
1399	Deposition of Richard II, king of England
1401	*Statute passed in England for burning heretics*
1407	*Lollard Bible is banned in England; Jan Hus emerges as reform leader in Bohemia*
1409	*Council of Pisa*
1410	Teutonic Knights defeated at the Battle of Tannenberg
1410	*Copies of John Wyclif's writings burned in Prague*
1411	King Sigismund of Hungary elected king of Germany
1413	*Jan Hus writes* De ecclesia
1414	Rebellion of Sir John Oldcastle
1415	Henry V wins Battle of Agincourt
1415	*Jan Hus condemned as a heretic at the Council of Constance and burned at the stake*
1417	*Martin V elected pope, restores papal authority in Rome and ends Great Schism*
1420	*Crusade against Hussites proclaimed*
1427	*Hussites defeat crusaders; Second Hussite Crusade proclaimed*
1428	*John Wyclif's body exhumed and burned*
1429	Rise of Joan of Arc
1431	Death of Joan of Arc
1431	*Council of Basel; Hussites defeat crusade again*
1434	*Taborites defeated by moderate Hussites and Catholics*
1436	*Hussites sign peace treaty; Bohemian Catholic Church established*
1439	*Pragmatic Sanctions of Bourges; Council of Ferrara-Florence meets*
1440	*Thomas à Kempis completes* Imitation of Christ
1440S	Invention of moveable type by Johannes Gutenberg
1444	Ottomans defeat Christian armies at the Battle of Varna
1453	Fall of Constantinople to Mehmed II the Conqueror; end of the Hundred Years' War
1455	Wars of the Roses begin
1483	Richard III usurps the throne of England
1483	*Torquemada becomes grand inquisitor in Spain*
1485	Battle of Bosworth Field and end of the Wars of the Roses; Henry VII founds Tudor dynasty
1492	Fall of Granada and expulsion of Muslims from Spain; Jews expelled from Spain
1516	Thomas More publishes *Utopia*
1517	*Martin Luther posts 95 Theses*

NOTES

Introduction

1. 'The Letter of Heribert,' translated by Guy Lobrichon in 'The Chiaroscuro of Heresy: Early Eleventh-Century Aquitaine as Seen from Auxerre,' in *The Peace of God: Social Violence and Religious Response in France around the Year 1000*, Thomas Head and Richard Landes, ed. (Ithaca, NY: Cornell University Press, 1992), p. 85.
2. Ibid.
3. Ibid. R. I. Moore, *The Origins of European Dissent* (Oxford: Blackwell, 1985), p. 198, notes that this formula is similar to one which, according to Cosmas the Priest, was used by the Bogomils.
4. 'The Letter of Heribert,' p. 85.
5. Ibid.
6. Ibid. The meaning of the miracle of the wine vat is explored fully in Claire Taylor, 'The Letter of Heribert of Périgord as a Source for Dualist Heresy in the Society of Early Eleventh Century Aquitaine,' *Journal of Medieval History* 26 (2000): 313–49.
7. Malcolm Lambert, *Medieval Heresy: Popular Movements from the Gregorian Reform to the Reformation*, 3rd edn. (Oxford: Blackwell, 2002), p. 36.

Chapter 1

1. John V. A. Fine, Jr, *The Early Medieval Balkans: A Critical Survey from the Sixth to the Late Twelfth Century* (Ann Arbor, MI: University of Michigan Press, 1993), pp. 106–81, provides a useful survey of events in ninth- and tenth-century Bulgaria.
2. Dmitri Obolensky, *The Bogomils: A Study in Balkan Neo-Manichaeism* (Cambridge: Cambridge University Press, 1948), p. 92.
3. Ibid., p. 112.
4. 'To Peter, King of Bulgaria, from Theophylact the Patriarch, Composed by John, *Chartophylax* of the Great Church,' in *Christian Dualist Heresies in the Byzantine World, c.650–c.1405*, trans. and ann. Janet and Bernard Hamilton (Manchester: Manchester University Press, 1998), p. 99.
5. The classic statement of this can be found in Steven Runciman, *The Medieval Manichee: A Study of the Christian Dualist Heresy* (New York: The Viking Press, 1961). A more recent survey of the history of medieval dualism, which does not posit an unconnected chain, is that of Yuri Stoyanov, *The Other God: Dualist Religions from Antiquity to the Cathar Heresy* (New Haven and London: Yale University Press, 2000).
6. For a general overview of the Paulicians, see Runciman, *The Medieval Manichee*, pp. 26–62, and Obolensky, *The Bogomils*, pp. 52–69. A different view of the Paulicians is offered by Nina Garsoian, *The Paulician Heresy: A Study of the Origin and Development of Paulicianism in Armenia and the Eastern Provinces of the Byzantine Empire* (The Hague and Paris: Mouton, 1967).

7. Peter of Sicily, *History of the Paulicians*, in *Christian Dualist Heresies*, p. 67.

8. For a translation of the anathemas, see *Christian Dualist Heresies*, p. 100.

9. The sermon has been translated in part or whole several times, most recently under the title 'The Discourse of the Priest Cosmas against Bogomils (after 972),' in *Christian Dualist Heresies*, pp. 114–34. The standard edition and translation into French is that of H.-C. Puech and A. Vaillant, *Le Traité contre les Bogomiles de Cosmas le Prêtre* (Paris: Institut d'Etudes Slaves, 1945).

10. Fine, *The Early Medieval Balkans*, p. 173.

11. Obolensky, *The Bogomils*, p. 104.

12. For the various translations of the Greek name 'Theophilos' see Stoyanov, *The Other God*, 164. The latest one can be found in *Christian Dualist Heresies*, pp. 114–34; the translation of 'Bogomil' is at p. 116.

13. 'The Discourse of Cosmas,' p. 116.

14. Ibid.

15. Ibid.

16. Ibid., p. 127.

17. Ibid., p. 126.

18. Ibid., p. 127.

19. Ibid., p. 128.

20. Ibid.

21. Stoyanov, *The Other God*, pp. 163–64.

22. 'The Discourse of Cosmas,' p. 130.

23. Ibid., p. 117.

24. Ibid., p. 118.

25. Ibid., p. 123.

26. Ibid., pp. 123–24.

27. Ibid., p. 131.

28. Ibid., p. 123.

29. Ibid.

30. Ibid., p. 125.

31. Ibid., p. 118.

32. Ibid., p. 125.

33. Ibid., p. 121.

34. Ibid., p. 119.

35. Ibid., p. 120.

36. Ibid., p. 129.

37. Ibid., p. 116.

38. Ibid., p. 132.

39. Ibid., pp. 132–33.

40. Ibid., p. 130.

Chapter 2

1. *Heresies of the High Middle Ages*, ed. and trans. by Walter L. Wakefield and Austin P. Evans (New York: Columbia University Press, 1991), p. 74. I have corrected the translation slightly.
2. The classic statement of this view is Runciman, *The Medieval Manichee*. It has recently been revived by Jean-Pierre Poly and Erich Bournazel, *The Feudal Transformation: 900–1200*, trans. Caroline Higgit (New York: Holmes and Meier, 1991), pp. 272–308.
3. This process is best described in Georges Duby, *The Three Orders: Feudal Society Imagined*, trans. Arthur Goldhammer (Chicago: University of Chicago Press, 1980), and in Poly and Bournazel, *The Feudal Transformation*.
4. Uta-Renate Blumenthal, *The Investiture Controversy: Church and Monarchy from the Ninth to the Twelfth Century* (Philadelphia: University of Pennsylvania Press, 1988), provides the best introduction to religious reform in the eleventh century.
5. Rodulfus Glaber, in *Rodvlfi Glabri Historiarum Libri Quinque: Rodulfus Glaber, The Five Books of the Histories*, edited and translated by John France (Oxford: Clarendon Press, 1989), 3: 6.9, pp. 126–27.
6. *Heresies of the High Middle Ages*, p. 75.
7. *Heresies of the High Middle Ages*, pp. 76–81, is the best translation of the account of Paul of St. Pere de Chartres.
8. Ibid., p. 77.
9. Ibid., p. 78.
10. Ibid., pp. 78–79.
11. Ibid., p. 81.
12. Ibid.
13. Heinrich Fichtenau, *Heretics and Scholars in the High Middle Ages, 1000–1200*, trans. Denise A. Kaiser (University Park, PA: Pennsylvania State University Press, 1998), p. 38.
14. *Heresies of the High Middle Ages*, p. 81.
15. Ibid., p. 76.
16. R. H. Bautier, 'L'Hérésie d'Orléans et le mouvement intellectuel au début du XIe siècle,' in *Actes du 95e Congrès National des Sociétés Savantes* (Rheims, 1970): *Section philologique et historique* (Paris, 1975), Vol. 1, pp. 63–88.
17. The growth of literacy after the year 1000 is the subject of numerous studies, the most important of which are those of Michael Clanchy, *From Memory to Written Record: England 1066–1307*, 2nd edn. (Oxford: Blackwell, 1993), and especially Brian Stock, *The Implications of Literacy: Written Language and Models of Interpretation in the Eleventh and Twelfth Centuries* (Princeton: Princeton University Press, 1983). Stock provides a useful analysis of the heresy at Orléans at pp. 106–20.
18. Stock, *The Implications of Literacy*, pp. 88–243.

Chapter 3

1. This matter is fully explored in Michael Frassetto, *Medieval Purity and Piety: Essays on Medieval Clerical Celibacy and Religious Reform* (New York: Garland Publishing, Inc., 1998).
2. *Self and Society in Medieval France: The Memoirs of Abbot Guibert of Nogent*, ed. John F. Benton (Toronto: University of Toronto Press, 1991), Book 3, Chapter 17, pp. 212–14.
3. The identification of Henry as a heresiarch was made by Moore, *Origins*, p. 83.
4. Marbod of Rennes describing Robert of Arbrissel, cited in Moore, *Origins*, pp. 84–85.
5. *Heresies of the High Middle Ages*, p. 109.
6. Ibid., pp. 108 and 109.
7. Ibid., p. 109.
8. Ibid.
9. Ibid., p. 110.
10. Ibid., pp. 110–11.
11. Ibid., pp. 111–12.
12. Ibid., p. 113.
13. Ibid., p. 114.
14. Ibid., p. 115.
15. Ibid., p. 116.
16. Cited in Moore, *Origins of European Dissent*, pp. 95–96.
17. *Heresies of the High Middle Ages*, p. 116.
18. Ibid.
19. Ibid., p. 117.
20. Ibid., p. 116.
21. Ibid.
22. Ibid., p. 117.
23. Ibid.
24. Ibid.
25. Cited in Moore, *Origins*, p. 95.
26. *Heresies of the High Middle Ages*, p. 122.
27. Ibid., p. 125.
28. Ibid.
29. Ibid.

Chapter 4

1. M. D. Chenu, *Nature, Man, and Society in the Twelfth Century: Essays on New Theological Perspectives in the Latin West*, ed. and trans. Jerome Taylor and Lester K. Little (Chicago: University of Chicago Press, 1968), p. 243.

2. Lester K. Little, *Religious Poverty and the Profit Economy in Medieval Europe* (Ithaca, NY: Cornell University Press, 1978), p. 120.

3. Ibid., p. 121.

4. Selections from the Laon Anonymous concerning the conversion of Valdes are translated in *Heresies of the High Middle Ages*, pp. 200–202.

5. Ibid., p. 201.

6. Ibid.

7. Ibid.

8. Quoted in Lutz Kaelber, *Schools of Asceticism: Ideology and Organization in Medieval Religious Communities* (University Park, PA: Pennsylvania State University Press, 1998), p. 138.

9. *Heresies of the High Middle Ages*, p. 210.

10. Ibid.

11. Ibid.

12. Ibid., p. 203.

13. Ibid., p. 204.

14. Ibid.

15. Ibid., p. 203.

16. Ibid., p. 206.

17. Ibid.

18. Ibid., p. 207.

19. Ibid.

20. Ibid.

21. Ibid.

22. The decree is translated in *Heresy and Authority in Medieval Europe: Documents in Translation*, ed. Edward Peters (Philadelphia: University of Pennsylvania Press, 1980), pp. 170–73.

23. Ibid., p. 172.

24. Ibid., p. 171.

25. Ibid.

26. *Heresies of the High Middle Ages*, p. 204.

27. Quoted in Euan Cameron, *Waldenses: Rejections of Holy Church in Medieval Europe* (Oxford: Blackwell, 2001), p. 42.

Chapter 5

1. A translation of this account appears as 'An Appeal from Eberwin of Steinfeld against Heretics at Cologne,' in Wakefield and Evans, *Heresies of the High Middle Ages*, pp. 127–32.

2. A translation of this account from the *Acta concilii Lumbariensis* appears under the title 'A Debate between Catholics and Heretics' in *Heresies of the High Middle Ages*, pp. 190–94.

3. Quoted in Jonathan Sumption, *The Albigensian Crusade* (London and Boston: Faber, 1978), p. 74.

4. Quoted in Dana C. Munro, *Urban and the Crusaders* (Philadelphia: University of Pennsylvania Press, 1985), p. 18.

5. Quoted in Joseph R. Strayer, *The Albigensian Crusades* (Ann Arbor, MI: University of Michigan Press, 1992), p. 90.

6. Quoted in Strayer, *The Albigensian Crusades*, pp. 90–91.

7. Particularly useful in the preparation of this chapter has been Lawrence Marvin's forthcoming study of the Albigensian Crusade and career of Simon de Montfort. I would like to thank him for sharing his work with me.

Chapter 6

1. 'The Summa of Rainerius Sacconi,' in Wakefield and Evans, *Heresies of the High Middle Ages*, p. 336.

2. Malcolm Lambert, *The Cathars* (Oxford: Blackwell, 1998), p. 151.

3. Quoted in Malcom Barber, *The Cathars: Dualist Heretics in Languedoc in the High Middle Ages* (London: Longman, 2000), p. 154.

4. The full story of the fall of Montségur is most dramatically told in Zoé Oldenbourg, *The Massacre at Montségur: A History of the Albigensian Crusade*, trans. P. Green (New York: Pantheon Books, 1962).

5. Barber, *The Cathars*, p. 182.

6. Quoted in Jean Duvernoy, *Le Catharisme*, Vol. 2: *L'Histoire des Cathares* (Toulouse: Edouard Privat, 1979), p. 322.

7. Lambert, *The Cathars*, p. 236.

8. René Weiss, *The Yellow Cross: The Story of the Last Cathars' Rebellion Against the Inquisition, 1290–1329* (New York: Vintage Books, 2002), p. 155.

9. Ibid., p. 108.

10. Ibid., pp. 108–109.

11. Ibid., pp. 109–10.

12. Lambert, *The Cathars*, pp. 250–51.

13. Barber, *The Cathars*, pp. 90–91.

14. Duvernoy, *Le Catharisme*, Vol. 2, p. 209.

15. Lambert, *The Cathars*, p. 246.

16. Quoted in Barber, *The Cathars*, p. 187.

17. Quoted in Barber, *The Cathars*, pp. 187–88.

18. Lambert, *The Cathars*, p. 239.

Chapter 7

1. Dante, *The Inferno* Canto 28, pp. 53–57, trans. Robert Pinsky (New York: The Noonday Press, 1994), p. 239.

2. Marjorie Reeves, *The Influence of Prophecy in the Later Middle Ages: A Study of Joachimism* (Notre Dame, IN: University of Notre Dame Press, 1993), p. 242.

3. Bernard Gui, *Manuel de l'Inquisiteur*, ed. and trans. by Guy Mollat (Paris: Champion, 1926), Vol. 1, 3:2, pp. 84–86. A helpful introduction to the activities of Bernard Gui is James Given's study 'A Medieval Inquisitor at Work: Bernard Gui, 3 March 1308 to 19 June 1323,' in *Portraits of Medieval and Renaissance Living: Essays in Memory of David Herlihy*, ed. Samuel K. Cohn, Jr and Steven A. Epstein (Ann Arbor, MI: The University of Michigan Press, 1996), pp. 207–32.

4. Lambert, *Medieval Heresy*, p. 221.

5. Joachim's ideas and influence are best studied in Reeves, *The Influence of Prophecy*.

6. Jeffrey Burton Russell, *Dissent and Order in the Middle Ages: The Search for Legitimate Authority* (New York: Twayne Publishers, 1992), p. 76.

7. Gui, *Manuel de l'Inquisiteur*, p. 78.

8. Ibid., p. 80.

9. Gordon Leff, *Heresy in the Later Middle Ages: The Relation of Heterodoxy to Dissent, c.1250–1450* (New York: Barnes and Noble, Inc., 1967), Vol. 1, p. 193.

10. Gui, *Manuel de l'Inquisiteur*, pp. 80–82.

11. Ibid., pp. 82–84.

12. Ibid., pp. 88–90.

13. Ibid., p. 90.

14. Russell, *Dissent and Order in the Middle Ages*, p. 76.

15. Reeves, *The Influence of Prophecy*, p. 246.

16. Gui, *Manuel de l'Inquisiteur*, p. 98.

17. Ibid., pp. 94–96.

18. Ibid., pp. 96.

19. Reeves, *The Influence of Prophecy*, p. 246.

20. Gui, *Manuel de l'Inquisiteur*, pp. 96–98.

21. *Popular Protest in Late Medieval Europe*, ed. and trans. Samuel K. Cohn, Jr (Manchester: Manchester University Press, 2004), p. 57.

22. Cohn, *Popular Protest*, p. 55.

23. Ibid., p. 56.

24. Ibid.

25. Gui, *Manuel de l'Inquisiteur*, p. 100.

26. Leff, *Heresy in the Later Middle Ages*, Vol. 1, p. 194.

27. Gui, *Manuel de l'Inquisiteur*, p. 106.

28. Ibid.

29. Gui's manual, pp. 108–18, contains a Latin edition and French translation of the letter.

30. Reeves, *The Influence of Prophecy*, p. 247.

31. Leff, *Heresy in the Later Middle Ages*, Vol. 1, p. 195.

Chapter 8

1. H. C. Lea, *A History of the Inquisition in the Middle Ages*, 3 vols. (New York: Harper, 1887), Vol. 2, p. 123.
2. A brief but useful summary of her life is Ellen L. Babinsky's 'Marguerite Porete,' in *Medieval France: An Encyclopedia*, ed. William W. Kibler and Grover A. Zinn (New York: Garland Publishing, Inc., 1995), pp. 588–89.
3. Peter Dronke, *Women Writers of the Middle Ages* (Cambridge: Cambridge University Press, 1984), p. 217.
4. Robert Lerner, *The Heresy of the Free Spirit in the Later Middle Ages* (Berkeley and Los Angeles: University of California Press, 1972; reprinted Notre Dame, IN: University of Notre Dame Press, 1991), p. 233.
5. Lerner, *The Heresy of the Free Spirit*, p. 203.
6. Quoted in Lerner, *The Heresy of the Free Spirit*, p. 1.
7. Lea, *History of the Inquisition*, Vol. 2, pp. 122–23; and Lerner, *The Heresy of the Free Spirit*, p. 5.
8. The best discussion of the early history of the Beguines is in Brenda M. Bolton, 'Mulieres Sanctae,' in *Women in Medieval Society*, ed. Susan Mosher Stuard (Philadelphia: University of Pennsylvania Press, 1976), pp. 141–58.
9. The best introductions to the Beguines are Herbert Grundmann, *Religious Movements in the High Middle Ages*, trans. Steven Rowan (Notre Dame, IN: University of Notre Dame Press, 1995), pp. 139–52, and Ernest W. McDonnell, *The Beguines and Beghards in Medieval Culture, with Special Emphasis on the Belgian Scene* (New Brunswick, NJ: Rutgers University Press, 1954).
10. Quoted in *Marguerite Porete: The Mirror of Simple Souls*, trans. and intro. Ellen L. Babinsky (New York: Paulist Press, 1993), p. 11.
11. Babinksy, 'Introduction,' *Mirror of Simple Souls*, p. 11.
12. Lerner, *The Heresy of the Free Spirit*.
13. Leff, *Heresy in the Later Middle Ages*, Vol. 1, p. 371.
14. *Mirror of Simple Souls*, ch. 140, p. 221.
15. Quoted in Babinksy, 'Introduction,' *Mirror of Simple Souls*, pp. 23–24.
16. Babinsky, 'Introduction,' *Mirror of Simple Souls*, p. 26, and Lerner, *The Heresy of the Free Spirit*, pp. 72–75, discuss the question of the copies and translations of Marguerite's *Mirror*.
17. Norman Cohn, *The Pursuit of the Millennium*, 3rd edn. (New York: Oxford University Press, 1970), p. 164.
18. Lerner, *The Heresy of the Free Spirit*, p. 75, and Babinsky, 'Marguerite Porete,' p. 588.
19. The figures are from Lerner, *The Heresy of the Free Spirit*, p. 201.
20. Dronke, *Women Writers*, p. 218.
21. Ibid.
22. Lerner, *The Heresy of the Free Spirit*, p. 202.
23. *Mirror of Simple Souls*, p. 79.

24. Ibid., ch. 1, p. 80.

25. Ibid., ch. 61, p. 138.

26. Ibid.

27. Convenient summaries of the stages can be found in Cohn, *The Pursuit of the Millennium*, p. 185, and in Lerner, *The Heresy of the Free Spirit*, pp. 202–203.

28. *Mirror of Simple Souls*, ch. 61, p. 138.

29. Ibid., ch. 118, p. 189.

30. Ibid.

31. Ibid., ch. 118, p. 190.

32. Ibid., ch. 118, pp. 190–91.

33. Ibid., ch. 118, p. 193.

34. Ibid., ch. 5, p. 83.

35. Ibid., ch. 85, p. 160.

36. Ibid., ch. 9, p. 87.

37. Ibid., ch. 52, pp. 129–30.

38. Lerner, *The Heresy of the Free Spirit*, p. 203.

39. *Mirror of Simple Souls*, ch. 43, p. 122.

40. Ibid., ch. 122, p. 200.

41. Lambert, *Medieval Heresy*, p. 204.

42. Leff, *Heresy in the Later Middle Ages*, p. 370.

43. Lerner, *The Heresy of the Free Spirit*, pp. 68–71, raises this possibility, but it has not been uniformly accepted, and Babinsky rejects the connection in her introduction to Porete's *Mirror*, pp. 24–26.

44. For general introduction to Philip, and for a discussion of the persecutions of Boniface and the Templars, see Joseph Strayer, *The Reign of Philip the Fair* (Princeton: Princeton University Press, 1980). The best studies of the Templars are those of Malcolm Barber: *The New Knighthood: A History of the Order of the Temple* (Cambridge: Cambridge University Press, 1995) and *The Trial of the Templars* (Cambridge: Cambridge University Press, 1993). On Philip's struggles against Boniface and the Templars, see James Given, 'Chasing Phantoms: Philip IV and the Fantastic,' in *Heresy and the Persecuting Society in the Middle Ages: Essays on the Work of R. I. Moore*, ed. Michael Frassetto (Leiden: Brill, 2006), pp. 271–89.

45. Lerner, *The Heresy of the Free Spirit*, p. 68.

46. Babinsky, 'Introduction,' *Mirror of Simple Souls*, p. 20.

47. Given, 'Chasing Phantoms,' p. 289.

Chapter 9

1. Quoted in Margaret Deanesly, *A History of the Medieval Church, 590–1500* (New York: Routledge, 1972), p. 222.

2. *Selections from English Wycliffite Writings*, ed. Anne Hudson (Toronto: University of Toronto Press, 1997), p. 1.

3. Russell, *Dissent and Order in the Middle Ages*, pp. 82–83.

4. A brief but useful survey of Wyclif's life is Anne Hudson, 'Wyclif, John,' in *Dictionary of the Middle Ages*, ed. Joseph Strayer (New York: Scribner, 1982–89), Vol. 12, pp. 706–11. H. B. Workman, *John Wyclif*, 2 vols. (Oxford: Clarendon Press, 1926), and Anthony Kenny, *Wyclif* (Oxford: Oxford University Press, 1985), are good full-length biographies.

5. Lambert, *Medieval Heresy*, p. 254.

6. K. B. McFarlane, *John Wycliffe and the Beginnings of English Nonconformity* (New York: The Macmillan Company, 1953), p. 70.

7. McFarlane, *John Wycliffe*, pp. 24–25.

8. Deanesly, *History of the Medieval Church*, 222.

9. *Medieval Philosophy*, ed. John Marenbon (New York: Routledge, 1998), p. 433.

10. Cited in Lambert, *Medieval Heresy*, p. 252.

11. *Medieval Philosophy*, p. 433.

12. Hudson, *English Wycliffite Writings*, p. 2.

13. Lambert, *Medieval Heresy*, p. 254.

14. Leff, *Heresy in the Late Middle Ages*, p. 496.

15. McFarlane, *John Wycliffe*, p. 60.

16. Lambert, *Medieval Heresy*, p. 253.

17. McFarlane, *John Wycliffe*, p. 63.

18. Ibid., p. 76; Kenny, *Wyclif*, p. 53.

19. Quoted in McFarlane, *John Wycliffe*, p. 78.

20. Ibid.

21. 'Pope Gregory XI to the Masters of Oxford: On Wyclif,' in Peters, *Heresy and Authority in Medieval Europe*, p. 271.

22. 'Pope Gregory to the Masters of Oxford,' p. 271.

23. McFarlane, *John Wycliffe*, p. 81.

24. Kenny, *Wyclif*, p. 59.

25. McFarlane, *John Wycliffe*, pp. 97–98.

26. Kenny, *Wyclif*, p. 91.

27. Quoted in Kenny, *Wyclif*, p. 91.

28. Quoted in Kenny, *Wyclif*, p. 92.

29. Michael Wilks, '*Reformatio Regni*: Wyclif and Hus as Leaders of Religious Protest Movements,' in *Schism, Heresy and Religious Protest* Studies in Church History, Vol. 9, ed. Derek Baker (Cambridge: Cambridge University Press, 1972), pp. 126–27.

30. McFarlane, *John Wycliffe*, p. 117.

31. Kenny, *Wyclif*, p. 94.

32. Quoted in McFarlane, *John Wycliffe*, p. 120.

33. Lambert, *Medieval Heresy*, p. 259, and Stephen E. Lahey, *Philosophy and Politics in the Thought of John Wyclif* (Cambridge: Cambridge University Press, 2003), p. 4.

34. Kenny, *Wyclif*, pp. 52–53.

35. Leff, *Heresy in the Later Middle Ages*, p. 546.

36. Ibid., p. 516.

37. Quoted in Kenny, *Wyclif*, p. 71.

38. Leff, *Heresy in the Later Middle Ages*, p. 518.

39. Kenny, *Wyclif*, pp. 70–71.

40. Quoted in Kenny, *Wyclif*, p. 76.

41. Quoted in McFarlane, *John Wycliffe*, p. 91.

42. Hudson, *English Wycliffite Writings*, p. 162. Selections of the Wyclifite Bible can be found in Hudson's volume, pp. 40–72, and the complete text can be found in J. Forshall and F. Madden, *The Holy Bible, containing the Old and New Testaments, with the Apocryphal books, in the earliest English versions made from the Latin Vulgate by John Wycliffe and his followers* (Oxford: Oxford University Press, 1850).

43. Quoted in Kenny, *Wyclif*, p. 62.

44. Leff, *Heresy in the Later Middle Ages*, p. 513.

45. McFarlane, *John Wycliffe*, pp. 94–95.

46. Leff, *Heresy in the Later Middle Ages*, p. 556.

47. Ibid., p. 559. For full accounts of the Lollards, see Lambert, *Medieval Heresy*, pp. 257–305; Leff, *Heresy in the Later Middle Ages*, pp. 559–605; and especially Anne Hudson, *The Premature Reformation: Wycliffite Texts and Lollard History* (Oxford: Oxford University Press, 1988).

48. Lambert, *Medieval Heresy*, p. 270.

49. Ibid., p. 273.

50. McFarlane, *John Wycliffe*, pp. 127–36.

51. The Council's condemnations have been translated in Peters's *Heresy and Authority in Medieval Europe*, pp. 274–77.

52. McFarlane, *John Wycliffe*, p. 120.

Chapter 10

1. Matthew Spinka, *John Hus: A Biography* (Princeton: Princeton University Press, 1968), p. 3.

2. Leff, *Heresy in the Later Middle Ages*, p. 608.

3. Ibid.

4. Lambert, *Medieval Heresy*, p. 313.

5. Spinka, *John Hus*, pp. 6–7.

6. Ibid., p. 19.

7. Kenny, *Wyclif*, p. 102.

8. *John Hus at the Council of Constance*, trans. Matthew Spinka (New York: Columbia University Press, 1965), pp. 26–28.

9. Russell, *Dissent and Order in the Middle Ages*, p. 89.

10. Spinka, *John Hus*, p. 22.

11. Ibid., pp. 23–24.

12. Ibid., pp. 24–25.
13. Quoted in Spinka's *John Hus*, p. 28.
14. Spinka, *John Hus*, p. 40.
15. Ibid., pp. 45–46.
16. Lambert, *Medieval Heresy*, p. 319.
17. Leff, *Heresy in the Later Middle Ages*, Vol. 2, p. 620.
18. *John Hus at the Council of Constance*, pp. 31–32.
19. 'John Hus: On Simony,' in *Heresy and Authority in Medieval Europe*, pp. 282 and 283.
20. Quoted in Lambert, *Medieval Heresy*, p. 322.
21. Quoted in Spinka, *John Hus*, p. 132.
22. Leff, *Heresy in the Later Middle Ages*, Vol. 2, p. 635.
23. Spinka, *John Hus*, p. 137.
24. Wilks, 'Wyclif and Hus as Leaders of Religious Protest Movements,' pp. 128–29.
25. Ibid., p. 129.
26. Quoted in *John Hus at the Council of Constance*, p. 45.
27. Quoted in Spinka, *John Hus*, p. 165.
28. Cohn, *The Pursuit of the Millennium*, p. 207.
29. Leff, *Heresy in the Later Middle Ages*, Vol. 2, pp. 658–59.
30. 'John Hus: On Simony,' p. 284.
31. Ibid., pp. 282–83.
32. For a full discussion of the Council, see C. M. D. Crowder, *Unity, Heresy and Reform, 1378–1460* (New York: St Martin's Press, 1977), *The Council of Constance*, ed. L. S. Loomis (New York: Columbia University Press, 1961).
33. *John Hus at the Council of Constance*, p. 73.
34. The list can be found in 'The Council of Constance, 1415: The Condemnation of Hus's Errors,' *Heresy and Authority*, pp. 286–89.
35. 'Peter of Mladoňovice: An Account of the Trial and Condemnation of Master John Hus in Constance,' in *John Hus at the Council of Constance*, p. 233.
36. For a full discussion of the revolt, see Howard Kaminsky, *A History of the Hussite Revolution* (Berkeley and Los Angeles: University of California Press, 1967). For the apocalyptic character of the revolt, see Cohn, *The Pursuit of the Millennium*, pp. 206–34.

BIBLIOGRAPHY

Arnold, John H. *Inquisition and Power: Catharism and the Confessing Subject in Medieval Languedoc.* Philadelphia: University of Pennsylvania Press, 2001.

Audisio, Gabriel. *The Waldensian Dissent: Persecution and Survival, c. 1180–c. 1570.* Claire Davison, trans. Cambridge: Cambridge University Press, 1999.

Babinsky, Ellen L. 'Marguerite Porete.' In *Medieval France: An Encyclopedia*, William W. Kibler and Grover A. Zinn, eds. New York: Garland Publishing, Inc., 1995, 588–89.

Babinsky, Ellen L., trans. and intro. *Marguerite Porete: The Mirror of Simple Souls.* New York: Paulist Press, 1993.

Baker, Derek, ed. *Schism, Heresy and Religious Protest.* Studies in Church History, Vol. 9. Cambridge: Cambridge University Press, 1972.

Barber, Malcolm. *The Trial of the Templars.* Cambridge: Cambridge University Press, 1993.

Barber, Malcolm. *The New Knighthood: A History of the Order of the Temple.* Cambridge: Cambridge University Press, 1995.

Barber, Malcolm. *The Cathars: Dualist Heretics in Languedoc in the High Middle Ages.* London: Longman, 2000.

Bautier, R. H. 'L'Hérésie d'Orléans et le mouvement intellectuel au début du XIe siècle.' In *Actes du 95e Congrès National des Sociétés Savantes* (Rheims, 1970) – *Section philologique et historique.* Paris, 1975, Vol. 1, 63–88.

Benton, F., ed. *Self and Society in Medieval France: The Memoirs of Abbot Guibert of Nogent.* Toronto: University of Toronto Press, 1991.

Biller, Peter. *The Waldenses, 1170–1530.* Ashgate: Variorum, 2001.

Biller, Peter and Anne Hudson, eds. *Heresy and Literacy, 1000–1530.* Cambridge: Cambridge University Press, 1994.

Blumenthal, Uta-Renate. *The Investiture Controversy: Church and Monarchy from the Ninth to the Twelfth Century.* Philadelphia: University of Pennsylvania Press, 1988.

Bolton, Brenda M. 'Mulieres Sanctae.' In *Women in Medieval Society*, Susan Mosher Stuard, ed. Philadelphia: University of Pennsylvania Press, 1976, 141–58.

Bredero, Adriaan. *Christendom and Christianity in the Middle Ages.* Grand Rapids, MI: William B. Eerdmans Publishing Company, 1994.

Cameron, Euan. *Waldenses: Rejections of Holy Church in Medieval Europe.* Oxford: Blackwell, 2000.

Chenu, M. D. *Nature, Man, and Society in the Twelfth Century: Essays on New Theological Perspectives in the Latin West*, Jerome Taylor and Lester K. Little, eds. and trans. Chicago: University of Chicago Press, 1968.

Clanchy, Michael. *From Memory to Written Record: England 1066–1307*, 2nd edn. Oxford: Blackwell, 1993.

Cohn, Norman. *The Pursuit of the Millennium: Revolutionary Millenarians and Mystical Anarchists of the Middle Ages*, 3rd edn., revised and expanded. New York: Oxford University Press, 1970.

Cohn, Norman. *Europe's Inner Demons: The Demonization of Christians in Medieval Christendom*, revised edn. Chicago: University of Chicago Press, 1993.

Cohn, Samuel K., Jr., ed. and trans. *Popular Protest in Late Medieval Europe*. Manchester: Manchester University Press, 2004.

Crowder, C. M. D. *Unity, Heresy and Reform, 1378–1460*. New York: St Martin's Press, 1977.

Deanesly, Margaret. *A History of the Medieval Church, 590–1500*. New York: Routledge, 1972.

Dronke, Peter. *Women Writers of the Middle Ages*. Cambridge: Cambridge University Press, 1984.

Duby, Georges. *The Three Orders: Feudal Society Imagined*. Arthur Goldhammer, trans. Chicago: University of Chicago Press, 1980.

Duvernoy, Jean. *Le Catharisme. I: La Religion des Cathares; II: L'Histoire des Cathares*. Toulouse: Edouard Privat, 1976 and 1979.

Fichtenau, Heinrich. *Heretics and Scholars in the High Middle Ages, 1000–1200*. Denise A. Kaiser, trans. University Park, PA: Pennsylvania State University Press, 1998.

Fine, John V. A., Jr. *The Early Medieval Balkans: A Critical Survey from the Sixth to the Late Twelfth Century*. Ann Arbor, MI: University of Michigan Press, 1993.

Forshall, J. and F. Madden. *The Holy Bible, containing the Old and New Testaments, with the Apocryphal books, in the earliest English versions made from the Latin Vulgate by John Wycliffe and his followers*. Oxford: Oxford University Press, 1850.

France, John, ed. and trans. *Rodvlfi Glabri Historiarum Libri Quinque: Rodulfus Glaber, The Five Books of the Histories*. Oxford: Clarendon Press, 1989.

Frassetto, Michael. *Medieval Purity and Piety: Essays on Medieval Clerical Celibacy and Religious Reform*. New York: Garland Publishing, Inc., 1998.

Frassetto, Michael, ed., *Heresy and the Persecuting Society: Essays on the Work of R. I. Moore*. Leiden: Brill, 2006.

Garsoian, Nina. *The Paulician Heresy: A Study of the Origin and Development of Paulicianism in Armenia and the Eastern Provinces of the Byzantine Empire*. The Hague and Paris: Mouton, 1967.

Given, James. 'A Medieval Inquisitor at Work: Bernard Gui, 3 March 1308 to 19 June 1323.' In *Portraits of Medieval and Renaissance Living: Essays in Memory of David Herlihy*, Samuel K. Cohn, Jr. and Steven A. Epstein, eds. Ann Arbor, MI: University of Michigan Press, 1996.

Given, James. *Inquisition and Medieval Society: Power, Discipline, and Resistance in Languedoc*. Ithaca, NY: Cornell University Press, 1997.

Given, James. 'Chasing Phantoms: Philip IV and the Fantastic.' In *Heresy and the Persecuting Society in the Middle Ages: Essays on the Work of R. I. Moore*, Michael Frassetto, ed. Leiden: Brill, 2006, 271–89.

Grundmann, Herbert. *Religious Movements in the Middle Ages*. Steven Rowan, trans. Notre Dame, IN: University of Notre Dame Press, 1995.

Gui, Bernard. *Manuel de l'Inquisiteur*. Guy Mollat, ed. and trans. Paris: Champion, 1926.

Hamilton, Bernard. *The Medieval Inquisition*. New York: Holmes and Meier, 1981.

Hamilton, Janet and Bernard Hamilton, eds. and trans. *Christian Dualist Heresies in the Byzantine World, c. 650–c. 1405*. Manchester: Manchester University Press, 1998.

Heymann, Frederick G. 'The Crusades against the Hussites.' In *A History of the Crusades* (Editor in Chief, Kenneth Meyer Setton), Vol. 3: *The Fourteenth and Fifteenth Centuries*, Harry W. Hazard, ed. Madison: University of Wisconsin Press, 1969–89, pp. 586–646.

Hudson, Anne. *The Premature Reformation: Wycliffite Texts and Lollard History*. Oxford: Oxford University Press, 1988.

Hudson, Anne. 'Wyclif, John.' In *Dictionary of the Middle Ages*. Joseph Strayer, ed. New York: Scribner, 1982–89, Vol. 12, 706–11.

Hudson, Anne, ed. *Selections from English Wycliffite Writings*. Toronto: University of Toronto Press, 1997.

Kaelber, Lutz. *Schools of Asceticism: Ideology and Organization in Medieval Religious Communities*. University Park, PA: Pennsylvania State University Press, 1998.

Kaminsky, Howard. *A History of the Hussite Revolution*. Berkeley and Los Angeles: University of California Press, 1967.

Kenny, Anthony. *Wyclif*. Oxford: Oxford University Press, 1985.

Lahey, Stephen E. *Philosophy and Politics in the Thought of John Wyclif*. Cambridge: Cambridge University Press, 2003.

Lambert, Malcolm. *The Cathars*. Oxford: Blackwell, 1998.

Lambert, Malcolm. *Medieval Heresy: Popular Movements from the Gregorian Reform to the Reformation*, 3rd edn. Oxford: Blackwell, 2002.

Lansing, Carol. *Power and Purity: Cathar Heresy in Medieval Italy*. Oxford: Oxford University Press, 1998.

Lea, Henry Charles. *A History of the Inquisition in the Middle Ages*, 3 vols. New York: Harper, 1887.

Leff, Gordon. *Heresy in the Later Middle Ages: The Relation of Heterodoxy to Dissent c. 1250–c. 1450*, 2 vols. New York: Barnes and Noble, Inc., 1967.

Le Goff, Jacques and Herbert Grundmann, eds. *Hérésies et sociétés dans l'Europe pré-industrielle, 11–18 siècles*. Paris: Mouton, 1968.

Lerner, Robert. *The Heresy of the Free Spirit in the Later Middle Ages*. Berkeley and Los Angeles: University of California Press, 1972; reprinted Notre Dame, IN: University of Notre Dame Press, 1991.

Le Roy Ladurie, Emmanuel. *Montaillou: The Promised Land of Error*. Barbara Bray, trans. New York: Vintage Books, 1979.

Little, Lester K. *Religious Poverty and the Profit Economy in Medieval Europe*. Ithaca, NY: Cornell University Press, 1978.

Lobrichon, Guy, trans. 'The Letter of Heribert' (in 'The Chiaroscuro of Heresy: Early Eleventh-Century Aquitaine as Seen from Auxerre'). In *The Peace of God: Social Violence and Religious Response in France around the Year 1000*, Thomas Head and Richard Landes, eds. Ithaca, NY: Cornell University Press, 1992, 85.

Loomis, L. S., ed. *The Council of Constance*. New York: Columbia University Press, 1961.

Loos, Milan. *Dualist Heresy in the Middle Ages*. Prague: Academia, 1974.

McDonnell, Ernest W. *The Beguines and Beghards in Medieval Culture with Special Emphasis on the Belgian Scene*. New Brunswick, NJ: Rutgers University Press, 1954.

McFarlane, K. B. *John Wycliffe and the Beginnings of English Nonconformity*. New York: The Macmillan Company, 1953.

Marenbon, John, ed. *Medieval Philosophy*. New York: Routledge, 1998.

Marvin, Lawrence. *The Occitan War: 1209–21* (Cambridge: Cambridge University Press, forthcoming).

Moore, R. I. *The Origins of European Dissent*. Harmondsworth: Penguin, 1977; reissued Oxford: Blackwell, 1985.

Moore, R. I. *The Formation of a Persecuting Society: Power and Deviance in Western Europe, 950-1250*. Oxford: Blackwell, 1987.

Moore, R. I., ed. *The Birth of Popular Heresy*. New York: St Martin's Press, 1976.

Mundy, John. *Men and Women at Toulouse in the Age of the Cathars*. Toronto: Pontifical Institute of Medieval Studies, 1990.

Munro, Dana C., ed. *Urban and the Crusaders*. Philadelphia: University of Pennsylvania Press (Translations and Reprints from the Original Sources of European History, Vol. 1:2), 1985.

Obolensky, Dmitri. *The Bogomils: A Study in Balkan Neo-Manichaeism*. Cambridge: Cambridge University Press, 1948.

Oldenbourg, Zoé. *The Massacre at Montségur: A History of the Albigensian Crusade*. P. Green, trans. New York: Pantheon Books, 1962.

Pegg, Mark. *The Corruption of Angels: The Great Inquisition of 1245–1246*. Princeton: Princeton University Press, 2001.

Peters, Edward. *Inquisition*. New York: Free Press, 1988.

Peters, Edward, ed. *Heresy and Authority in Medieval Europe: Documents in Translation*. Philadelphia: University of Pennsylvania Press, 1980.

Poly, Jean-Pierre and Erich Bournazel. *The Feudal Transformation: 900–1200*. Caroline Higgit, trans. New York: Holmes and Meier, 1991.

Reeves, Marjorie. *The Influence of Prophecy in the Later Middle Ages: A Study of Joachimism*. Notre Dame, IN: University of Notre Dame Press, 1993.

Roach, Andrew P. *The Devil's World: Heresy and Society, 1100–1300*. London: Longman, 2005.

Runciman, Steven. *The Medieval Manichee: A Study of the Christian Dualist Heresy*. New York: The Viking Press, 1961.

Russell, Jeffrey Burton. *Dissent and Reform in the Early Middle Ages*. Berkeley and Los Angeles: University of California Press, 1965.

Russell, Jeffrey Burton. *Dissent and Order in the Middle Ages: The Search for Legitimate Authority*. New York: Twayne Publishers, 1992.

Southern, R. W. *The Making of the Middle Ages*. New Haven: Yale University Press, 1953.

Spinka, Matthew. *John Hus: A Biography*. Princeton: Princeton University Press, 1968.

Spinka, Matthew, trans. *John Hus at the Council of Constance*. New York: Columbia University Press, 1965.

Stock, Brian. *The Implications of Literacy: Written Language and Models of Interpretation in the Eleventh and Twelfth Centuries*. Princeton: Princeton University Press, 1983.

Stoyanov, Yuri. *The Other God: Dualist Religions from Antiquity to the Cathar Heresy*. New Haven and London: Yale University Press, 2000.

Strayer, Joseph. *The Reign of Philip the Fair*. Princeton: Princeton University Press, 1980.

Strayer, Joseph. *The Albigensian Crusades*. Ann Arbor, MI: University of Michigan Press, 1992.

Sumption, Jonathan. *The Albigensian Crusade*. London and Boston: Faber, 1978.

Taylor, Claire. 'The Letter of Heribert of Périgord as a Source for Dualist Heresy in the Society of Early Eleventh-Century Aquitaine.' *Journal of Medieval History* 26 (2000): 313–49.

Taylor, Claire. *Heresy in Medieval France: Dualism in Aquitaine and the Agenais, 1000–1249*. Woodbridge: The Boydell Press, 2005.

Wakefield, Walter L. *Heresy, Crusade and Inquisition in Southern France, 1100–1250*. London: George Allen and Unwin, Ltd., 1974.

Wakefield, Walter L. and Austin P. Evans, eds. and trans. *Heresies of the High Middle Ages*. New York: Columbia University Press, 1991.

Waugh, Scott L. and Peter Diehl. *Christendom and Its Discontents: Exclusion, Persecution, and Rebellion, 1000–1500*. Cambridge: Cambridge University Press, 1996.

Weiss, René. *The Yellow Cross: The Story of the Last Cathars' Rebellion against the Inquisition, 1290–1329*. New York: Vintage Books, 2002.

Wilks, Michael. '*Reformatio Regni*: Wyclif and Hus as Leaders of Religious Protest Movements.' In *Schism, Heresy and Religious Protest*, Derek Baker, ed. Studies in Church History, Vol. 9. Cambridge: Cambridge University Press, 1972, 126–27.

Workman, Herbert. *John Wyclif: A Study of the English Medieval Church*, 2 vols. Oxford: Clarendon Press, 1926.

INDEX

ACKNOWLEDGEMENTS

Although it would be rather contrary to a volume on heresy, not to recognize those responsible for its completion would be most heretical indeed, and so I must thank those who have made it possible. I should like to thank all those at Profile Books for the assistance they have provided and their efforts to correct the many infelicities of style I have committed in these pages. I would like especially to thank John Davey and Peter Carson for their patience and continued support for a project that has taken longer than expected. I owe a debt of gratitude to Claire Taylor, who suggested that I take up this project and who has helped me shape my own understanding of heresy in the Middle Ages. I would not have been able to complete this volume without the continued support and encouragement of Jill and Olivia, who have suffered more than a few interruptions in family life so that I could finish this book, and it is to them that I am most thankful.